PARLIAMENT
AND PUBLIC OWNERSHIP

PARLIAMENT AND PUBLIC OWNERSHIP

BY

A. H. HANSON

*Reader in Public Administration
at the University of Leeds*

PUBLISHED FOR

THE HANSARD SOCIETY BY

CASSELL · LONDON

CASSELL & COMPANY LTD
35 Red Lion Square · London WC1
and at
MELBOURNE · SYDNEY · TORONTO
JOHANNESBURG · CAPE TOWN · AUCKLAND

———

First Edition April 1961
Second Edition January 1962

Printed by J. W. Arrowsmith Ltd., Bristol
1061

PREFACE

THE subject of this essay is more limited than the title might perhaps suggest. It is not concerned at all with the views of parliamentarians and political parties on the extent of nationalization; nor does it discuss the many proposals that have been made for improving the internal organization of the nationalized industries. It is solely concerned with what is sometimes rather inappropriately called parliamentary 'control' over the nationalized industries that have been actually established and given the shape of public corporations. It attempts to study this by describing and analysing the evolution of the enterprise-minister-parliament relationship during the course of the last thirty-five years.

To keep the subject within manageable proportions, the term 'nationalized industry' has been given a restrictive interpretation. Bodies such as the British Broadcasting Corporation and the Colonial Development Corporation, which are not industries in the ordinary sense of the word, have been excluded. Among the modern nationalized industries, attention is concentrated on the National Coal Board, the British Transport Commission, the Electricity Boards, the Gas Boards, and the Civil Airways Corporations.

While every effort has been made to present the facts fully and fairly, so that the reader may draw his own conclusions from them, it would be too much to hope that the views which the author has developed during the course of this investigation have never led him away from the path of strict impartiality. For the very 'presentation' of factual material implies an hypothesis about its significance, and hypotheses are always liable to take charge of their begetters. All the author can say is that he has been constantly aware of this danger and that he makes no claim that his conclusions, concentrated in the last chapter, are either self-evident or irrefutable. On the contrary, he hopes that they will provoke lively discussion.

LEEDS 1960   A.H.H.

ACKNOWLEDGEMENTS

MY best thanks are due to the Hansard Society, for commissioning this work, and to its Chairman, Commander Sir Stephen King-Hall, for his friendly encouragement.

I am deeply grateful to Mr. David Pring, M.C., a Senior Clerk of the House of Commons, who gave me far more of his time and knowledge than I had any right to expect. Of the many others who helped me, special thanks are due to: The Right Hon. Sir Toby Low, K.C.M.G., C.B.E., D.S.O., T.D., M.P.; Mr. Austen Albu, M.P.; Sir Keith Joseph, Bt., M.P.; Mr. Philip Chantler (Ministry of Power); Mr. W. C. Gawthorne (Ministry of Transport); Mr. Arthur Bond (Yorkshire Electricity Board); Mr. A. H. A. Wynne (National Coal Board); Dr. F. Ridley (University of Liverpool); Professor J. E. Hodgetts (Queen's University, Kingston, Canada); and Mr. T. Kewley (University of Sydney).

These gentlemen, of course, are in no way responsible for either my mistakes or my opinions.

Her Majesty's Stationery Office has kindly given me permission to quote from Parliamentary Debates, Reports and Acts.

CONTENTS

I

Democracy and Bureaucracy

THE relationship between Parliament and the nationalized industries is often discussed as though it were an entirely new problem. In some respects it is, but in others it is no more than a special aspect of a problem as old as constitutional government: the relationship between the legislature and the executive. This wider and older problem itself has, however, been given new urgency by twentieth-century developments. With the ever increasing complexity and specialization of the executive function, the task of ensuring that the organs which conduct it are subject to adequate democratic control, through parliamentary institutions, becomes more and more difficult to accomplish.

Inevitably, the means to its accomplishment are the subject of acute controversy. Broadly, the debate is between those who believe that existing institutions can be adapted for the purpose without radical alterations and those who consider that thorough-going reforms are required. But this debate about 'means' rests on certain assumptions, shared by the participants, which first of all ought to be examined, as they have already been challenged on many occasions. The most fundamental of them is that parliamentary control of the executive, which has diminished, not only ought to be increased, but *can* be increased without effects on efficiency—and therefore on welfare—which would be sufficiently adverse to cause people to question the value of democratic institutions themselves. Those who challenge this assumption generally argue that we already have a 'managerial' society, and that the kind of democracy that the advocates of increased parliamentary powers regard as desirable is in fact incompatible with it. It is this argument that needs to be looked at, briefly, before the specific problem of parliament and the nationalized industries can be usefully approached.

1

The new 'democratic realism', if it may be so called, has found an exceptionally able exponent in the American economist, Joseph Schumpeter. In that masterpiece of political thought, *Capitalism, Socialism and Democracy*, he argues that the only kind of democracy that can possibly co-exist with modern capitalism or modern socialism is one which restricts the role of the people to that of periodically electing the party which is to rule them. After demolishing the 'classical' doctrines of democracy and exposing their irrelevance to the phenomena of contemporary political life, he defines the democratic method as 'that institutional arrangement for arriving at political decisions in which individuals acquire the power to decide by means of a competitive struggle for the people's vote'. It has nothing to do with the fictitious conception of the 'will of the people', and is indeed incompatible with any significant degree of popular participation in the governmental process. Once the politician has been put in office, voters must understand that 'political action is his business, not theirs', and must renounce a whole number of tempting activities, such as 'bombarding MPs with letters and telegrams', which cannot formally be disallowed by the constitution. Furthermore—and most significant for the inquiry in which we shall be engaged—the politician himself must understand the limitations of his effective authority; for the bureaucracy, formally his servant, is in fact a 'power in its own right', entitled to enjoy exemption from political 'meddling'. In particular, the main economic agencies—including the nationalized industries—must be 'sufficiently exempt in the fulfilment of their current duties from interference by politicians, or for that matter by fussing citizens' committees or by their workmen' i.e. 'from the atmosphere of political strife', as to display 'no inefficiencies other than those associated with the term bureaucracy'.[1]

This may be described as 'positive managerialism', in so far as Schumpeter, implicitly agreeing with Engels that freedom lies in the recognition of necessity, is clearly of the opinion that, as managerialism is inevitable, we might as well decide to like it.

[1] See *Capitalism, Socialism and Democracy* (Fourth Edition) Allen and Unwin, Ltd., London 1954, pp. 269–91. I have chosen Schumpeter as an example, not because of the originality of his views, but because of the clarity and forthrightness with which he expresses them. The sources of his presentation of the historical development of capitalism, upon which his political theories are founded, are to be found in Sombart and Weber.

What might be called 'negative managerialism', on the other hand, sees the alleged necessity, deplores it, and attempts to resist it without hope of success. Its spirit is that of Mark Pattison, who said 'Socialism is inevitable, and I hate it'. The germs of this attitude may be found in Burckhardt and de Tocqueville, and it received its clearest expression from Max Weber, at the beginning of the present century.

> 'It is utterly ridiculous', he wrote, 'to see any connection between the high capitalism of today . . . and democracy or freedom in any sense of these words. Yet this capitalism is an unavoidable result of our economic development. The question is: how freedom and democracy in the long run are at all possible under the domination of a highly developed capitalism? Freedom and democracy are only possible where the resolute will of a nation not to allow itself to be ruled like sheep is permanently alive. We are "individualists" and partisans of "democratic" institutions "against the stream" of material constellations.'[2]

Only the Russians have claimed the ability to reconcile, through their Soviet institutions, 'the democracy of the toiling masses, which surges like a spring flood overflowing all banks, with iron discipline at the time of work, and with direct subordination to the will of one person, the Soviet director . . .'; and the claim is patently false. Under cover of ultra-democratic slogans, they have followed a 'historical necessity' which has led them to the most stark and uncompromising of all contemporary forms of managerialism. Hence the disillusion of those who vainly imagined that the proletarian dictatorship, having reduced administration to 'the extraordinarily simple operations of watching, recording and issuing receipts', and having drawn the masses into 'constant and . . . decisive participation in the democratic administration of the state',[3] would usher in a régime combining the best features of Athenian democracy with the spirit of William Morris's *News from Nowhere*.

[2] Gerth and Mills (Eds.): *From Max Weber—Essays in Sociology*, Routledge & Kegan Paul Ltd., London 1948, p.71. It hardly need be added that Weber is here using 'capitalism' in the sense of 'industrialism'.

[3] Lenin: *State and Revolution*, Little Lenin Library, London 1933, p.78, and *Selected Works*, Vol. VII, p. 231.

Indeed, only when the very idea of a rigid historical necessity, ruthlessly moulding human activities and institutions, is rejected, and the ability of men and women, within wide limits, consciously to choose the type of régime under which they are to live is boldly asserted, does the discussion become anything but one-sided. It is only then, too, that the magnitude of the task—of which the theme of this book provides a specialized example—can be fully grasped. For it is perfectly true that we are in the grip of certain forces which are not, in themselves, favourable to the development of democratic institutions. Bureaucracy, in its widest sense, is one of the inevitable and irreversible consequences of the technological revolution of the nineteenth and twentieth centuries. Democracy is not, as we now know to our cost. A modern-type administrative apparatus is a special and unique response to the demands of a developed industrial civilization; but political democracy, of the kind that we enjoy in Western Europe, is by no means the product of the same kind of necessity. So far, industrialism has proved compatible with a variety of governmental systems, and there is no evidence to suggest that parliamentary democracy provides it with the most appropriate political 'shell'. Otherwise we should not habitually speak of the struggle to *preserve* democracy, and think of it as a precious bloom liable to wither in the absence of tender and persistent care. Almost instinctively we regard the great dynamic forces of modern civilization as hostile to democracy, and talk of the need to establish safeguards, erect barriers etc., to prevent them from eroding it. We never, on any account, use similar language about the apparatus of public administration, because we know full well that it is the toughest, best-established and most self-perpetuating of modern political institutions, which can be relied upon to strike deeper and deeper roots the further the technological revolution, the soil in which it flourishes, proceeds.

In this sense, belief in freedom and in the capacity of democratic parliamentary institutions to cope satisfactorily with the novel problems of an economy undergoing a permanent revolution is a particularly bold assertion of faith. For, as E. H. Carr has said, mass democracy, as the political counterpart of mass industrialism, is 'a difficult and hitherto largely uncharted territory'.[4] It is within

---

[4] *The New Society*, Macmillan, London 1951, p. 76.

4

the context of this general problem that the specific one discussed in this book must take its place.

There is also a narrower, more overtly party-political, context in which it needs to be seen. In this country, the Labour Party, as the great partisan of the extension of the functions of the state as economic organizer and provider of 'welfare', has tended to defend bureaucracy as its chosen instrument and to disregard or gloss over the constitutional consequences of a shift in the centre of gravity from Westminster to Whitehall (and indeed to Hobart House too). Time and time again, official Labour spokesmen have expressed their suspicion of proposals to make the executive more subject to the supervision of Parliament. They were lukewarm, to say the least, about the proposal to establish a Statutory Instruments Committee, and agreed to the re-establishment of the Estimates Committee after the war, only with a certain reluctance and rather bad grace. They rejected Lord Campion's proposals, made before the Select Committee on Procedure in 1946, to strengthen the financial control of the House of Commons by combining the Estimates with the Public Accounts Committee. They voted against the setting up of a Select Committee to examine the Reports and Accounts of the nationalized industries. They failed, in many cases, to see that a vital issue of principle was at stake in the Crichel Down affair. The reason for this attitude is not difficult to discover. It was expressed, with unusual precision and clarity, by a Labour spokesman in the debate on the motion to establish a Select Committee on Statutory Instruments (May 1944). This Member, Mr. Moelwyn Hughes, opposed the motion on the grounds that the proposed Committee would be 'the thin end of the wedge for the obstruction of necessary post-war legislation'. The examination of Statutory Instruments, he said, was 'only an excuse to cover obstruction and delay'. Delegated legislation, far from being inimical to, was 'to a large extent responsible for the liberty of the individual', as regulations under the Factories Act for the protection of machinery, orders under the Workmen's Compensation Acts about notifiable diseases, bye-laws relating to sanitation, water, housing etc. all bore witness.

'Because I am not satisfied', he continued, 'with the motives of those who are now pleading for the need of further restrictions upon delegated legislation, or that their motive is the liberty of the subject, but because I am satisfied that what they want to do is to obstruct as far as they can the necessary social legislation of this country, I regret the concession which the Government have made.'[5]

Although the attitude of the Labour Party—and indeed of both parties—towards these matters has changed considerably of recent years, it is still broadly true to say that for many Labour people the 'menace of bureaucracy' is an invention of the Conservatives to scare the timid away from socialism and to make the administration of a Welfare State more difficult. They feel that as long as the departments of state and other governmental agencies are controlled, immediately or ultimately, by Ministers, who are responsible to Parliament, which is responsible to a democratic electorate, no harm can come of giving more and more power to the official. On the contrary, it makes democracy more positive and creative, by removing vital decisions from the hands of people who are actuated by private interests and placing them in the hands of those who are professionally devoted to the service of the public.

Conservatives, on the other hand, as partisans of free enterprise, have tended to view bureaucracy with deep suspicion. The older type of Conservative, who has now almost disappeared, regarded every conferment of discretionary authority on an official as a restraint, *ipso facto* unjustifiable, on individual liberty, which, in A. V. Dicey's classic words, was incompatible with 'the exercise by persons in authority of wide, arbitrary, or discretionary powers of constraint'. All 'extraordinary' powers, and particularly those involved in the exercise of delegated legislation and in the establishment of administrative jurisdiction, undermined the dual principles of the Sovereignty of Parliament and the Rule of Law. Excessive faith in the virtues of state action created a situation in which the checks and balances of the British Constitution virtually ceased to operate. Modern Conservatives, of course, know as well as anyone else that the Diceyan view of the Constitution is outdated, and are prepared to give officialdom a scope for discretionary action that would have horrified their predecessors. Their political creed, however, still enables them to emphasize what socialists would call the 'negative', as distinct from the 'positive'

[5] H.C. Deb., Vol. 400, cols. 278–80.

aspects of individual liberty, and hence inclines them to look with favour upon proposals to bring bureaucratic action more closely under the control both of Parliament and of the Courts of Common Law. It is, of course, this very fact, together with the suspicion that Conservative anti-bureaucratism is highly partisan and selective, that has caused the Labour Party to oppose, or at least to refrain from actively supporting, schemes for the strengthening of parliamentary control which, on the face of things, look eminently desirable from a democratic point of view. Thus the association of a controversy about constitutional and democratic principle with a policy struggle between the two main political parties has made for considerable confusion in the public mind.

The confusion has been made worse confounded by the fact that neither party has been united on the issue. This applies particularly to the Labour Party. At no time in the history of the labour movement in this country has the bureaucratic—perhaps one might today call it the 'Morrisonian'—type of socialism gone unchallenged. There has always been a trend of opinion, deriving its inspiration variously from Owenite and Rochdale forms of co-operation, from the utopian quasi-medievalism of William Morris, from the direct democracy of the nonconformist sects, and from continental and transatlantic syndicalism, which has looked upon bureaucracy and socialism not as allies but as enemies. It achieved its greatest influence during the years immediately following the end of the First World War, when, in its Guild Socialist forms, it affected even the official policy of the Labour Party.[6] Its exponents contributed little to the understanding of parliamentary democracy, as their efforts were directed towards the establishment of what they regarded as democracy within industry, through the achievement of 'workers' control'. Many of them, indeed, expressed a studied lack of interest in the mechanics of 'bourgeois' parliamentarism, which they looked upon as obsolescent.[7] But among those

[6] See D. N. Chester: *Management and Accountability in the Nationalised Industries*, in *Public Administration*, Vol. 30, 1952.

[7] As late as 1933, G. D. H. Cole, the most important figure among the Guild Socialists, expressed the opinion that a 'socialist government will not be able to spare several hundreds of its picked men to sit day after day in Parliament listening to one another talk, when it will need for vital administrative and pioneering work every competent Socialist on whom it can lay its hands'. (Cripps and others: *Problems of a Socialist Government*, Gollancz, London 1933, p. 173).

of the 'left' who continued to have faith in parliamentary institutions, there was a parallel, if weaker, demand for a transformation of parliamentary procedure calculated to 'democratize' the House of Commons in much the same way as the Guild Socialists would have democratized industry. Its most consistent spokesman was Fred Jowett, one of the leaders of the Independent Labour Party, who, impressed by the virtues of the committee system in local government as a means of bringing administration under the direct and continuous control of the representatives of the people, advanced proposals for the 'municipalisation' of the House of Commons itself, through the establishment of a series of all-party committees which would take over the executive powers of ministers and reduce the Cabinet itself to the status of a kind of 'general purposes' committee.[8] Thus, on the socialist left, there was an anti-bureaucratic trend no less determined and extreme than that on the conservative right to which Lord Hewart, in his *New Despotism*, and C. K. Allen, in his *Bureaucracy Triumphant* gave expression—but, of course, with entirely different objects and an entirely dissimilar philosophy.

Between the extremes, moreover, there was to be found a great variety of liberal, moderate socialist and 'left' conservative opinion which, while accepting the necessity of bureaucratic institutions and welcoming the material benefits which they made possible, was deeply disturbed at the prospect of a servile state and anxious to find ways and means by which public opinion and group volitions could be given more effective and more continuous expression. Some advocated the creation of a 'social' or 'industrial' parliament —a Webbsian idea rather unexpectedly taken up by Mr. Winston Churchill in his Romanes Lecture of 1929 and more recently revived by Mr. Christopher Hollis. Others attempted to draw the teeth of the demand for workers' control by popularizing the idea of industrial co-partnership or of advisory industrial councils on the Whitley pattern. Thinkers as differently inspired as Harold Laski and Ramsay Muir recommended modifications of the 'Jowett Plan' which would equip the House of Commons with a network of advisory, as distinct from executive, committees. In

[8] For an account of the 'Jowett Plan', see A. H. Hanson: *The Labour Party and House of Commons Reform*, in *Parliamentary Affairs*, Vol. 10, No. 4 and Vol. 11, No. 1, Autumn 1956-7 and Winter 1957-8.

devious ways, the pluralist political philosophy, conceived by Gierke and Figgis and developed by Duguit and Laski, was extending its influence. The Webbs themselves, long regarded by Guild Socialists and syndicalists as the apostles of bureaucratic socialism, devised, in that strange but persuasive work, *A Constitution for the Socialist Commonwealth of Great Britain*, a scheme of 'multiform democracy', visualizing 'a community so variously organized, and so highly differentiated in function as to be not only invigorated by a sense of personal freedom, but also constantly swept by the fresh air of experiment, observation and verification'.[9]

In attempting to summarize these manifold cross-currents in the great debate about bureaucracy, it is sometimes difficult to know whether to use the present or the past tense. All the elements of the controversy are still with us, and none of the issues have been clearly and finally decided. But the emphasis has changed considerably, and there has at least been some degree of simplification. It would seem, for instance, that only a few slightly eccentric—if professionally distinguished—thinkers, such as Professors Hayek and Keeton, continue to regard bureaucracy itself as an unmitigated evil. Hewart's *New Despotism* is now of historical interest only, and Sir Carlton Allen has considerably modified his former uncompromising views. On the Labour side, the demand for 'workers' control' or 'joint control', although still voiced by two nationally-important trade unions, no longer causes much excitement; the Jowett Plan is as dead as the Dodo, and the younger intellectuals of moderate socialist persuasions, such as R. H. S. Crossman and Anthony Crosland,[10] show an awareness of the problems of combining managerial with democratic institutions in a predominantly collectivist society which was almost absent in the writings and speeches of Herbert Morrison and his supporters. There are very few of any political persuasion who continue to think in terms of radical changes in existing political institutions, either by way of reversion to a 'Diceyan' past or by way of a jump into an ultra-democratic future in which the bureaucrat will be reduced to the humble, passively obedient role which was

[9] Longmans, Green & Co. Ltd., London 1923, p. 356.
[10] See R. H. S. Crossman: *Socialism and the New Despotism* (Fabian Tract No. 298); Anthony Crosland: *The Future of Socialism*, Jonathan Cape, Ltd., London 1956, Chaps. 14 and 23.

envisaged for him by the architects of the Paris Commune. Those seriously concerned with the problem of bureaucracy now tend to concentrate their attention on (a) the development of certain specific features of our parliamentary system, such as the Select Committee, and the strengthening of the apparatus of local self-government, and (b) improvements in the means of defending the individual against bureaucratic arbitrariness, through, for instance, a rationalization of our system of administrative tribunals, and the introduction of supervisory machinery capable of providing the British citizen with the kind of protection that the Frenchman obtains from the Conseil d'Etat and the Scandinavian from the Ombudsman. We have also learnt something of the lesson taught by Weber and Schumpeter, in so far as we recognize much more clearly than some of us once did that representative institutions are subject to certain inescapable limitations, which must be understood unless we are to make a nonsense of representative democracy. Admittedly, there is no firm agreement about the precise location of these limits, but at least there is a wide appreciation of the importance of, first, finding out just *what* the representative institution can accomplish most effectively, and then organizing it for the pursuit of precisely these purposes, and of no others. For the recent history of many countries, of which France is perhaps the most outstanding, has powerfully underlined the fact that to extend the representative's jurisdiction to fields in which he possesses no competence and where his intervention can produce nothing but confusion and frustration is to jeopardize public confidence in the democratic principle itself.

Nevertheless, the problem that we attempted to define in the first few paragraphs of this chapter is still very much with us, and powerful echoes of the specific controversies of inter-war and immediately post-war periods persist. In no field of administration is this more evident than in that of the nationalized industries; for the entry of the state into industrial ownership and entrepreneurship has raised issues of peculiar complexity for a democratic society. In order to understand these issues in their contemporary setting, it will first be necessary to give some account of their historical development, against a background of the more general ideological and political struggles which we have endeavoured to analyse.

II

The Idea of the Public Corporation

OUR understanding of these issues will perhaps be assisted by a small digression into the field of semantics. For the word 'bureaucracy', which we have hitherto used in an undefined way, may be given at least three separate meanings.

In the preceding pages, definition was hardly necessary, because it was obvious from the context that the word was being used in its traditional or Weberian sense, as meaning simply the professionalized apparatus of public administration. Employed in this manner, the word is purely descriptive, without valuational overtones. But the very fact that the control of 'the bureaucracy' is a 'problem' leads us naturally to a second use of the term, which has, at least for democrats, an element of judgment attached to it. In this second sense, bureaucracy means the effective determination of policy by the personnel of the administrative apparatus, which has become, not merely 'a power in its own right', but the repository of real sovereignty within the system of government, to the detriment of the powers that *ought* to be wielded (according to democratic theory) by Parliament, the Ministers of the Crown, and the Courts of Common Law. This is the 'bureaucracy' for the destruction of which Lord Hewart, Sir Carlton Allen, and Professors Hayek and Keeton have sharpened their swords and against whose solid ranks the Guild Socialists attempted to mobilize the forces of the wage-slaves. The third meaning of the word is, however, the most widespread one, and that which almost invariably carries with it pejorative implications. 'Bureaucracy', in this sense, is a *modus operandi* in the conduct of public affairs of a kind to which 'bureaucrats' (in the original sense) are said to be addicted. 'Bureaucratic' administration, as popularly conceived, is characterized by slowness, circumlocution, caution, and excessive devotion to routine and

11

precedent—in fact all those things that we summarize in the useful expression, red tape.

The problem discussed in general terms in Chapter 1 is simply that of controlling 'the bureaucracy' (sense 1) in such a way as to prevent it from becoming 'a bureaucracy' (sense 2). This has been the special concern of those who, from their various points of view, are anxious to maintain the principle of undivided ministerial responsibility and to reinforce the effectiveness of parliamentary supervision of the administrative apparatus. It is clear, however, that in attempting to solve it one incurs the danger of actually *reinforcing* 'bureaucracy' in its third sense. The reason for this is well known; for there is evidence (much of it coming from the civil servants themselves) to suggest that the defects of 'bureaucracy' (sense 3) are at least partly caused by the device of ministerial responsibility to Parliament, in so far as this means that every decision that a civil servant makes is taken in the name of the minister and as such may become the subject of parliamentary questions, debates or inquiries. These defects, therefore, are to some extent a product of parliamentary democracy itself—from which it seems reasonable to conclude that the more democratic one's parliamentary system becomes the more serious they are likely to be.

Business-like efficiency in administration, therefore, would appear to be incompatible, at least to some degree, with democratic control. Because we are democrats, however, we have been satisfied with something less than business-like efficiency in our normal governmental services, regarding its partial sacrifice on the democratic altar as necessary for the preservation of a particular kind of political life. But can we be equally satisfied when the state itself goes into business? That is the question which the nationalization of industry brings to the fore. The answer has generally, although not universally, been to the effect that state businesses should first and foremost be business-like, and hence need to be exempted from the full force of ministerial responsibility, Treasury control and parliamentary supervision.

The making of this important exception to what is generally regarded as a basic principle of the British constitution does not represent so sharp a break with tradition as might first appear. For by the inter-war period, when controversies about

12

nationalization began to take a practical turn, Britain already had considerable experience in the use of *ad hoc* administrative bodies, partly or totally autonomous. Most of these, admittedly, had been established, not to ensure greater efficiency, but to remove certain aspects of administration from the field of politics, on grounds of public policy. But to insulate the nationalized industries from the political struggle was also one of the objects of those who advocated their autonomy; and hence the experience, both positive and negative, of the older *ad hoc* bodies seems fully relevant to the issue under discussion.

In some cases, the establishment of an autonomous or semi-autonomous body was quite obviously legitimate and necessary, even on the strictest of democratic principles, and was accepted as such by informed public opinion. No-one has ever suggested, to my knowledge, that ministers should be responsible to parliament for the quasi-judicial decisions taken by such bodies as the Civil Service Commissioners or the Area Traffic Commissioners. In other cases, the legitimacy of the *ad hoc* principle was more open to question, because the bodies concerned had executive (or advisory-cum-executive) functions as well as quasi-judicial ones. But where much of the agency's time was consumed in adjudicating between rival claims or in deciding individual cases within the framework of law or regulation, the demand for a measure of 'insulation' was inevitably strong. Bodies which fall, or have fallen, within this class include the University Grants Committee, the Development Commission, the Dyestuffs Advisory Licensing Committee, the Import Duties Advisory Committee, the Electricity Commission and the Coal Mines Reorganisation Commission.[1] Trusteeship bodies, concerned with 'the management of property on behalf of others', such as the Charity Commissioners and the Estates Committee of the Ecclesiastical Commission, also had a strong claim to autonomy on grounds of public policy; but here again there were inevitably marginal cases. The Forestry Commission of 1919 (subsequently absorbed into the Ministry of Agriculture) is quoted by Mr. Greaves as one of these.[2]

[1] This miscellaneous list, which could be considerably extended, is quoted from H. R. G. Greaves: *The Civil Service in the Changing State*, Harrap & Co., London 1947, p. 112.
[2] 'Whether or not the management of land for the purpose of producing a commodity like timber can be properly regarded as more the function of a

[*footnote continued on page 14*]

In spite of difficulties occasionally experienced 'at the edges', autonomous or semi-autonomous bodies whose functions are predominantly quasi-judicial or trustee in character have caused little controversy. This may have been due less to the nature of their functions than to the fact that their field of operations was not being trampled over by political partisans. For whenever the *ad hoc* principle has been applied to politically-controversial fields of administration (in other words, when the attempt has been made to de-politicize something essentially political) the agency concerned has always had a very rough passage. But, as might be expected, this has been particularly the case when autonomy has been given to a body with more-or-less straightforward administrative functions, comparatively unsullied by any element of the quasi-judicial or of trusteeship.

The classic example, of course, is the Poor Law Commission of 1834. Ten years' experience, during which the Commissioners were almost continuously at the centre of a political storm, finally convinced the government that a mistake had been made in constituting them as an independent body, uncontrolled by a Minister and unrepresented in the House of Commons. Indeed, the Commissioners themselves found their position an intolerable one.

Sir George Cornewall Lewis, writing to Grote at the time when the Amending Act of 1847 was being passed, said: 'Parliament is supreme; and we cannot be better governed than Parliament is willing to govern us. It is in vain for a body of subordinate functionaries to attempt to enforce, on such a subject as the Poor Law, opinions which are repudiated by the majority of the Sovereign legislature.'[3]

Britain repeated this experience, and confirmed its lessons, with the Board of Health of 1848–1854, despite the fact that a government representative, the Head of the Department of Woods and Forests, was one of its members. Difficulties of the same kind—although more easily and readily solved—arose in 1934, when the

---

[*footnote continued from page 13*]
trustee than of commercial management may be open to question, but the holding and development of property by a body combining trustee and technical qualifications seems to have been the governing purpose in those responsible for establishing the Commission.' (*ibid.*, p. 113.)

[3] Quoted from S. and B. Webb: *English Poor Law History: Part II—The Last Hundred Years*, *Vol. 2*, Longmans, Green & Co. Ltd., London 1929, p.186.

centenary of the Poor Law Commissioners was 'celebrated' by the establishment of the Unemployment Assistance Board, concerned with a very similar subject. In this case, Members of Parliament violently criticized an administration which, although operating under regulations which had received the Minister's approval and had been confirmed by Parliament, was not subject to ministerial direction in its 'day-to-day' operations, which consisted of deciding entitlements to relief for able-bodied unemployed who had exhausted their insurance benefits. Constitutionally, the essence of the trouble was that the regulations themselves could be changed only on the initiative of the Board itself, and not on that of the Minister. If the Board had been adamant, an exceptionally nasty situation could have arisen, at a time when the roads of the country were resounding with the tramp of hunger-marchers. As it was, the 'old boy' method worked.

'As a consequence of that Debate', said the Minister, 'I represented to the Chairman of the Board opinions and detailed cases which had been conveyed to me both during discussion by Members of this House and subsequently by other Members and outside bodies.'[4] The Board, thus pressed, 'asked' the Minister to suspend the Regulations.

This incident, now almost forgotten except by historians and constitutional lawyers, shows that, even if there had been no nationalized industries, we should not have escaped our twentieth century controversies about the *ad hoc* principle. For the increasing complexity of twentieth century administration and the difficulty of adapting to new tasks an apparatus of central and local government that had become set in a rather rigid mould together ensured that attempts would be made to 'de-politicize' and 'de-bureaucratize' certain branches of the public service—particularly, of course, the more novel ones. Thus, even while the nineteenth century crop of 'statutory authorities for special purposes' was being gathered into the capacious barns of the central departments and local councils

[4] H.C. Deb., 5s., Vol. 297, col. 968, as quoted in W. I. Jennings: *Parliament*, Cambridge 1936, p. 81. Of *ad hoc* agencies operating in politically controversial fields, Mr. H. R. G. Greaves has written: 'Between 1832 and 1914, from the Poor Law Commission and Board of Health to Mr. Lloyd George's Road Board, the only noteworthy fact about them is that they *failed* and were absorbed by State Departments under ministerial responsibility'. (*Political Quarterly*, Vol. 16, 1945, p. 67.)

(the last important ones to be harvested being the School Boards in 1902 and the Boards of Guardians in 1929), a new crop was vigorously springing up. Not surprisingly, these developments were regarded with suspicion by those who remembered the fate of some of the earlier experiments, such as the Poor Law Commission and the Board of Health. 'We regard with apprehension', wrote the MacDonnell Commission on the Civil Service (1914), 'the creation of any authority having large public funds at its disposal which is outside effective ministerial control and parliamentary supervision'.[5] 'There should be no omission', added the 'Haldane' Committee on the Machinery of Government (1918), '. . . of those safeguards which ministerial responsibility to Parliament alone provides'.[6]

In respect of a whole range of services, therefore, the question arose of the legitimacy, desirability and possibility of dispensing with normal democratic safeguards in order (a) to improve their administrative efficiency and (b) to exempt them from political 'interference' or 'meddling'. The apparent contradiction between democratic administration and good administration had to be resolved either in favour of one of these principles, or by some kind of compromise which would establish a new balance between them. Nowhere was this contradiction more acute than in the sphere of the nationalized industries. For here one was confronted with a new kind of state activity which offered the possibility of devising fresh forms of administration rather than of revamping old ones. Here, moreover, one was concerned with a subject of central rather than of peripheral constitutional and administrative significance—or likely to become such as the state extended its entrepreneurial responsibilities. Inevitably therefore, nationalized industries became the centre of a peculiarly complicated controversy: a controversy in which the critics of 'bureaucracy', in both of the pejorative senses that we have defined, found themselves taking up positions that looked oddly untypical.

The most outstanding peculiarity of this dispute is that the very people, i.e. Conservatives and Liberals, who expressed most vocally and persistently their apprehensions about 'bureaucracy' (sense 2) became the original protagonists of independence from

[5] *Fourth Report*, pp. 76–7.
[6] *Cmd.* 9230 of 1918, p. 11.

16

ministerial control and parliamentary supervision for the nationalized industries. In this field, in fact, they shifted their attack away from 'bureaucracy' in sense 2 and towards 'bureaucracy' in sense 3. The reasons for this shift are well known. Departmental administration, with its concomitants of Treasury control and subjection to civil service regulations, was held to be incompatible with that commercial efficiency which should be a nationalized industry's predominant, if not sole, aim. Likewise, ministerial responsibility, being the main source of those inefficiencies characteristic of 'bureaucratic' administration, could not be superimposed on a commercial-type organization without disastrous results. Thirdly, if an industry was to be run on sound business principles, it must be exempt from the political meddling of those whom Mr. Frank Pick impolitely described as 'inquisitive and irresponsible guardians of the public interest'.

These views were held with particular strength by members of the business community, anxious that such nationalized industries as might be necessary (the fewer the better, of course) should be run by businessmen and not by civil servants, who were regarded as having convincingly displayed their lack of business capacity when operating economic controls during the First World War. The public sector businessman, it was held, could never give of his best, or even be induced to remain in the public service, unless he were left free to do his job in much the same way as he was accustomed to do it in his own enterprise. He must be free, not merely to devise the most suitable structures and procedures (within the broad limits of his statutory assignment), but also to carry on day-to-day administration without having constantly to be looking over his shoulder at ministerial mentors and parliamentary critics. To ensure his enjoyment of these facilities and privileges, the nationalized industry must be given the status of an autonomous public corporation.

As both the Conservatives and the Liberals were predominantly 'business' parties, their sympathy for such views was assured, and the autonomous public corporation became the pattern for the three major inter-war nationalizations, Electricity, Broadcasting and London Transport. Indeed, in the 1930s, enthusiasm for autonomy reached the point where Parliament was prepared to deny to the Minister even the right of appointing the members of a public corporation. By the London Passenger Transport Act of 1933, this right was placed in the hands of 'appointing trustees'. Autonomy, in fact, was carried to 'extraordinary lengths'. Of the inter-war public corporation Mr. Lincoln Gordon said:

'Only in its method of appointment, its constitutional incapacity to derive profit from the undertaking, and the very narrow provision for control by Parliament, Ministers, and special supervisory and quasi-judicial tribunals, is its independence, within that field as defined by Parliament, in any way modified.'[7]

Yet agreement on the carrying of autonomy to such extraordinary lengths was well-nigh universal, despite the warnings of the MacDonnell Commission and the Haldane Committee. The legitimacy of the public corporation as an administrative device and the desirability of keeping it independent were stressed, for instance, by several of this country's most distinguished economists.

Professor Pigou, in his *Economics of Welfare*, said that the *ad hoc* Board or Commission had the advantage of overcoming no less than 'four disadvantages' of 'municipal or national representative assemblies, as organs for the control or operation of business'. These were: (1) that the latter bodies were 'primarily chosen for purposes other than that of intervention in industry'; (2) that the 'fluctuating make-up of a national government or of a town council' was difficult to reconcile with consistency of managerial policy; (3) that 'the areas to which public authorities are normally allocated' were determined by 'non-commercial considerations'; and (4) that 'regular governmental agencies' were 'liable to injurious forms of electoral pressure'.[8]

Painting a broader picture, Mr. J. M. Keynes, in *The End of Laissez-Faire*, suggested that progress lay in 'the growth and recognition of semi-autonomous bodies within the state . . . bodies which in the ordinary course of affairs are mainly autonomous within their prescribed limitations, but are subject in the last resort to the sovereignty of the democracy expressed through parliament'.

[7] Lincoln Gordon: *The Public Corporation in Great Britain*, Oxford 1937, p. 7.
[8] Macmillan & Co. Ltd., Fourth Edition, London 1932, pp. 333–4.

The corporation, he continued, was 'a mode of Government which had never ceased to be important and sympathetic to our institutions', and in support of this somewhat questionable statement he instanced the Universities, the Bank of England, the Port of London Authority and 'even perhaps the railway companies'.[9]

Further support for the autonomous public corporation came from that very carefully-prepared and influential document, the Liberal 'Yellow Book' of 1928, produced under the supervision of an Executive Committee that included among its members Sir Walter Layton, E. D. Simon, Lloyd George, J. M. Keynes, Ramsay Muir, Sir Herbert Samuel and Sir John Simon. This expressed firm opposition to 'state trading' in the form of 'national undertakings operated by the Central Government itself', advocated the use of the corporation as the nearest public equivalent of the joint stock company, and stressed, as its main advantage, 'a greater detachment from politics and political influence'.[10]

Above all, one of the minor ironies of history ensured that the Labour Party itself, together with the main part of the trade union movement, should move over to the same side of the fence; for it is well known that Mr. Herbert Morrison, himself the progenitor of the London Passenger Transport Board, succeeded during the course of the 1930s in converting his party to the public corporation idea. That idea, it must be remembered, was rather different from the one that later found expression in Labour's post-war nationalization statutes; for Morrison, at this time, consistently advocated an autonomy no less complete than that held desirable by his political opponents. 'The Board', he wrote, 'must have autonomy and freedom of business management. It must not only be allowed to enjoy responsibility; it must even have responsibility thrust down its throat'.[11] By 1935, he had persuaded the greater

[9] The Hogarth Press Ltd., London 1926, pp. 41–2. The reader will gather from these quotations that Keynes was considerably less than his usual lucid self in his treatment of this problem. Nevertheless, his 'striking words' were quoted with approval by the T.U.C. in its evidence to the 'Macmillan' Committee. See summary of that evidence in T.U.C. *Report*, 1931, para. 295.

[10] *Britain's Industrial Future, being the Report of the Liberal Industrial Enquiry*, London 1928, pp. 67, 76. The authors of this Report tentatively suggested that it 'would have been better' if the Post Office itself had been established as an 'ad hoc administrative body'. Viscount Wolmer, in *Post Office Reform* (1932), demanded that it should be transformed into one.

[11] *Socialisation and Transport*, Constable & Co. Ltd., London 1933, p. 170.

part of the labour movement, not merely of the superiority of the public corporation as a form of nationalization and of the necessity of appointing its members solely on grounds of ability and experience, but of the desirability of giving it exemption from parliamentary and ministerial inquisition into its day-to-day administrative behaviour. Thus, for the orthodox Labour man, the C.E.B., B.B.C., P.L.A. and L.P.T.B. ceased to be examples of 'capitalist nationalization' and became patterns of socialization. Mr. Morrison himself, one may parenthetically note, has never ceased to call the nationalized industries 'socialized industries', always to the scandal of the more left-wing of his political colleagues.

Irrespective of its merits or demerits, Morrison's proselytizing achievement seems a remarkable one to those familiar with Labour's previous attitudes on this question. By the 1930s, Labour had moved far from the fluid empiricism to which its former leading 'backroom boy' on nationalization questions had thus given expression in the early 1920s:

> 'The constitution of the industry may be "unitary", as is (for example) that of the Post Office, or it may be "federal", as was that designed by Mr. Justice Sankey for the coal industry. Administration may be centralised or decentralised. The authorities to whom it is entrusted may be composed of representatives of the consumers, or of representatives of professional associations, or of state officials, or of all three in several different proportions. Executive work may be placed in the hands of civil servants, trained, recruited and promoted as in the existing State Departments, or a new service may be created with a procedure and standards of its own. The industry may be subject to Treasury control, or it may be financially autonomous. The problem is, in fact, of a familiar, though difficult, order. It is one of constitution making.'[12]

It had moved even further from the ideas of workers' control, as propagated by the Guild Socialists, and of joint control, as embodied in the mines and railways nationalization bills and in *Coal and Commonsense*.

[12] R. H. Tawney: *The Acquisitive Society*, Bell & Co. Ltd., London 1921, pp. 141–2.

Yet the evolution of its ideas, if unexpected, was a perfectly natural one. Labour, although in favour of increased state intervention and therefore (it might be argued) *ipso facto* of increased bureaucratic powers, had its own reasons for disliking political control of industry. Its policies for the nationalization of the mines and the railways were formulated when prospects of a socialist government seemed remote; hence it tended to think of parliamentary and ministerial powers as being exercised by 'capitalist' parliaments and 'capitalist' ministers. Moreover, despite the Webbs the ordinary Labour man could hardly fail to regard the civil service as an alien body, because of the class-origins of its top-level personnel. Unlike the businessman, he did not doubt its competence; what he doubted was its impartiality—and not entirely without justice, in the light of the long and bitter struggle for recognition by the Post Office unions, which seemed to suggest that the civil servant could be a task-master as hard as any capitalist. Thirdly, it must be remembered that, in the early 1920s, 'industrial democracy' was more than a slogan; it was a deeply felt need. Guild Socialists had convinced most active trade unionists, and indeed a significant section of the Labour leadership, that wage-slavery could be ended only by the establishment of some form of producers' self-government. These industrial democrats, of course, could not contemplate the running of industry by civil servants with anything but aversion, and they could hardly become excited about pettifogging questions of how much or little supervisory authority Ministers and Members of Parliament should possess. The rank-and-file industrial democrat, if he ever considered the matter at all, in all probability answered 'The less the better'. His more sophisticated leaders, when compelled to consider the issue (which did not happen often) were liable to display more than a trace of confusion.[13]

If one subtracts from this complex of ideas the third, workers' control, one is left with an ideological basis fully capable of providing support for the autonomous public corporation as understood by Mr. Morrison and created by the inter-war Conservative

---

[13] See A. H. Hanson: *The Labour Party and the House of Commons Reform*, Part I, in *Parliamentary Affairs*, Vol. 10, No. 4, Autumn 1956-7, pp. 464–5, and the references to the Minutes of Evidence of the 'Sankey' Commission on the Coal Industry, there quoted.

governments. Morrison's political achievement was to recognize this, and also to realize, sooner than many of his colleagues, that workers' control was in fact 'subtracting' itself. The defeat of the General Strike in 1926 had put an end—as hindsight now enables us to recognize—to the apocalyptic hopes from which the Guild Socialists and their more moderate fellow travellers had derived their strength. Trade Unions tended to become ultra-cautious, concentrating their energies on preserving the standards of life of their members in economic circumstances where militancy was at a discount. The Labour Party was solemnly and sedately grooming itself, under Ramsay MacDonald's leadership, for a second period of office. Only a small minority held strongly to the old ideas, although political inertia and attachment to the familiar slogan ensured that they continued to be embodied, for the time being, in the rather vague programmes of industrial reorganization then current.

By the late 1920s, signs and portents of their decline had become abundant, and the idea of the autonomous public corporation was steadily gaining support. Even before the controversy about the London Passenger Transport Bill, the resolution of which in Mr. Morrison's favour was perhaps the decisive event in the process of ideological transition, individual labour leaders had given their allegiance to the new conception of nationalization. William Graham, sometimes regarded as the pioneer of the Corporation in the Labour Party, had suggested that the B.B.C's charter should become the model for subsequent public enterprises. James Maxton had introduced a Bill to give the Bank of England public corporation status. At the Labour Party Conference, Philip Snowden went on record for the public corporation, and even some of the union leaders, in their evidence before the Royal Commission on Transport (1929–31) indicated that they were having new thoughts on the management of nationalized industries and that, like Clement Attlee in 1926, they no longer considered themselves 'pinned down' to 'any particular form of nationalization'.[14]

[14] H.C. Deb., 5s. Vol. 199, col. 1440. Two years later Emanuel Shinwell and John Strachey worked out a remarkably prophetic plan for the nationalization of the coal industry under an autonomous public corporation. The miners' leaders, however, were not ready for it, and its authors, after circulating it in mimeographed form, did not continue to press for its adoption. Indeed, it remained entirely forgotten until its 'rediscovery' by the present author in 1953. (See A. H. Hanson: *Labour and the Public Corporation*, in *Public Administration*, Vol. 32, Summer 1954, pp. 203–9.)

For those who continued to cling to the old ideas, the unkindest cut of all came from the most distinguished of the former advocates of workers' control, G. D. H. Cole, who, in his *Next Ten Years in British Social and Economic Policy*, published in 1929, admitted that Guild Socialism had been largely mistaken and advocated the running of industry by the 'expert' almost as enthusiastically as he had formerly advocated its running by the workshop delegate. Dismissing Guild Socialism in its original form as 'a theory of representation run mad', he claimed that its main virtue was merely that it had 'killed dead . . . the old Collectivism which thought of the mechanism of nationalization as a mere extension of the political government of the State, and proposed to hand over the running of industries to Civil Service departments under political heads'. Management, he now considered, was 'essentially an affair of experts', to whom, 'within the limits of the broad control of policy by the State', it was 'indispensable to give . . . a wide discretionary power and a liberal freedom to experiment with new methods'. Such discretion and freedom could be achieved only by 'delegating powers to independent and responsible bodies of Commissioners, already adopted in the case of electricity and the railways' and 'likely to play a very large part in the working out of the new socialism'. Even the immediate supervision of such 'Commissions', he considered, should not be placed in the hands of Parliament, because 'spasmodic parliamentary intervention . . . does more harm than good'. Instead, he proposed the establishment of a superior 'Power and Transport Commission', along the lines suggested by the policy statement, *Coal and Commonsense*, to co-ordinate 'one group of controlling Commissions', and above this another expert co-ordinating body, a 'Board of National Investment'. Although he also suggested changes in the organization and procedure of the House of Commons to enable it to exercise its ultimate supervisory powers more effectively, his stress throughout was on the autonomy of his proposed heirarchy of Commissions. It is significant that nowhere in this plan of administrative reform did the Minister or the Cabinet appear to be involved. Indeed, the *machinery* through which Parliament traditionally exercised its supervision of administrative agencies, the device of ministerial responsibility, was not mentioned at any stage of a fairly lengthy exposition.

23

In this now-forgotten work we see most clearly and logically set out the thought processes whereby Labour became converted to the public corporation idea. Apart from a taste for clumsy and unworkable superstructures, typical of Cole's prolific scheme-making at its weakest, there is little to distinguish the views of the ex-Guild-Socialist in 1929 from those of Mr. Morrison in 1933, as expressed in his *Socialisation and Transport*.

Characteristic of Labour thought at this period is Cole's lack of real concern with ministerial control and parliamentary supervision. The same blindness to what was to become a major issue is evident in the 'nationalization' debates of the Trades Union Congresses and Labour Party Conferences of the early 1930s, when the labour movement, ashamed of the vagueness and flabbiness of the policies which were widely regarded as responsible for its disastrous defeat in 1931, was attempting to work out a detailed and realistic programme. It is significant that, in these debates, the very lively opposition to Morrison's ideas was entirely directed at the expert and non-representative character of the corporation and never at the corporation's insulation from political control. Both sides, in fact, assumed that, once the profit motive had been abolished and the right people appointed to the Board, neither the Minister nor Parliament need display more than occasional interest in its affairs.

Although in some disagreement, which was never completely resolved in the 1930s, about the extent of workers' participation, both the Labour Party and the T.U.C., in their official resolutions, came down heavily on the side of autonomy. The Resolution on 'The National Planning of Transport', adopted at the Labour Party's Leicester Conference in 1932, demanded that 'the general direction and day-to-day management' of a nationalized industry 'should be endowed with a strong sense of initiative and responsibility' and 'therefore be freed from unnecessarily detailed Ministerial and Parliamentary supervision once the broad principles of policy have been laid down by the statute creating the new machinery'.[15] The proposed National Transport Board, it continued, must be subject only to such unspecified 'Ministerial and other

---

[15] This faith in the power of 'statutes' to lay down the policies to be pursued by nationalized industries is characteristic of Labour Party and trade union statements on nationalization at this period.

direction as may be laid down by Statute'; for 'to make a political Minister, subjected as he is to Parliamentary and electoral pressure, responsible for settling facilities, charges and prices, wages and salaries, appointments, and so on, would involve him in the most embarrassing situations and would add an unpleasing feature to parliamentary elections'. As for Parliament, its functions should be 'to lay down the general lines on which the industry should be run, but normally not to interfere in the detailed direction or in the complicated day-to-day problems of commercial management'.[16]

In a general report on 'Public Control and Regulation of Industry and Trade' (1932), the General Council of the Trades Union Congress expressed its views on the subject thus:

'It is doubtful, according to modern Socialist ideas, whether there is ever any advantage in conducting an industry or a commercial service by the method of direct state operation i.e. by a Government Department. State activities such as the general supervision and administration of national education, public health, postal service, and trade, as well as the older functions in relation to foreign affairs, finance and the rest, are obviously different in kind from the operation of services like Transport, Coal-Mining, etc. The former are typical Governmental functions which cannot be divorced from the machinery of State and Parliament. The latter are really commercial undertakings, whose business is production, not regulation and supervision.

The idea that socialization and public control of industries necessarily mean administration directly by a Government department dies hard, but it is dying in every country. The importance of flexibility and expert management on the one hand, and of freedom from party political domination on the other hand, has so far been recognised that (as in the Labour Government's London Passenger Transport Bill) the tendency

---

[16] *Report*, pp. 11–13. A few paragraphs later there is an even vaguer formulation, viz. 'In any reconstitution of the Board or dealing with its affairs in Parliament, it would be the duty of the Minister to satisfy himself that the proper principles were being carried out and that the direction and management were efficient, but subject to this he could not interfere, except as regards his own statutory powers'. (*Ibid.* p. 14.)

is to secure public control and the elimination of the profit motive while keeping the actual management in the hands of a body not susceptible to party political pressure and interference.'[17]

Subsequent reports on the nationalization of specific industries did nothing to amplify these views. In the Reports on the Socialization of the Iron and Steel Industry (1934) and on the Socialization of the Cotton Industry (1935) there is not the briefest reference to the parliament-minister-enterprise relationship, while the Report on the Socialization of the Coal Industry (1936) simply repeats the view already expressed in the Labour Party Report on Transport, saying that the nationalization statute 'should, as far as practicable . . . define the respective responsibilities of the Minister of Mines and the Corporation' and that 'the corporation would be responsible for the effective direction and control of the industry, subject to any limitations or ministerial checks as may be laid down by Statute'.

Belief in the possibility and desirability of separating economic administration from political government (reminiscent of Engels's famous distinction between the 'government of persons' and the 'administration of things') was almost universal, particularly among the trade unionists. At the T.U.C. of 1932, C. G. Cramp, the Railwaymen's Secretary, supporting the Executive Committee's 'Control of Industry' report (a document which gave little satisfaction to the advocates of workers' control), said:

'There are some of us who are very dubious about the political control of industry . . . I do not believe that you can deal with industry adequately by having it in the hands of party politicians. We do not want in this country the jobbery which exists in some cases on the other side of the Atlantic.'

At the same Congress Ben Turner, of the Textile Workers, moved a resolution requesting the General Council to submit a report on industrial organization which would 'give consideration to the problem of the separation of the political and economic

---

[17] The T.U.C. had already expressed similar views in the evidence it had given to the 'Macmillan' Committee. See the Summary of its Evidence in the T.U.C. *Report* of 1931, para. 292.

functions, and the establishment of a representative industrial authority to control and coordinate industry'. Seconding, Maurice Hann of the Shop Assistants drew favourable attention to Winston Churchill's proposals for the establishment of an economic sub-parliament and told those who had been blaming the politicians for the state of British industry: 'It is no use railing against the House of Commons or against the Labour Government; you are asking them to accomplish something which I think it is impossible to accomplish through the political machinery entirely'. The resolution was carried. Unlike Cramp, Hann was a workers' control man, who, at the 1933 T.U.C., supported Charles Dukes's 'industrial democracy' resolution. On this occasion he revealed, in the following words, the close association in his mind between workers' control and political insulation:

> 'If the principle of democracy were to prevail, the unions must have the right beyond question to elect the people they considered fit to sit on the controlling boards of socialized industries. They could not permit the appointments to be made by political ministers.'

In the same debate, another prominent trade unionist, Jagger of the Distributive and Allied Workers, attacked Morrison's reliance on the 'administrator and technical expert', not on the grounds that these specialists would be insufficiently subject to ministerial control and parliamentary supervision, but because their place 'was not at the top but below, and acting under the instructions of the *workers* who should direct the policy'.

By the 1930s, then, there was substantial agreement between the political parties, at least at the official level, on the need to insulate the nationalized industries from political control by setting them up as public corporations over which ministers should possess no more than strictly limited and clearly defined powers. It is pertinent to ask why this agreement remained substantially unbroken and why the status of the industries then nationalized was not attacked in the way that of previous *ad hoc* administrative bodies, such as the Poor Law Commission and the Board of Health, had been.

It is not sufficient to say that the pre-war public corporations, in contrast with the post-war ones, were responsible for only a very small sector of the country's economic life. This, of course, is true, but it is also true that at least one of the corporations, the Central Electricity Board, had a key role to play in Britain's economic development, in so far as it was responsible for the construction and operation of the national electricity grid. More important was the fact that the operations of these bodies rarely raised vital constituency issues. One must also remember that, in the pre-war climate of opinion, Members were perhaps less prepared than they are today to consider themselves competent to discuss business matters, which they tended to regard as technical mysteries. An even more important factor would seem to be the *success* of the pre-war corporations as commercial concerns. For their Conservative originators, this was a matter of legitimate pride; for the Labour Party, it 'proved' that socialism, even thouhg limited by Conservative prejudice and the vested interests of private business to a comparatively narrow field, was not only a possible but a superior method of industrial organization. This, one may judge, particularly in the light of subsequent experience, was the fundamental reason why the fears regarding the 'irresponsibility' of the public corporation, expressed by certain Members in the 1926 debates on the Electricity Bill, became allayed, and why the nationalized industries did not become involved in political crises of the kind that made the life of the Poor Law Commission nasty and that of the Board of Health short.

It is not surprising, therefore, that Members rarely protested with much vigour against the limitations of their opportunities to debate the affairs of the public corporations. Even such opportunities as were available were not frequently used. Up to 1937, Members had 'never availed themselves of the opportunity to discuss the Port of London Authority, like any other subject, on the adjournment or a Private Member's Motion'.[18] The Central Electricity Board, although frequently the subject of Questions, was rarely debated on Ministry of Transport Estimates, only once on a Private Member's Motion, and never on the Adjournment.[19] Although parliamentary discussion of the London Passenger

[18] Lincoln Gordon: *op. cit.* p. 35.
[19] T. O'Brien: *British Experiments in Public Ownership and Control*, London 1937, p. 82.

28

Transport Board was more frequent, the reason for this was simply that nearly every year it had to promote private bill legislation, in order to obtain the compulsory powers that it required. Parliamentary Questions about the Board's affairs were 'not . . . at all numerous' and never did it become the subject of a 'full dress debate'.[20]

In general, then, satisfaction with the performance of the Boards made it easy for Members to agree with the 'philosophy' of public enterprise proposed to them by Mr. Hore-Belisha, the Minister of Transport, during a debate on the affairs of the Central Electricity Board:

> 'It is surely in the philosophy of instituting great public boards to administer public utilities that we should give those boards something approximating to the business latitude which is allowed to ordinary boards in conducting private business. If every step that they take is to be looked upon with lack of confidence, and if it is to be suggested that their day-to-day transactions are to be closely scrutinized . . ., their capacity to bring about the public good for which we look to them will be severely hampered. The Central Electricity Board is not a profit-making concern. It has a single-minded purpose and a sole duty of guarding the common interest.'[21]

Only the B.B.C., which was a very special kind of public enterprise, sailed rather frequently into rough parliamentary waters. The day-to-day administrative duty of this corporation was to produce radio programmes, about which Members had widely-differing and sometimes violently-held opinions. Moreover, if its geographical coverage was inadequate, as was bound to be the case when demand was tending to outstrip supply, constituents were liable to be aroused. Hence the opportunities for discussion available were comparatively widely used, and Members sometimes chafed at the limitations on ministerial responsibility.[22] To

[20] *Ibid.* p. 272.
[21] H.C. Deb., 5s., Vol. 295, col. 1132, 29 Nov. 1934, quoted in Gordon: *op. cit.* p. 112.
[22] See *ibid.* pp. 176–82. The extent of ministerial responsibility for B.B.C. programmes was thus defined by Sir William Mitchell-Thomson, the Postmaster-General, in 1928: 'In the ordinary matters of detail and day-to-day
[footnote continued on page 30]

this extent the B.B.C. was the exception that proved the rule, giving point to Mr. O'Brien's cautious prophecy that if the 'functions and responsibility' of a corporation such as the C.E.B. ever came to be extended the parliamentary calm in which it lived might well be disturbed.[23]

What, above all, preserved the belief, in the 1930s, that nationalized industries could be run 'non-politically' was that the idea of national economic planning had not up to that time found any significant practical expression. Although interest in it had been greatly stimulated by the joint impact of the World Economic Crisis of 1929–33 and the planning experiences of the Soviet Union, it remained unacceptable to the majority of Conservatives, and even the Labour Party's ideas on the subject lacked precision. Moreover, there was a widespread opinion, rather typical of the times, that such planning organs as might be needed could themselves be given *ad hoc* status and removed to some distance from the sphere of politics. We have already seen that this was G. D. H. Cole's opinion in 1929. It also finds expression in that very influential book, *The Next Five Years*, *An Essay in Political Agreement*, published in 1935 under the signatures of a great array of distinguished people, including prominent members of the Conservative, Liberal, National Liberal and National Labour Parties. Here is proposed the establishment of a National Development Board, 'charged with the duty of promoting a long-range programme of national development and conservation, and a programme of useful public works available for use whenever required', and of a National Housing Commission, with 'a whole-

---

[*footnote continued from page 29*]

working, the governors are absolutely masters in their own house. I do not interfere and do not seek to interfere with their absolute freedom in those respects . . . If any honourable member of the (Supply) Committee, therefore, is desirous of making remarks on the character of the programmes, all I have to say is that I shall faithfully see that what he says is conveyed to the British Broadcasting Corporation and the governors thereof; but . . . I firmly refuse to have any responsibility for these details . . .

As regards matters of general policy . . . I am prepared to take a certain measure of responsibility—because, of course, we must retain a measure of control over larger matters of policy.'

This must have been one of the first statements in which the now-familiar unclarity of the distinction between 'general policy' and 'day-to-day administration' was made manifest.

[23] *Ibid.* p. 80.

time chairman of high standing and expert knowledge, with a status different from that of the head of a branch of a Government Department'. Admittedly, the authors are insistent that these bodies should work under the direction of, and in closest collaboration with, a ministerial Government Planning Committee, but nevertheless indicate that they should enjoy some kind of specially-protected status. The National Development Board, for instance, is to be a 'self-financing' body, deriving its funds, not from the budget, but from earmarked taxes, from the Road Fund and from 'a tax imposed on property values enhanced by public action', while the constitutional position of the National Housing Commission is specifically compared with that of the London Passenger Transport Board. A not dissimilar view was expressed by Hugh Dalton, in his *Practical Socialism for Britain* (1935), a book fairly representative of 'middle-of-the-road' Labour thought in the 1930s. Somewhat cautious and ambiguous—although perhaps less so than G. D. H. Cole—about the roles of Ministers and Parliament, Dalton suggests that his State Planning Department (a staff agency of the Cabinet Economic Planning Committee) should 'stand a little detached from' ordinary political life, in much the same manner as a public corporation.

Thus neither planners nor anti-planners saw any need to limit the autonomy of the public corporation. The anti-planners saw its task as the straightforward commercial one of fitting its operations into the framework of a more or less self-regulating economy; the planners were anxious to extend the principle of autonomy, which seemed to be working well in the existing public corporations, to the planning machinery itself, Dalton, indeed, juxtaposed 'the plans of the different corporations' with 'the larger national plan', implying that the change of scale had no qualitative significance.

It may be admitted that, in the works we have quoted, there were certain incidental or parenthetical indications that these lines of advance might involve difficulties for constitutional and democratic government. Cole, for instance, wrote: 'Many Socialists . . . will doubtless express the fear that the creation of this great network of administrative machinery will in effect give us Socialism without democracy, and place society in the hands of the expert rather than of the representatives of the ordinary man'. But he did not appear to share these apprehensions. The authors of *The Next Five Years* said that they 'realized the difficulties, as to ambiguous authority, etc.' involved in their proposal to establish a National Housing Commission, but immediately expressed their conviction 'that the new economic tasks confronting the government in our time necessitate an extension of the machine of government by the association, under appropriate conditions, of specialized bodies with a different constitution and status from the customary branches of Government Departments'.

By and large, such difficulties were emphasized only by a handful of writers who, although professionally or academically concerned with politics, were somewhat off-centre in the intellectual environment of the 1930s. Among them were Hugh Molson,[24] Ivor Jennings[25] and Stafford Cripps[26].

None of these, however, saw the essential issues as clearly and sharply as the Australian professor, F. A. Bland, who proclaimed: 'Political blackmail assumes many forms, but I suggest that the most sinister fashion in which it can operate is through a Commission which the public believes to be independent of political control'. On the 'dilemma' of the public corporation, he wrote:

'The fact is that the statutory government corporation is out of harmony, if not quite inconsistent, with the old theory of parliamentary government and ministerial responsibility. That theory asserted that the government ought to be called to account for everything that happened. But ought it to be called to account for the acts of a Corporation which Parliament has created with a "responsible management"? And if the Government cannot be called to account for the actions of the Corporation, how is the Corporation itself to be kept in harmony with public opinion?'[27]

In the totally changed circumstances of the post-war world, this question, which so many people of so many different persuasions had chosen to disregard, again became the subject of lively debate.

[24] *Parliament and the Independent Boards*, in *The Nineteenth Century*, Vol. 123, January 1938.

[25] *Parliamentary Reform*, Gollancz, Ltd., London 1934.

[26] *Democracy Up-to-Date*, Allen & Unwin, Ltd., London 1939.

[27] *Some Implications of the Statutory Corporation*, in *Australian Quarterly*, Vol. 9, No. 2, June 1937.

III

Ministerial Powers
and Parliamentary Opportunities

As far as the subject of this study is concerned, the situation after 1945 contained two new elements. The first was the acceptance by almost all sections of opinion of the need for economic planning of some kind, together with the knowledge and experience of planning techniques that had been acquired during the war-time. The second was the accession to office of a Labour Government, backed by a large parliamentary majority and committed to the policy of nationalizing some of Britain's major and basic industries.

If the economy was to be planned and the public sector greatly extended, new thinking about nationalization would have to take place, sooner or later; for war-time experience dispelled the illusion that planning could be a non-political function and it was obvious —or should have been—that a basic industry, nationalized and geared to the requirements of a national plan, could not possibly enjoy the kind of autonomy which had been given to the pre-war public corporations.

To say that Labour was fully conscious of the implications of 'planning plus extended nationalization' would be an exaggeration. Nevertheless, one point had become firmly established in the minds of those responsible for framing post-war policies: that ministerial powers over nationalized industries would have to be made more comprehensive.

As far as one can discover, this need was first clearly stated in the T.U.C. document entitled *Interim Report on Post-War Reconstruction* (1944), where it was presented as what the authors apparently regarded as a minor amendment to the 1932 policy statement, *Public Control and Regulation of Industry and Trade*, whose 'main argument for the establishment of Public Corporations'

33

they thought to be sufficiently important and sufficiently valid to quote in full. After supplementing this with some general remarks about the composition and method of appointment of the boards, they continued as follows:

> 'It will be necessary also to provide for the ultimate responsibility of the managements of socialized industries to a Minister in order to ensure the proper co-ordination of their policies and that the industries are conducted in full accordance with the Government's general plans for the maintenance of employment, the control and the location of industry, and the furtherance of socially desirable expansions of consumption.'

Later in the Report, under the heading of 'Selection of Workpeople's Representatives', the same point was put rather more strongly, viz:

> 'Ultimate control over the policy and direction of a public industry must be exercised by Parliament as representatives of the community in general. Public control must be secured by the definite responsibility of a Minister to Parliament for the industry's affairs. This in turn must be ensured by placing the administration of the industry in the hands of persons responsible to the Minister for that administration.'

Nowhere was there any indication that the T.U.C. realized that it was, in effect, demanding a fundamental change in the pre-war constitutional status of the public corporation, or that it saw any possibility of contradiction between 'definite responsibility to Parliament for the industry's affairs' and 'management in the hands of a body not susceptible to party political pressure and influence'. The leaders of the trade union movement, who ignored this problem in the 1930s, were only half aware of its existence even in 1944.

The need for stronger ministerial powers, however, was well understood, and accordingly provided for in the first major nationalization measure, the Coal Industry Nationalization Act of 1946. We may disregard the numerous specific provisions for ministerial intervention which are scattered throughout the Act, as these are mainly concerned with the process of transforming the coal industry from a private into a public concern. The main 'novelties' are gathered together in Section 3, which reads as follows:

(1) The Minister may, after consultation with the Board, give to the Board directions of a general character as to the exercise and performance by the Board of their functions in relation to matters appearing to the Minister to affect the national interest, and the Board shall give effect to any such directions.

(2) In framing programmes of reorganization or development involving substantial outlay on capital account, the Board shall act on lines settled from time to time with the approval of the Minister.

(3) In the exercise and performance of their functions as to training, education and research, the Board shall act on lines settled as aforesaid.

(4) The Board shall afford to the Minister facilities for obtaining information with respect to the property and activities of the Board, and shall furnish him with returns, accounts and other information with respect thereto and afford him such facilities for the verification of information furnished, in such manner and at such times as he may require.

The vagueness of these clauses, and the virtual impossibility of securing their enforcement by legal action, must have been profoundly shocking to the more old-fashioned kind of parliamentary draughtsman. Their general tenor, however, is quite clear. The National Coal Board is to manage the industry,[1] but ultimate responsibility for policy is the Minister's.

When these clauses were being debated in the House of Commons[2] the Conservative Opposition was quick to remind the Labour

[1] Its duties are defined as '(a) working and getting the coal in Great Britain, to the exclusion (save as in this Act provided) of any other person; (b) securing the efficient development of the coal-mining industry; and (c) making supplies of coal available, in such quantities and at such prices, as may seem to them best calculated to further the public interest in all respects, including the avoidance of any undue or unreasonable preference or advantage.'
[2] H.C. Deb., Vol. 418, 29th January 1946.

Party of its previous advocacy of autonomy for the public corporation, and to accuse it of inconsistency. Contrasting Mr. Morrison's
statements on ministerial function in *Socialisation and Transport*
with Mr. Shinwell's in the current debate, Mr. Anthony Eden said:
'I have a slight suspicion that the Rt. Hon. Gentleman is trying
to make the best of both worlds, that he is trying to tell those
behind him that he could use wide powers to introduce the Socialist
control of industry, while he can reply to critics over here that the
Board is an entirely independent enterprise, only subject to general
direction.'

Severer strictures came from a back-bencher, Mr. J. S. C. Reid
(Glasgow, Hillhead), who pointed to the now famous 'general
directions' clause as a potential source of trouble, saying 'that
this bill makes it possible for the Minister to be the complete
dictator of the mining industry. It enables the Minister to use the
Board as a mere facade, behind which he can retire when convenient.'[3]

Prophetically, he claimed that nobody could ever know whether
a particular decision had been taken by the Board 'on industrial
grounds', or forced upon the Board 'by the Minister on political
grounds'. He was less prophetic, however, in attributing this
ambiguity to the failure of the Bill to provide for the publication
of general directions—an omission subsequently rectified by a
Lords' amendment which the Government accepted.

Replying for the Government, Mr. Morrison expressed the
view that Parliament would 'find a way', issued one of his oft-
repeated warnings against 'meticulous political interference',
and somewhat ambiguously prophesied that in 'a high proportion
of cases' the use of the general direction would 'not be necessary
at all'. It was left to Mr. Gaitskell, in the Third Reading Debate,
to attempt a closer definition of what the Government had in mind.
He began by drawing a distinction between two enterprises which
he regarded as being at opposite ends of the scale. On the one
hand, there was the Post Office.

'There we have a trading organization; but it is entirely
financed by the State, and is completely controlled by a
Minister of the Crown responsible to Parliament for all its
details, and its employees are civil servants'.

[3] *Ibid.* col. 798.

At the opposite end, the London Passenger Transport Board.

> 'The Board has finance of its own, not backed by State credit. The Minister has not even the power of appointment to the Board, and Parliamentary control is remote in the extreme, and scarcely arises at all, except when the Board happens to have to come to Parliament for fresh powers.'

Other existing state enterprises occupied various points between these two extremes. For instance, 'the Central Electricity Board is not so far from Ministerial control as is the London Passenger Transport Board; the British Overseas Airways Corporation is still nearer to what I may call the Post Office alternative.'[4]

Enunciating a general principle, Gaitskell said: 'As we tend towards greater Parliamentary control, so we dispense with the extent of statutory control'. In this scale, the Coal Board would occupy a 'mid-way' position. There was general agreement that the Minister should have powers over training, education, safety, health, research, borrowing, and the form of the accounts, and his control over capital expenditure was an essential feature of economic planning. 'I do not believe', he concluded, 'that there is any real disagreement on all this. No-one really wants the Minister to interfere in the day to day affairs of the National Coal Board'.[5]

But Mr. Macmillan, the Opposition spokesman, remained unconvinced. He criticized the relevant provisions of the Bill firstly on the ground that they did nothing to solve the problem of creating 'an economic democracy parallel with the political

[4] B.O.A.C. was not mentioned in the last chapter, because it was constituted on the eve of the war and never came into effective operation. Of the B.O.A.C. Act, Mr. D. N. Chester writes:

'It contained many more references to Ministerial control than did, for example, the London Transport Act, 1933. The Act provided for Ministerial approval for certain types of action which the B.O.A.C. might have wished to take, e.g., operating an internal air service, or acquiring or constructing an aerodrome. Some of the main provisions for Ministerial control were to apply only so long as the Government were subsidising the Corporation, or making payments under a Treasury guarantee, e.g. Ministerial control was required for capital expenditure in this period.' (*The Nationalised Industries, an Analysis of the Statutory Provisions*, Allen & Unwin, Ltd., 2nd Ed. London 1951, p. 13.)

[5] H.C. Deb., Vol. 423, cols. 46–8.

democracy which has come to its full estate'. Developing a positively syndicalist line of thought, which consorted rather oddly with his Conservatism, he said:

'This Bill vests ownership of all the colliery undertakings in a board of nine men—nine men not elected by, not even containing, a single representative of the mining community. It is not nationalization in the old sense of the word . . . This is not Socialism; it is State capitalism. There is not too much participation by the mineworkers in the industry; there is far too little. There is not too much syndicalism; there is none at all . . . To the men, the new owners will mean the Board. However gifted or eminent they may be, they will be more remote and more soulless than the the old owners.'

His second criticism was that the Board would 'have neither the authority and independence of a statutory company or public utility organization, nor the proper position of a Minister in a ministerial department.'[6] Much more was to be heard of these criticisms during subsequent years.

As is well known, the Coal Industry Nationalization Act set the pattern for the post-war minister-enterprise relationship, to the extent that such a relationship could be prescribed in terms so ill-defined. The provisions of subsequent nationalization acts differ in detail, but not in principle. In no case was the vital clause empowering the Minister to issue 'general directions' omitted. Details, of course, varied considerably, as a result of the differences in the structures established by statute for the various nationalized industries. Coal, where the Minister exercised his supervisory authority over a single national Board responsible for the whole industry, provided the simplest and most straightforward example of the new relationship—a model, as it were. Electricity, on the other hand, presented a picture of much greater complexity as a result of the creation, in addition to a Central Electricity Authority, of 12 partially autonomous and independently appointed Area Boards with distributing functions. In the original Act of 1947 the Central Authority was empowered to give to the Area Boards

6 *Ibid.* cols. 132–6.

directions similar in scope to those which it was liable to receive from the Minister—for the purpose of 'co-ordinating the distribution of electricity by the Area Boards and exercising a general control over the policy of the Boards'. The Minister, nevertheless, retained the right to issue orders direct to the Area Boards in respect of certain matters. He could, for instance, vet their 'general programmes' for training, education and research, control the disposal of such assets as they might possess which were 'not connected with the distribution of electricity', and order them to provide him with information and opportunities for verifying it.[7]

In Gas, the most completely 'federalized' of all the nationalized industries, he was empowered to give 'directions of a general character' to the Area Boards generally, to a particular Area Board, and to the Gas Council itself. The reorganization and development schemes of *each* Area Board, moreover, were to be in accordance with 'a general programme settled . . . from time to time with the approval of the Minister'. Their research, training and education programmes, however, were to be settled merely 'in consultation' with the Minister. (Gas Act, 1948.)

In addition to these general powers, the Minister received a great variety of specific ones, varying in number and importance from statute to statute. Indeed, a listing of these formal powers might give the impression that there was little that the industry could do without consulting the Minister and obtaining his approval at one stage or another. During the second reading of the Gas Bill, Mr. Brendan Bracken noted that 'in twenty-eight places it empowered the Minister to make regulations, in nineteen places it empowered him to give directions, and in twenty places it gave him powers of approval'.[8] A mere listing of powers, however,

[7] These provisions were altered by the Electricity Act, 1957, to correspond with the new structure given to the industry by that Act. By Section 8, the Minister received the power (1) to give general directions to the newly-constituted Electricity Council and to *any* of the Electricity Boards (including the Generating Board) in England and Wales; (2) to approve measures of reorganization and works of development involving substantial capital outlay proposed by *each* of the Boards, in consultation with the Electricity Council. It was also provided that the Boards might be required to supply information, not only to the Electricity Council, but 'if the Minister so requires, to the Minister'.

[8] *Nationalised Industry: The Powers of the Minister*, Acton Society Trust London 1951, p. 2.

gives a false impression; for many of them were included simply to facilitate the complicated process of bringing the Act into effect and were of a kind that any important 'reform' measure was bound to contain, while others were not dissimilar from those to be found in pre-war nationalization acts, such as the Electricity Act and the London Passenger Transport Act. Nevertheless, certain 'specific' powers went well beyond any precedent. By the 1947 Transport Act, for instance the Minister was authorized, 'after consultation with the Commission', to direct them 'to discontinue any of their activities, dispose of any part of their undertaking, dispose of any securities held by them, call in any loan made by them or exercise any power they may possess to revoke any guarantee given by them'. In addition, he might by order provide for the 'number and names' of the Executives to which the Commission was expected to delegate certain of its powers, and each scheme of delegation was made subject to his approval. The Commission's Area Road Passenger Transport schemes and Harbour schemes were also subject to Ministerial approval by order, and its 'co-ordinating' powers with regard to coastal shipping were made subject to such directions as the Minister thought fit, after consultation with a Coastal Shipping Advisory Committee.[9]

The reason for these extensive 'specific' powers is obvious. The Transport Commission had not been presented with the whole of British transport, as the Coal Board had been with all—or nearly all—British coal. The anticipated co-existence of a public with a private sector, uncertainty as to where the boundary between the two should run, and the alleged desirability of close co-ordination between them, meant that, in default of a long series of complicated and time-consuming amending Acts, the area of the Transport Commission's jurisdiction had to be left vague. The decisions that

[9] These provisions were substantially modified by the Transport Act of 1953, the most important of all measures for the amendment of a nationalization act. An interesting feature of this Act, from the standpoint of ministerial powers, is its provisions for the reorganization of the railways. By Section 16, the Transport Commission is required to formulate a reorganization scheme, and to submit it to the Minister, who, after consultation with representatives of persons likely to be affected, is to confirm it with or without modifications, *by order*, and not simply by the signification of his approval. This order takes the form of a Statutory Instrument requiring the positive confirmation by resolution of each House of Parliament. A scheme may be amended or revoked on the initiative of the Commission, *via* the same procedure.

would have to be made in these matters, however, were clearly of such economic and political importance that they could not be simply confided to an *ad hoc* body. The latter might propose— and indeed was the only body with the necessary specialized knowledge to do so—but it was up to the Minister with the approval of Parliament to dispose. Hence, the post-war Transport Commission could not be placed on the same footing as the pre-war London Passenger Transport Board, for the greater the number of enterprises that were drawn into the nationalization net, the more numerous and important became the political, as distinct from the purely technical, decisions that had to be taken.

Civil Airways were also subject to unusually stringent (if not unusually detailed) ministerial powers. By the Civil Aviation Act of 1946 the Minister was empowered to limit, by order, the powers of any of the corporations 'to such an extent as he thinks desirable in the public interest, by providing that any power of the corporation specified in the order shall not be exercisable except in accordance with a general or special authority given by him'. He might also 'direct' that the aircraft used by the corporation should 'be registered in some part of His Majesty's dominions'.

At the beginning of each financial year each corporation had to submit to him (a) 'a programme of the air transport services which the corporation propose to provide during that year and of the other activities in which the corporation propose to engage during that year and (b) an estimate of the revenue to be received by the corporation during that year and of the expenditure to be incurred by them on revenue account during that year'.

In the light of this information, the Minister and the Treasury would decide 'whether any Exchequer grant should be made to the corporation concerned for the year in question, and, if such a grant is to be made, the basis on which the amount thereof is to be calculated'. The Act also contains unusually lengthy sections on 'Accounts and Audit' and 'Annual Report and periodical returns'. These latter provisions were obviously justified by the fact that the corporations, at that time and for some years to come, were heavily dependent upon annual Exchequer Grants. The former ones, together with the many specific ministerial powers authorized by other measures, such as the Air Navigation Acts, owed their existence to certain features peculiar to this nationalized industry, such as the dependence of its operations on international agreements.

Any attempt to give a fuller account of ministerial powers over the post-war nationalized industries would be inappropriate in this context, as we are concerned with general principles rather than with matters of detail, and as the reader seeking further information may readily find it in Mr. D. N. Chester's invaluable booklet, *The Nationalised Industries, An Analysis of the Statutory Provisions* and may also consult the Appendix to the Acton Society's pamphlet, *The Powers of the Minister*. In subsequent chapters, the general rather than the specific powers of the Minister are the ones that will receive emphasis, because these constitute the major novelty in post-war nationalization measures, so far as enterprise-minister-parliament relationships are concerned, and it is these that have been the source of so much difficulty and controversy. Nevertheless, it is useful to remind ourselves that the specific powers are both extensive and important, because a great deal of the discussion that has taken place has tended to assume that only the existence of general powers has made possible greater and more continuous parliamentary control of the affairs of the nationalized industries. In point of fact, many of the questions and debates with which we shall be dealing have been stimulated by the exercise of specific powers which, as illustrated, are in some cases far more extensive than in pre-war days and not infrequently exercisable by orders which bring into operation the provisions of the Statutory Instruments Act of 1946.

The extension of ministerial responsibility, along the lines we have indicated, has necessarily increased Parliament's opportunities for intervention, by way of Question and Debate; and the importance and political sensitivity of the newly-nationalized industries, together with the fact that nationalization itself has been politically controversial, has ensured that these opportunities should be used to the full.

The most important occasions for parliamentary discussion were, of course, provided by the nationalization bills themselves. They can hardly be described, however, as opportunities for the exercise of parliamentary *control* (whatever that rather ambiguous expression may mean), because the House of Commons was then discussing the very powers that it proposed to confer on itself—

42

deciding, in fact, on how much parliamentary 'control' there should actually be. But amending legislation, more important and frequent than was perhaps originally envisaged, has often provided the House with a chance to consider the affairs of a nationalized industry fairly comprehensively and at some length. Major amending legislation, such as the Air Corporations Act and Coal Industry Act of 1949, the Transport Act of 1953 and the Electricity Act of 1957, enables Members to raise almost any point they wish that is relevant to the industry concerned. The same may be said of the short bills, which are presented to the House almost annually, to permit a nationalized industry to raise further capital, and of the very important Act of 1956, together with its subsequent re-enactments, prescribing that the industries should henceforward obtain their capital funds from 'below the line' budgetary sources. The Act temporarily subsidizing the Transport Commission, by advancing to it large sums of capital on which it was excused, for several years, from making payments of interest, also provided an occasion for wide-ranging debate. Further opportunities are provided, from time to time, by Private Bills, such as those which the Transport Commission has to promote rather frequently in order to give itself the power to interfere with certain property rights. Although the content of such Bills is very limited, the Speaker has ruled that the scope of debate on them may be fairly wide. The Acton Society's prediction, made in 1949, that debates on legislation relative to the nationalized industries 'are likely to occur rarely', has thus hardly been borne out by events.[10] Since then, the following Acts dealing with the nationalized industries have been passed: Air Corporations Act, 1949; Coal Industry Act, 1949; Coal Mining (Subsidence) Act, 1950; Coal Industry Act, 1951; Transport Act, 1953; Air Corporations Act, 1953, Gas and Electricity (Borrowing Powers) Act, 1954; Transport Charges (Miscellaneous Provisions) Act, 1954; Electricity Reorganization (Scotland) Act, 1954; Transport (Borrowing Powers) Act, 1955; Transport (Disposal of Road Haulage Property) Act, 1956; Coal Industry Act, 1956; Air Corporations Act, 1956; Electricity Act, 1957.

The most regular occasion for formal and comprehensive debate is provided by the annual submission to the House of Commons,

[10] See *Nationalised Industry: Accountability to Parliament*, Acton Society Trust, London 1950, p. 17.

by the Minister, of the Report and Accounts of a nationalized industry. There is no rule, however, that Reports and Accounts shall always be discussed, and indeed those of the gas industry have never been the subject of a separate motion. As only three days are normally provided for 'Reports and Accounts' debates, it follows that only some of the nationalized industries can be covered in this way each year. It has become standard practice for the Government, at the request of the Opposition, to propose the 'neutral' motion that 'this House takes note of the Annual Report and Statement of Accounts' of whatever industry has been selected through consultation 'behind the Speaker's chair', and to provide time (usually about six hours in the case of a major nationalized industry) for this motion's debate. The Opposition does not usually move an Amendment, but may do so if it feels particularly strongly about the Government's behaviour towards the nationalized industry during the period under review.

Supply Days may also be used to debate the nationalized industries, on the Vote for the appropriate ministry, if the Opposition wishes to use for this purpose the time which, by convention, is placed at its disposal. Another, less frequent, occasion for important and wide-ranging debate has been the ministerial presentation of long-term plans for the development of the fuel and power industries and the transport industry. The Queen's Speech, 'Welsh' days, 'Scottish' days, motions for the Adjournment (half-hour, urgency, and recessional), and motions for the confirmation or 'prayers' for the annulment of Statutory Instruments have offered further—although more restricted—opportunities. Once, as we shall see, the House has held a debate on a general direction. Finally, there are Questions, the scope of which has been the subject of considerable and occasionally rather bitter controversy.

These are the main occasions when the House as a whole considers the nationalized industries; but no summary of its opportunities would be complete without reference to two Select Committees. The Reports and Accounts, when laid on the Table, are automatically available for consideration by the Public Accounts Committee, which used occasionally to examine them and take evidence. As the financial records of the industries were not open to expert examination by the Comptroller and Auditor General however, the Committee was deprived of the services of its watch-dog in respect of these particular accounts, and consequently could not do very much about them. Hence, since the establishment of the Select Committee on Nationalized Industries (Reports and Accounts), the Public Accounts Committee has given up the attempt, gratefully surrendering the function of examination and report to the new body, whose simple and vague terms of reference enable it to range as far and as wide as it wishes. The work of both of these Select Committees will be the subject of detailed inquiry in Chapter VI.

How was it originally envisaged that ministerial responsibility for and parliamentary supervision of the nationalized industries would work? To answer this question is not easy, for the more intelligent parliamentarians on both sides realized that a field so new and experimental was wide open for the development of conventions the precise shape of which could hardly be predicted. What actually happened, however, was certainly not expected by the promoters of the post-war nationalization acts, although, as we have seen, it was forecast in general terms by some of their Conservative critics. Certainly, the general impression one receives from a perusal of the nationalization debates is that, despite the introduction of the 'general directions' clause, Labour Ministers and Members did not envisage that the enterprise-minister-parliament relationship would be fundamentally different from the pre-war one. Autonomy was still the watchword, and one was given a broad picture of an industry left free, for most of the time, to 'pursue the public interest in all respects', and having only occasional contact, of a rather formal kind, with a comparatively remote ministerial master. Statutory approvals, of course, would have to be applied for and received, and from time to time—particularly, perhaps, when the Board and the Minister failed to see eye to eye on an important matter of general policy—there would be a direction, delivered in writing and later reproduced in the Annual Report. As for Parliament, it would debate the general progress of the nationalized industries at rather infrequent intervals and from time to time hold the Minister to account for the exercise of his statutory powers. The relationship, perhaps, would not be quite so cut-and-dried as this summary of it suggests, but the general feeling, undoubtedly, was that once the Minister had performed his essential task of appointing the most competent people to run the industries' affairs, they ought to be left to get on with the job without very much ministerial or parliamentary interference.

All this was a mere pipe-dream. Both the short-term and the long-term situations proved to be quite different from those envisaged. In the short run, of course, trouble could be quite reasonably expected. Until the Conservative Party could decide just how much nationalization it was prepared to accept, the newly-nationalized industries were bound to constitute battle-grounds over which nationalizers and anti-nationalizers fought their wordy warfare, without too much respect on either side for the somewhat intangible constitutional conventions that were supposed to limit the scope of the conflict. Faced with grave shortages of equipment and manpower, the industries could give scant satisfaction to the consumer, whose self-appointed champions on the Opposition benches, smarting under the impact of the greatest electoral defeat they had ever experienced, were hardly in a mood to respond to appeals that they should give the newly-appointed managers a chance to show what they could do.

Although these somewhat prolonged birth-pangs were later assuaged, it had become abundantly clear, by the early 1950s, that even under more normal circumstances the post-war nationalized industries could not become depoliticized to the extent that the pre-war ones had been. The public interest which they were supposed to follow was too important to be left to the more-or-less autonomous judgement of *ad hoc* bodies, and their day-to-day decisions had so many policy implications that it was difficult to say where administration left off and policy began. The Minister, whether he liked it or not, became deeply and continuously involved, and invariably acted as the spokesman of the industries in the House and before the public, defending them from attack and implying that *his* policy was to be judged by *their* performance. More surprisingly to those who falsely imagined that constitutional practices could be prescribed by statute, all this happened without the issue up to 1952 of a single general direction of any significance, with the result that Parliament naturally began to wonder who precisely was responsible for what and to suspect the existence of a Hewart-type conspiracy between minister and enterprise to evade democratic controls.

One incident, in particular, gave Parliament an early insight into the peculiarities of the situation that was developing. In July 1948, the 'Clow' Committee recommended that there should be seasonal variations in electricity charges for domestic consumers. The object was to avoid load-shedding by the Electricity Authority's generating stations during the winter months. After the Authority had announced its acceptance of this recommendation, the Minister was asked, in the House of Commons, what directions he had given 'for the application of the Clow Committee's proposals for seasonal variations of domestic charges'. In his reply, he said that he had given no directions, but had simply asked the Electricity Boards to put the recommendations into effect.[11] In subsequent answers, defending the decision, he continued to suggest that there was complete agreement on the matter between the Electricity Authority and himself.[12] But in the summer of 1949, the B.E.A., in its First Report and Accounts, stated that it had been 'reluctant to implement the proposed differential charge', the 'efficacy' of which it had doubted.

'The apprehensions of the Authority and the Area Boards', it continued, 'proved to be well-founded. As the winter progressed, no evidence was forthcoming of any appreciable effect on peak loads even in the case of districts with a predominantly domestic load. The consumption of electricity outside the peak load period was, however, adversely affected; and further, there were many cases of serious financial hardship among smaller consumers. There was a growing volume of public protest, and it became clear that in spite of the care that had been taken to explain the nature, reasons and effects of the proposals, the goodwill between the electricity supply industry and its consumers, which had been built up over many years, was being jeopardised. As soon, therefore, as the ineffectiveness of the proposal in relation to the peak load problem became apparent, the Authority and the Area Boards, with the support of the Consultative Councils which had in the meantime been set up, made strong representations to the Minister

[11] H.C. Deb., Vol. 457, 14th November 1948, Written Answers, col. 128.
[12] H.C. Deb., Vol. 461, Written Answers, cols. 181–2; Vol. 463, cols. 538–9; Vol. 466, cols. 732–3.

that the differential should be discontinued at the end of the nine months period.'[13]

On 11th July 1949, the Minister announced that he did not intend to 'ask' the B.E.A. to repeat the experiment in the winter of 1949–50.[14]

Here was one of the first clearly-authenticated cases of the use of 'old boy' methods. That the decision was the Minister's and that the B.E.A. regarded itself as bound by it was fully apparent from the fact that the Authority felt unable to rescind the differential on its own initiative, without obtaining his approval. Yet, although this was a matter of considerable public importance, the Minister had issued no direction, and had allowed the British Electricity Authority to incur most of the odium for what those of us with recollections of the winter of 1948–9 remember as an unpopular policy. Furthermore, the truth about this incident would never have been revealed if the British Electricity Authority, braving the wrath of the Minister, had not chosen to 'spill the beans' in its Report.

The Affair of the Clow Differential is here presented not as typical but as symptomatic. We just do not know how many similar 'affairs' there have been, any more than we know the number of unrecorded 'Crichel Downs'. It showed that the Minister was intervening in a sphere of decision-taking somewhere between policy and day-to-day administration, and doing so by methods which made the enforcement of his responsibility to Parliament very difficult. Some, at least, of the autonomy which was supposed to be the birthright of the public corporation had been quietly transferred to him. It appeared, therefore, that there was arising between the enterprise and the minister a relationship which was new, unforeseen and constitutionally dangerous. Consequently, the 'Clow' case reinforced the arguments of those who were already claiming (a) that the constitutional position of the nationalized industries needed to be redefined, and (b) that more effective and less capricious forms of parliamentary supervision needed to be devised.

During the passage of years since the 'Clow' dispute, the informal, ill-defined and constitutionally 'messy' minister-enterprise

---

[13] British Electricity Authority: *First Report and Accounts*, August 1947–March 1949, H.C. Paper 336 of 1948–9, paras. 355 and 357.

[14] H.C. Deb., Vol. 467, cols. 6–8.

relationship then revealed has become almost *de rigueur*. The Conservatives who, when in opposition, criticized it most violently, seem to have made it their very own. Indeed, it could be argued that a new and unexpected constitutional convention is in the process of consolidating itself. For none of the guardians of constitutional chastity expressed any sense of outrage when Sir John Maud, in the smoothest of civil service manners, revealed to the Select Committee on Nationalized Industries (Reports and Accounts) the full intimacy of the relations between the National Coal Board and the Ministry of Power.[15] Nor was there anything in the nature of an outcry when Sir Ian Horobin, on behalf of the Minister of Power, rejected the Select Committee's proposal that the Minister's 'gentlemen's agreement' with the National Coal Board about coal prices should be replaced by formal 'approval' machinery.[16]

But the periodical complaints about this situation that arise in the House of Commons are evidence of continued uneasiness. Government spokesmen themselves have sometimes admitted that it is an unsatisfactory one for the Boards, as well as for Ministers and parliamentarians. There may, of course, be reasons for believing that the new conventions will, in the long run, come to be generally accepted; for the British constitution has an unrivalled capacity for the quiet assimilation of novelties of all kinds. 'Give things an opportunity to settle down' is a comfortable and complacent doctrine but nevertheless one that can sometimes be recommended. It does not, however, exempt the *status quo* from reasoned criticism, and there is a great deal in the particular *status* with which we are here concerned which both merits criticism and is receiving it. Furthermore, the argument that those things which have become, or are likely to become generally accepted, are necessarily the best possible under the circumstances is a poor one, far too often employed.

In the discussion which occupied the first part of the last chapter we saw that the nationalized industries presented in a peculiarly acute form one of the most important problems of democratic government, viz. how to control 'the bureaucracy' without making it into 'a bureaucracy' in the popular, red-tapish sense. The

[15] H.C. 187–I of 1957–8, Minutes of Evidence, Qs. 28–32.
[16] See below, p. 153.

particular bureaucracy here under examination is the administrative and managerial personnel of the nationalized industries. It is alleged that too much political control will compel these people to follow cautious, unenterprising, unimaginative civil-service-type routines which are quite incompatible with the efficient management of large commercial concerns. Too little political control, on the other hand, will enable them to avoid democratic responsibility and build up an *imperium in imperio* of dangerous dimensions. Clearly, the problem *as thus stated* can be solved only by compromise—and so indeed it has been solved, if one can talk in terms of a solution in these comparatively early days. We have stretched the meaning of our nationalization statutes to allow the Minister to exercise powers much wider than those originally envisaged by the men who drew up the statutes and by the Parliament that passed them; but we hope that he will exercise them reasonably and do not try to insist, by meticulous legislative provision, that everything he does should be open to parliamentary and public inspection. This is one way; but it is not necessarily the best way. In trying to get the best of both possible worlds, we may have got the worst: red tape without responsibility. It is also possible that our whole thinking on the subject has got into a rut, in so far as, up to the present, we have merely attempted to adapt pre-war institutions and pre-war procedures to the qualitatively new requirements of the post-war age, and have failed to profit sufficiently from the experience in this field of other countries, less deeply devoted than ourselves to constitutional traditions. A further—and even more serious—possibility is that the very terms in which we have posed the problem are wrong, and that the dilemmas with which we imagine ourselves to be confronted are not the real ones.

These are questions which demand serious and sustained inquiry. Some attempt will be made to answer them in the last chapter of this book, but first the materials for an answer must be assembled. Our immediate task is to subject the existing forms of parliamentary 'control' of the nationalized industries to a more detailed analysis, beginning with one of the most controversial, the Question.

IV

Questions

MR. HUGH MOLSON, one of the pioneers of new forms of parliamentary control over the nationalized industries, once described the Question as 'casual, capricious, superficial and inconclusive'. Mr. Baird, who from the other side of the House supported Molson's campaign, called it 'completely ineffective'.[1] There is much to be said for these rather unorthodox views, and no one, I think, would suggest that the Question has provided the House with the most useful of the devices for keeping the nationalized industries under supervision. Nevertheless, the Question provides our inquiry with a useful *point d'appui*, because (1) it was in connection with the allowability of specific types of Question that the issue of ministerial and parliamentary powers was originally and most sharply raised; and (2) it was the very failure of the Question to elicit the kind of information to which Members considered themselves entitled that sparked off the debate on other forms of control.

On the admissibility of Questions generally, Erskine May says the following:

> 'Questions addressed to Ministers should relate to the public affairs with which they are officially connected, to proceedings pending in Parliament, or to matters of administration for which they are responsible.'[2]

In the light of this general principle, Questions 'raising matters under the control of bodies or persons not responsible to the Government' are categorized as inadmissible. 'Certain public

[1] H.C. Deb., Vol. 458, col. 1731; Vol. 435, col. 2304.
[2] *Parliamentary Practice*, Sixteenth (1957) Edition, p. 356.

corporations' are quoted among the examples of such bodies or persons.[3]

In ordinary circumstances, the application of these rules causes little difficulty. Even for public corporations, in pre-war days, the dividing line between the admissible and the inadmissible was fairly clear, in so far as the respective duties of the corporation, the Minister, and various *ad hoc* supervisory bodies (such as the Electricity Commissioners) were closely defined by statute. The 'general directions' provisions of the post-war nationalization statutes, however, created an entirely new and extremely fluid situation. As the extent of ministerial responsibility largely depended on the Minister's own interpretation of a vaguely-worded clause, admissible and inadmissible Questions could not be defined in advance. All the Table could do was to let through Questions on subjects that *prima facie* engaged ministerial responsibility, see whether the Minister was prepared to accept responsibility, and then disallow all subsequent Questions similar to those which he had rejected as relating to 'matters for the Board'.

Not unnaturally in the political circumstances of 1946, the Opposition was prepared to throw consistency to the winds and try to make the Minister accept responsibility for as much as possible; while the Government, quite reasonably suspecting the Opposition of employing the Question for the purpose of discrediting the very principle of nationalization, was determined to interpret ministerial responsibility as restrictively as it could.

The game began some three months before the first of the major nationalization acts became operative. On 8th October 1946, in answer to Mr. Crossthwaite-Eyre, the Minister of Fuel and Power, Mr. Shinwell, refused to disclose the salaries of members of Divisional Coal Boards, on the grounds that 'under the Coal Nationalization Act the National Coal Board is given full freedom . . . to settle its own organization and the terms on which it engages staff, in the same way as other statutory and commercial undertakings'. Having no official responsibility for the matter, he declined to give information about it.[4] During subsequent months, he also denied responsibility for and refused to give information about the following:

[3] *Ibid.* p. 360.
[4] H.C. Deb., Vol. 418, cols. 723, 798.

(a) The ages of members of the Divisional Coal Boards;
(b) the allocation of the global sum of £10,000 assigned to
members of the National Coal Board for their expenses; (c)
the amount and cost of transport in London provided for
Coal Board members; (d) the number of staff employed by
the N.C.B.; (e) the qualifications and experience of the members of the Divisional Coal Boards; (f) the number of non-
industrial staff employed by the Board; (g) the purchase of
Himley Hall by the Midland Divisional Coal Board; (h) the
employment of private firms for underground surveying and
their charges; (i) the total cost of Vesting Day celebrations;
(j) the number of workers employed in adapting Sherwood
Lodge as the East Midlands Divisional Coal Board's headquarters; (k) the material and cost of N.C.B. flags; (l) merchants' contracts; (m) damage by subsidence in West Bridge-
ford; (n) the use of former private property by the N.C.B. in
Edinburgh; (o) the allocation of contracts of service by the
N.C.B.; (p) a Coal Board poster alleged to contain 'provocative and crude political propaganda'; (q) the number of staff
in the South West Division, and the number of Powell-
Duffryn employees who had received employment from the
Board; (r) the making of *ex-gratia* payments to Durham
miners by the N.C.B. 'in connection with the recent strikes';
(s) the purchase of houses by the Board (Mr. Boyd-Carpenter:
'the expenditure of large sums of money on the purchase of
large and luxurious houses for senior officials'); (t) the removal
of colliery office furniture for the benefit of the Divisional
Boards.[5]

This list clearly shows that many questions were being asked
simply to throw as much dirt as possible at the newly-nationalized
industry, particularly by spreading rumours about its administrative extravagance and bureaucratic top-heaviness. Many of
them, moreover, referred to matters which were unmistakably
within the field of day-to-day administration and for which no
self-respecting Minister, acting within the terms of reference set

[5] A. H. Hanson: *Parliamentary Questions on the Nationalised Industries*, in
Public Administration, Vol. 29, Spring 1951, p. 53, and references to Hansard
there given.

by the nationalization act, could possibly agree to take responsibility. Mr. Shinwell's refusal to give information, however, was open to criticism, for there was nothing to prevent him from using the well-worn 'I am informed by the Board . . .' formula, and his silence, which could be interpreted as arising from the fact that there were things that he wished to hide, may have defeated its own purpose by giving the rumours wider currency. It could also have been argued—and indeed was argued—that some of the Questions, although having day-to-day matters as their immediate targets, raised more general issues which could conceivably become the subjects of general directions. If, for instance, the Coal Board was in fact employing excessive numbers of non-industrial staff, or failing to discharge its responsibilities with regard to mining subsidence, or using its publicity machine to disseminate political propaganda, could the Minister reasonably claim that these were not matters for his consideration? Before long, the Minister himself was compelled to admit that what was superficially a day-to-day decision could give rise to a general issue affecting the national interest. Asked about the Coal Board's administration of the miners' cottages which it owned, he first employed the 'I am informed' formula. Then, when pressed by a Supplementary to say 'as a matter of policy whether he proposed to continue a system under which a man retains a cottage so long as he is employed, and loses it when he is no longer employed', the Minister replied:

> 'That is a matter within the jurisdiction of the National Coal Board—but if as a result of the activities of the National Coal Board some acute controversial issue arises affecting the public interest, I may have to intervene'.[6]

In general, however, Mr. Shinwell interpreted the Morrisonian doctrine very strictly—more strictly, in fact, than Morrison himself had interpreted it in *Socialisation and Transport*, where he stated that the Minister should normally answer on behalf of the Board, even while accepting no responsibility for the content of his reply.[7] This strictness would have been more tolerable to inquisitive

[6] H.C. Deb., Vol. 434, col. 638.
[7] *Socialisation and Transport*, Constable & Co. Ltd., London 1933, pp. 172–3.

Members if it had been consistent; but it was not. Sometimes, provoked beyond endurance, he would decide that rumour-killing was, after all, part of his function. Thus, in answer to a Question about the number of staff employed at the London Headquarters of the National Coal Board, he said, after first covering himself by pointing out that this was a matter for the Board:

'In view . . . of the recent statement in the Press that the Headquarters staff of the Board had reached the alarming total of 11,000, the Board have asked me to let the House know the truth'.

Then, having stated the facts, he indicated in reply to a supplementary question that information about the Coal Board's staff would not, in future, be 'automatically' available, and concluded, rather ambiguously, that whether a Question was answered or not depended on its 'merits'.[8]

In an Adjournment Debate on 21st October 1947, Sir John Mellor, whose persistent sniping from the Conservative back benches was one of the features of this Parliament, alleged that the Minister 'had elected to pick and choose the Questions which he would answer, apparently according to his taste and fancy'.[9] It did indeed look like that, but there may have been more consistency in Mr. Shinwell's practices than at first appeared; for one must remember that the Minister had powers and responsibilities, not only under the Coal Industry Nationalization Act, but under the Ministry of Fuel and Power Act, 1945, the Acts relating to health and safety in the mines, and the Defence Regulations. Hence his preparedness to answer Questions about such day-to-day matters as pit ponies (Coal Mines Act, 1911), underground gasification (Ministry of Fuel and Power Act, 1945), exports, stocks and the disposal of 'washery slurry' (Defence Regulations). But in between these and the ones that he rejected on the grounds that his responsibility was not engaged by any Act of Parliament or instrument of delegated legislation lay a miscellaneous and disorderly collection of Questions to which he replied 'on behalf of the Board', having decided, apparently, that these related to matters

[8] H.C. Deb., Vol. 436, cols. 2148–50.
[9] H.C. Deb., Vol. 443, col. 45.

on which information *could* be given without undermining the Board's administrative autonomy. Thus, the 'I am informed by the National Coal Board' gambit preceded factual answers on the following subjects:

> (a) Screening; (b) 'tied' cottages; (c) alleged attempts by the Board to prevent its employees from taking part in public work; (d) pay arrangements for night-shift workers; (e) the lighting of colliery sidings; (f) the number of miners transferred to the North Staffordshire area; (g) the re-employment of miners receiving compensation payments; (h) the object of the magazine 'Coal' and its anticipated size of circulation; (i) the extent to which the regrouping of collieries had effected economies of personnel; (j) the recruitment by the National Coal Board of engineering graduates; (k) the maintenance of local holiday customs; (l) the refusal of the National Coal Board in Notts to allow 'private enterprise' to pick coal from dirt tips; (m) the number of vacancies for coal face workers in South Wales; and (n) the progress achieved in the re-employment of partially disabled miners.[10]

It is possible that some of these matters were regarded as coming in the category of training and education, or within the scope of the Defence Regulations, or under the heading of miners' welfare. If so, it is difficult to see why the Minister was not prepared to accept responsibility as well as to give information—unless it was felt that they were all marginal cases, where he ought to tread cautiously so as to avoid creating precedents. Perhaps they were all matters of principle, as one who was concerned with the preparation of the answers once suggested to me? If so, the 'I am informed' formula is even more difficult to understand. On any interpretation of the Minister's statutory powers, it is not easy to see why these were selected for answer while other, very similar ones, were rejected. The fact is, of course, that the Minister and his civil service advisers were attempting to feel their way through a field scattered with imperfectly-discerned booby-traps—now advancing, now retreating, now hesitating, all the time fearful lest, by making the wrong move, they might set off a series of parliamentary detonations

[10] Hanson: *op. cit.* p. 56, and the references there given.

which would rock the incomplete and experimental structure of the National Coal Board to its foundations.

The Table itself was in a similar dilemma. Although not concerned, like the Minister and his advisers, with protecting the nationalized industry, it was very anxious to preserve consistency and at the same time allow for flexibility. In order not to set too rigid a precedent, and to allow the Minister himself the opportunity of deciding on the extent to which his responsibility was engaged, it would occasionally let through Questions which, according to the record of those to which answers had already been refused, were on the borderlands of 'Order'. The Minister, equally in doubt, would then devise as non-committal an answer as he could. As I have written elsewhere:

> It was all rather difficult, and *Hansard* provides occasional evidence of a state of chronic indecision. Miners' coal allowances, for instance, were subject to Defence Regulations and embodied in wages agreements. The Minister could alter the terms of the Regulations, if he so wished, but did not regard himself as competent to interfere with wages by general direction. His dilemma is reflected by the fact that he gave straightforward answers to two Questions on this subject, countered a third with 'I am informed . . .', and finally proclaimed that the matter was one for the National Coal Board, while expressing his 'personal opinion' that the allocations should be maintained during the fuel shortage. On being asked whether it was not a subject on which he was competent to issue general directions, he replied, 'It is in the national interest to see that the miners get a fair and square deal'.[11]

The trial and error process continued, under slightly calmer circumstances, when Mr. Gaitskell took over the Ministry of Fuel and Power. Like the former Minister, Gaitskell was determined not to give too much away. Asked by Sir John Mellor whether he intended to continue his predecessor's policy with regard to the answering of Questions, he replied that power and responsibility must march together, and that if he tried to obtain, for the benefit of the House, too much information, 'he would in fact be producing just that kind of bureaucratic paralysis which it was the

[11] *Ibid.* p. 56.

intention of the Act to avoid'. He would not be able to stop at giving information; he would have to anticipate supplementary Questions, and 'from this he would be led inevitably to intervene and control'. At the same time, he admitted that the distinction between day-to-day and policy matters was by no means clear, and proceeded to point out to Members that the existence of the 'general directions' clause gave them an opportunity which few of them, up to that time, had recognized or seized, viz.: 'to ask him, (i.e. the Minister) and expect a reply, why he has not made a direction on something which the Member thought he ought to have made a direction.'[12]

In practice, too, Gaitskell proved more flexible and conciliatory than Shinwell. He engaged in some effective rumour-killing,[13] used the 'I am informed' formula rather more frequently, and often passed on to the Board Questions which he felt demanded an answer but not a ministerial one. He also, on several occasions, used the device of wording an answer in such a way as to leave the extent of his responsibility deliberately vague. Did the Minister expect difficulty in selling 15 million tons of coal abroad?—'I *think* we can leave that matter to the National Coal Board to settle.' Would the emphasis be on long-term rather than on short-term contracts?—'There again we must *to some extent* leave that to the National Coal Board.' Would the Minister use his planning powers to give directions that no colliery should be closed unless all fit men under fifty-five could be found work in industry?—'I *think* we can leave these matters to the National Coal Board and the National Union of Mineworkers to settle'.[14]

Mr. Gaitskell's accession to office coincided with a reduction in the number of Coal Board Questions appearing on the Order Paper. This, however, was by no means entirely to be explained by the fact that the new Minister's parliamentary manners were less provocative than those of the old. It was partly due, no doubt, to the dying down of the coal crisis, and one may surmise that Conservative back-benchers felt that persistent attacks on the Minister and the Board were yielding decreasing political dividends. But probably more important was the fact that the Table had by

[12] H.C. Deb., Vol. 443, cols. 49–50, 74–7.
[13] See, for instance, H.C. Deb., Vol. 446, Written Answers, col. 258.
[14] Hanson: *op. cit.* p. 58.

this time accumulated abundant precedents for the rejection of Questions similar in nature to those previously refused by the Minister. As the body of precedent was built up, it became more and more difficult for Members to obtain from the Minister even a denial of responsibility for an alleged day-to-day matter; for their Questions, unless dealing with matters for which ministerial responsibility was clear or with those for which the minister had not already disclaimed responsibility, never even reached the Minister's desk. Many found this situation intensely frustrating, and hence began to direct their attack on the rules governing the eligibility of Questions. Frustration was increased by three additional factors, viz. (a) that the transfer of an industry to public ownership actually *decreased* Members' opportunities to inquire into the details of its administration, in so far as many of the government's former 'emergency' powers over it, being then transferred to the Board, ceased to be matters of ministerial responsibility; (b) that, in 1947, two further industries, electricity and transport, were added to the nationalized list, and that one of these, transport, was at the very centre of political controversy; and (c) that the Minister responsible for bringing the Transport Act into operation and for supervising the Transport Commission, Mr. Barnes, was even 'stickier' than Mr. Shinwell—a 'most skilful refuser and persistent evader of questions'.[15]

The first major attack on the 'eligibility' rules was made at Question Time on 4th December 1947. Mr. Morrison used the opportunity to reiterate his well-known views on the subject, and the Speaker to make a statement which, although not free from ambiguity, offered no real concession. After admitting that the problem was 'rather difficult', and referring to the 'usual practice' and the 'precedents of the last war', he said:

'The Minister is always entitled on public grounds to refuse to give an answer. That is perfectly clear. If he refuses to give an answer, that is the Minister's responsibility, and it has nothing to do with me. Therefore, I cannot authorise the Table to go behind the Minister and insert a Question a second time. The . . . remedy is to put down a motion of censure on

[15] *Nationalised Industry: Accountability to Parliament*, Acton Society Trust, London 1950, p. 7.

59

the Minister . . . for refusing to reply. That is outside my control'.[16]

These exchanges were followed, in February 1948, by a full-scale debate on ministerial responsibility for nationalized industries,[17] which was notable for Captain Crookshank's attempt to secure the acceptance of revised rules on the admissibility of Questions. He considered that there should be no restriction on the right of Members to put Questions on the Order Paper, that it was the Minister's and not the Table's duty to decide whether a Question should be answered or not, and that in the performance of that duty the Minister should have regard to the distinction between day-to-day management, which was not Parliament's concern, and day-to-day *administration*, which was. To illustrate this rather new and over-subtle distinction, Captain Crookshank took the example of a hypothetical late train. If it was late once, that could be the result of bad management; if it was late persistently, there must be something wrong with the administration of the railway line. He concluded by asking the Speaker to show 'great generosity . . . in the matter of the admissibility of Questions', and by demanding that 'factual, statistical, non-controversial, nonpolitical information which can be obtained by the Minister should be given to Members if they want it.' Although supported by speakers from all three parties, Crookshank did not dislodge even a brick from the solid Morrisonian wall; hence it was inevitable that the dispute should break out again with renewed vigour. Several Members attempted, without success, to persuade the Speaker to modify his previous rulings, and one Member, Mr. Teeling, occupied 42 minutes of adjournment time with a matter of detail on which his Question had been refused.[18]

It was electricity load-shedding that eventually brought matters to a head; for the existing rules were made to look merely ridiculous when Members found themselves unable to question the Minister about a serious electricity breakdown, affecting a considerable part of the country. Even Mr. Morrison could not now deny that the eligibility of Questions was a problem that ought to be

[16] H.C. Deb., Vol. 445, cols. 565–71.
[17] *Ibid.* Vol. 448, cols. 391–456.
[18] See below, p. 80-1.

'considered'.[19] His promise to consider it, made on 26th May, was followed, five days later, by an announcement from the Speaker that the whole matter of Questions on the nationalized industries was under discussion between Mr. Morrison and himself.[20] On 7th June 1948, the Speaker proposed the new and more liberal ruling which is still in force.

'It is the rule against the repetition of Questions already answered, or to which an answer has been refused', he said, 'that has had the largest share in excluding Questions . . .'

'I have come to the conclusion that in the case of an entirely novel branch of administration, such as that relating to the nationalised industries, the strict application of the Rule might operate more harshly than either Ministers or Members generally would wish. I am, therefore, prepared to make a suggestion which I hope will recommend itself to the House, for the power of dispensing with its recognised rules belongs to the House alone and not to me.

'I propose to leave the Rule which excludes Questions on matters outside Ministerial responsibility unchanged. But I am prepared, if it is generally approved, to exercise my discretion to direct the acceptance of Questions asking for a statement to be made on matters about which information has been previously refused, provided that, in my opinion, the matters are of sufficient public importance to justify this concession. "Public importance" is one of the tests for Motions for the Adjournment of the House under Standing Order No. 8, and in my experience is not an unduly difficult test to apply.'[21]

Although criticized by several Conservative and Liberal Members, this proposed ruling was accepted by the House without debate. It opened a chink in the ministerial armour, but not a very big one, and disputes about the admissibility of Questions continued, although with considerably less vigour. There were still complaints about the difficulty of eliciting from Ministers straight-

[19] See H.C. Deb., Vol. 451, cols. 208–16.
[20] H.C. Deb., Vol. 451, cols. 642–4.
[21] H.C. Deb., Vol. 451, cols. 1635–43.

forward items of information about the nationalized industries,[22] and on 5th April 1950, Mr. Henderson-Stewart, after alleging that the present government policy whereby Ministers refuse to answer parliamentary Questions dealing with the day-to-day administration of nationalized industries frequently deprives Members of the opportunity of challenging Ministers on matters of public importance', suggested that the whole problem should be referred to an all-party committee for examination and report.[23]

Within two years, and as a result of a change of government, Mr. Henderson-Stewart's proposal had been put into effect. When the Conservatives took office, in November 1951, there was ten-days' interregnum during which the policy of the Labour Ministers in refusing to seek information for the benefit of parliamentary questioners automatically lapsed. Questions asking for such information could therefore get through to the Order Paper. Few Members, however, realized the existence of these new opportunities before the door was closed again—oddly enough by Captain Crookshank himself, now Leader of the House—on 12th November. But in closing one door, by stating that the practice of the former Government would be for the present continued, he simultaneously opened another, by announcing the impending appointment of a Select Committee to consider the whole matter of Questions on nationalized industries.[24] When actually appointed, on 4th December, this Committee was given much wider terms of reference, viz. 'to consider the present methods by which the House of Commons is informed of the affairs of the nationalized industries and to report what changes, having regard to the provisions laid down by Parliament in the relevant statutes, may be desirable in these methods'. The first of its two Reports, however, was devoted entirely to the matter of Questions.

The main value of this Report lay, not in its few and extremely cautious recommendations, but in the Minutes of Evidence annexed to it. There, for the first time, the officials of the House put

[22] See, for instance, H.C. Deb., Vol. 472, cols. 407–8, 453–5; Vol. 473, cols. 1187–90; Vol. 482, cols. 13–20, 207–8, 524–6.
[23] H.C. Deb., Vol. 473, cols. 1189–92.
[24] H.C. Deb., Vol. 493, cols. 648–50. Later, in evidence to the Select Committee, Captain Crookshank admitted that he had changed the views which he had expressed to the House in 1948. (*Report from the Select Committee on Nationalised Industries*, 1952, H.C. 332–I, p. 78, Q. 715.)

on full record the principles on which they acted in deciding the admissibility of Questions, and the chairmen of three nationalized industries expressed their reactions to this form of parliamentary inquisition. The officials' evidence, although voluminous, simply provided useful chapter-and-verse documentation for practices with which Members of the House were already generally familiar, and underlined the fact that a Minister's readiness to accept responsibility or to provide information was often a function of his own individual will or caprice. This emerged most clearly from the evidence given by Mr. Gordon, the Second Clerk Assistant, on the subject of ministerial answers on 'dirty coal'.

'The previous Minister of Fuel and Power', he said, 'answered on the subject of dirty coal on which there was a large number of complaints. We have now many fewer complaints about that, and the last answer we had to a similar Question which we put down, because the previous Minister regularly answered such Questions, was . . . "This is a matter for the Coal Board". Consequently, that shuts out, as far as we are concerned, the subject of dirty coal. If it is a matter for the Coal Board we can no longer put these Questions down because the Minister is no longer willing to answer them. That is a Question of a type now fully answered for this Session.'

The chairmen provided powerful, if not entirely disinterested, support for the views about the Question that Mr. Morrison, himself a witness, once again expressed. Lord Hurcomb, Lord Citrine and Sir Hubert Houldsworth were agreed that any extension of ministerial responsibility such as would be implied by a liberalization of the existing rules about Questions could have only an evil effect on the efficiency of the industries for which they were responsible.

'If a station master or someone in the provinces knew that what he had said or done or what he was doing was being made the subject of questions in Parliament, of course it would have an effect on his mind; and, speaking from the purely commercial angle, I think it has a bad effect,' said Lord

Hurcomb. 'To the public servant who is used to it, no; it may be a stimulus. But it would not work that way with a staff of 800,000 people up and down the country. It does not have that effect . . . I feel that in a big machine people who have to deal with a great many matters in their own discretion and often urgently would to some extent be paralysed if they thought they were going to be put under the harrow later in Parliament; and their instinct would drive them to say "We will not settle this ourselves; we will refer it to one above".'

In a later answer, he followed this up by denouncing the centralizing tendency of parliamentary Questions:

'The inevitable effect of constant Parliamentary Questions is to centralise. It undoes all that we have been endeavouring to do in the way of decentralising. We are always attacked for not decentralising, but the attack is not well founded. We have decentralised. The Commission does not seek to know anything about 90 per cent. of what goes on, but of course if the Minister is being asked Questions, he has to ask them for information, and then at once you begin to undo all that. It is a thing which puzzles me. There are so many critics who attack us for over-centralisation, and then almost in the same breath they want to impose on us arrangements which can only lead to a very heavily over-centralised system.'

Citrine was equally categorical:

'My experience', he said, 'is that one of the hardest things to do in a big organisation is to get people to take responsibility. There is a tremendous . . . fear of doing something which may be setting a precedent. . . We have striven hard for four years to try to get people to realise that they cannot expect everything to be done at the centre. In other words, we have pursued a policy of decentralisation. We have been saying to people, "We will accept a percentage of mistakes, we will not tell you what that percentage is. We will not guarantee we will excuse you a particular mistake, but we do not expect

perfection. We want you to take your responsibilities". I assure
you I feel certain, from my conversations with the people who
are running private industry, that this is not peculiar to
nationalisation; they have the same trouble to get people
ready to take decisions in commercial organisations. That
is a factor. I am certain, as sure as I am here, that what would
happen would be this: if all our day-to-day activities were
reviewed in Parliament, were liable to Questions and so on,
we should get the Civil Service mentality; we would never
make any mistakes, but, by Jove, what we did would take the
devil of a long time.'

Like the other two chairmen, Houldsworth said that he would
'deprecate' the admission of Questions on matters of 'day-to-day
management', considering that 'one of the gravest dangers in the
conduct of a nationalized industry was fear of taking decisions
because of the danger of public criticism of those decisions'. He
made it clear, moreover, that his interpretation of 'day-to-day'
was a pretty wide one. Asked whether he would describe the
employment of Italian labour in the mines as a matter of day-to-
day management or as one of policy, he replied that it was one 'on
which opinions might differ', but a 'good illustration' of where, he
hoped, 'the discretion would err on the side of treating it as day-to-
day management'. As for 'proposals to start opencast operations
in a new district', he 'conceded' that it was 'not a matter in which
the Coal Board alone could claim to have the deciding voice', but
only because 'agricultural interests as well as coal interests were
involved'.

These views, perhaps, gave no cause for surprise, but it was useful
to have them on record, and they provided powerful ammunition
for Mr. Morrison and his fellow-thinkers. Those, on the other hand,
who suspected that in this matter incantation was tending to replace
clear thinking, could derive comfort from the statement by Mr.
Noel-Baker, a former Minister of Fuel and Power and a politician
distinguished for his intelligence and integrity, to the effect that he
had found Questions 'not hampering' but 'valuable as a means of
securing improvement'. The Minutes of Evidence also provided
the heterodox with some confirmation of Noel-Baker's view that
the effect of questioning on 'the initiative of people on the

perimeter' was by no means as clear as the three Chairmen had suggested, but on the contrary 'very obscure'.[25]

But whatever the preconceived notions of some of its members may have been, the Select Committee obviously could not ignore the weight of the three chairmen's evidence, supported as it was by both the actual Leader and the former Leader of the House. Accordingly, its Report recommended that there should be no widening of the field of parliamentary Questions. Only in one matter did it recommend a change, expressing its conviction that 'the present method of placing the onus of determining in the first place whether a Question which is not obviously ruled out. . . . should be placed upon the Order Paper should not rest upon the Clerks at the Table'.[26]

> 'Where the identical Question, or the same Question in slightly different terms', it said, 'has been previously asked, the Clerks at the Table are clearly obliged to refuse it. But in the case of questions which are not obviously matters of repetition or matters of detailed administration the questions should be allowed to appear on the Order Paper and the Minister would have to answer or refuse to answer on the floor of the House.'

No action was taken on this innocuous recommendation, although it did receive brief discussion in the House, on a Private Member's Motion, introduced by Sir Edward Boyle,[27] which ran as follows:

> 'That this House, whilst recognising that the public corporations which control the Nationalised Industries should enjoy that large degree of independence in matters of current administration which is vital to their efficiency as commercial undertakings; none the less urges that Hon. Members should not be precluded from placing Questions on the Question Paper relating to the nationalised industries, provided that

---

[25] *Ibid.* p. 81, Q.733. Mr. Noel-Baker, it should be noted, was not a witness, but a member of the Select Committee.

[26] i.e. by the terms of the statute.

[27] H.C. Deb., Vol. 508, cols. 1989–2018, 19th November 1952.

both the subject matter of any such Question is not confined to administrative detail, and the same Question has not previously been asked.'

The 'exclusion of whole blocks of Questions from the Order Paper', he considered, was 'a serious matter'. To avoid it, more latitude was required. 'A number of individual cases', he said, could 'add up to a rather more important question of administration on which the Minister might be very glad indeed to make a statement'. There was, furthermore, an 'intermediate class of case' which went beyond 'one isolated point of detail' and involved 'a rather wider issue'. Among the concessions he suggested to cover these points, the most important was that the Speaker should take into account 'not only the intrinsic importance of the Question, but also the number of Hon. Members who are interested in it'.

The debate was notable for Mr. Noel-Baker's reiteration and amplification of the views about Questions that he had already given in evidence to the Select Committee. He believed that the parliamentary Question was 'a very powerful instrument of public control', well worth the time and trouble and money that it cost. Although he endorsed the exclusion of matters of administrative detail, he considered that when the Minister was in any doubt as to the appropriateness of a particular Question, he ought to err on the side of latitude and give a reply. As in his evidence, he strongly stressed the positive value of Questions and Debates as means to the improvement of administrative efficiency.

'Speaking from my own experience', he said, 'I would say that thanks to the debates and the Questions which were put, a large number of matters were dealt with which otherwise might not have been dealt with so expeditiously or so well by the nationalised boards. In the first six months that I was at the Ministry of Fuel and Power, 343 Questions passed the Table, of which 250 were on the nationalised boards and on allied questions of administration. As a result, more speedy action was taken about manpower in the mines, about dirty coal, about stopping competitive advertising between electricity and gas, and about power cuts, and I believe that the great increase in coal output in 1950–51, when the miners gave us that three million extra tons, was largely due to proceedings in this House.'

Another contribution worth noting was that from Sir Herbert Williams, one of the most persistent of questioners on matters of administrative detail. He admitted to having been persuaded by the Select Committee of the error of his ways. 'I started off', he said, 'on the assumption that we ought to take the lid right off, but the evidence has convinced me that to do so would produce an intolerable situation.'

Sceptical Members might have suggested—but did not actually suggest—that the replacement of a Labour by a Conservative Government could also have borne some responsibility for Sir Herbert's conversion.

In his reply to the debate, the Minister of Fuel and Power (Mr. Geoffrey Lloyd), while promising to discuss the Select Committee's Report with his colleagues, made no concessions to those Members who had asked for greater latitude. He emphasized how much work was involved in the preparation of answers even to ordinary parliamentary Questions, the subject matter of which was 'directly within the control of the Department concerned'. When the information had to be supplied by a 'big public corporation' further difficulties arose, as in the recent 'Scarcroft' case. As a result of that case, the Minister had 'had to tighten up still further the precautions which had to be observed for the absolute accuracy of the information supplied to the Department for the service of this House'. It had to be remembered that the people concerned with supplying such information were not 'used to working like civil servants in the knowledge that every single act they took might be questioned'. Freer questioning, therefore, could only increase their problems and add to their burdens.

Whether the Scarcroft case really illustrated the inability of people not 'used to working like civil servants' to cope with the parliamentary Question is open to debate. It might perhaps be more appropriately held to illustrate the distaste on the part of people engaged in breaking the law for parliamentary investigations (whether by Question or any other method) of their activities. However, it is important enough, in the present context, to warrant a brief narrative description.

QUESTIONS

This affair, which culminated in the prosecution of the Chairman and Vice-Chairman of the Yorkshire Electricity Board for contravening Defence Regulation 56A, was brought to light as a result of persistent parliamentary questioning by a Conservative back-bencher, Mr. Donald Kaberry. Mr. Kaberry's original Question asked for information about (a) the amount of the licence or other permit granted for the extension of the Y.E.B.'s headquarters at Scarcroft, near Leeds; (b) the date of the licence; and (c) the amount that had actually been spent or the value of the work done.

Mr. Noel-Baker, then Minister of Fuel and Power, gave the first two items of information requested. To the third he replied: 'I am informed that these sums have been spent and that the work is now complete'. It subsequently transpired that this last part of the answer was incorrect, in so far as the Y.E.B. had spent considerably in excess of the sums authorized. After an Adjournment Debate on the subject, the Attorney-General, Sir Hartley Shawcross, announced in reply to Questions by Sir Waldron Smithers and Mr. Kaberry that he had put the matter in the hands of the Director of Public Prosecutions. Later, he revealed that inquiries had shown a *prima facie* case of infringement of the Regulations and that criminal proceedings were being initiated. After the trial and condemnation of the Y.E.B.'s Chairman and Vice-Chairman, the new Minister of Fuel and Power, Mr. Geoffrey Lloyd, who was careful to exonerate his predecessor, Mr. Noel-Baker, from all personal blame, set on foot an inquiry, conducted by Sir G. Russell Vick, Q.C., to discover who was primarily responsible for the inaccuracy of the original information supplied to the House. After receipt of the report of this inquiry, Mr. Lloyd said in the House:

'I think a fair summary of his conclusion is to say that the main responsibility for the incorrectness of the information ... must rest on the senior officers of the Yorkshire Electricity Board ... But though misled by this information, the Departmental officers concerned must bear some responsibility for allowing a draft reply to go forward when it should have been obvious that no satisfactory reply could at that time be given.'[28]

[28] Those wishing to follow the development of the Scarcroft case from the parliamentary record should consult H.C. Deb., Vols. 482, 484, 485, 491 and 496.

From the above it will be clear that the more general conclusions drawn from the Scarcroft experience by Mr. Lloyd about the likely effects of freer parliamentary questioning on the nationalized industries were, to say the least, rather exaggerated. In reality, all that the case proved was (a) that those responsible for running a nationalized industry, if engaged in some shady deal, will do their best to conceal the fact from their Minister, even to the extent of providing him with false information; (b) that, in such circumstances, the civil servants through whom the information is transmitted will sometimes have the wool pulled over their eyes. Both conclusions are obvious, and have very little to do with the problems that we are examining.

After Sir Edward Boyle's motion of 19th November 1952, no further attempt to raise the general subject of the admissibility of Questions on the nationalized industries was made until 10th July 1956. Mr. Hobson (Labour, Keighley) then asked the Prime Minister if he would give instructions to responsible Ministers 'to answer questions about matters arising in the annual reports and accounts of the appropriate industries'. After the Prime Minister had replied that no change was called for, Mr. Hobson, in a supplementary, revealed the source of his worry.

> 'It really is becoming most important', he said, 'particularly with regard to the accounts of Cables and Wireless, where, on page 19, there is shown the revenue from subsidiary companies, and it is impossible to find out which are the subsidiary companies, even by reference to the Schedule of the Act. Will the right hon. Gentleman look at this matter again?'

The Prime Minister expressed his sympathy and said rather vaguely that if the House was to have a debate, the matter might be considered.[29]

It was in the autumn of 1959 that the question of Questions came back to somewhere near the centre of the political stage. This was partly due to the fact that the organization of British Railways was about to enter the melting pot, with the result that Members were more than usually curious about the affairs of the Transport Commission. Equally important was their desire to 'try out' the attitude

[29] H.C. Deb., Vol. 556, col. 193.

70

of the new Government, a practice encouraged by the suggestions in Conservative election propaganda that the time was coming when the board-minister relationship would need to be looked at anew.

As Leader of the House, Mr. Butler blew hot and cold. In a 'Business' discussion on 29th October, he suggested that the 'assumptions' under which the Speaker and the Table acted were open to question and would be the subject of 'consultation'.[30] A week later, in reply to Mr. Mellish's suggestion that the time had come 'when Ministers should accept full responsibility in Parliament for these Questions', he said:

> 'In this House we have to pay regard to the recent Report of our own Select Committee on the Nationalised Industries. We drew attention to the difficulty of unbridled Questions about the nationalised industries and also to some of the other difficulties, and we indicated the manner in which Questions might conveniently be asked. We must pay attention to the report of our own Select Committee in deciding procedure on this matter.'[31]

During the next few months several Members on both sides of the House showed a desire to slip the noose in which the eleven-year-old Speaker's ruling had caught them. Among them was Mr. Francis Noel-Baker (Labour, Swindon), the son of the former Minister of Fuel and Power whose mild unorthodoxy on the subject has already been noted. Having failed to get satisfactory answers from Mr. Marples, the Minister of Transport, about the B.T.C's utilization of its railway workshops, he raised the matter on the adjournment and used the occasion to demand that Questions on nationalized industries should be entirely freed[23]. Many Opposition Members, he said, were 'beginning to be apprehensive about the relationship between many nationalized boards and the general public'. That was why they were pressing 'for a clearer acknowledgement of Ministerial responsibility for the working of these nationalized boards' and why they hoped that during the

[30] H.C. Deb., Vol. 612, col. 380.
[31] *Ibid*. col. 1206.
[32] H.C. Deb.,Vol. 613, cols. 363–74, 19th November 1959.

lifetime of the existing Parliament they would be able to get answers to Questions 'covering some of the detailed work of these great nationalized industries'. The actual situation appeared to be that some of the nationalized industries were 'not more accountable to the general public, but less accountable than some private firms'.

The Parliamentary Secretary to the Ministry of Transport (Mr. John Hay), in his reply, carefully refrained from expressing any opinion on this part of Mr. Noel-Baker's speech, but made it clear that he and the Minister regarded certain matters, of which railway workshops were one, as 'entirely . . . for the Commission'.

On February 25th 1960, at the end of 'Business of the House', Mr. Butler made his promised statement, which ran as follows:

'Hon. Members have recently inquired about the scope for Questions on the nationalised industries.

'With your permission, Sir, may I say that we must adhere to the view that Ministers can answer Questions only on matters for which they have a recognised responsibility? Otherwise, they would inevitably find themselves encroaching upon the managerial functions entrusted to the nationalised boards.

'Ministers would, of course, answer for the matters which the industries are required by Statute to lay before them, and for appointments, finance and matters on which they themselves have statutory powers and duties. In addition, they may from time to time be concerned with other questions of broad policy affecting the industries.

'There is no hard and fast formula by which these matters could be identified and opened to Questions in the House, but provided Questions on the Paper relate to Ministers' responsibilities for matters of general policy, they will consider sympathetically the extent to which they can properly reply.'

This somewhat cryptic utterance provoked two questions from Mr. Gaitskell, who asked about the extent to which Ministers would be prepared to procure information for the benefit of Members, and about the practice whereby certain Questions were refused by the Table. Mr. Butler cautiously replied that 'Ministers wished to supply as much information as it is possible to provide if it does not contradict what I was saying', and that the 'difficult task' of interpreting the rules relating to the allowability of Questions was for Mr. Speaker.

Appealed to by Mr. Gaitskell, the Speaker could only reiterate the existing doctrine, with the following rather obscure 'gloss':

> 'Of course, if Ministers were to say at any one time that they would now be willing to answer Questions in a category in which they had not been willing to answer them before— I mean not by means of a private communication to the Table—then that would change the application of the rules of the House in that instance.
>
> 'I do not know how to change that, and, of course, it would be quite unworkable if Ministers were to give an *ad hoc* assent relating to a particular Question in a hitherto refusable category. I cannot help the House further than that. The Table must have some consistent principle by which it operates.'

Mr. Peart (Labour, Workington) then underlined the obvious by saying that there had 'been no change'. In response to questions by him, Mr. Driberg, and Mr. Silverman, Mr. Butler admitted that there was 'no very great extension', but rather curiously suggested that his statement with regard to 'Ministers' responsibility for matters of general policy' constituted a 'new point'.

Mr. Shinwell then asked for some definition of 'general policy'.

> 'A variety of issues have emerged', he said, '. . . on which Members desire to have information, and it is quite invidious that they should be compelled to write to the nationalised boards for information and very often not receive answers in reply.'

Mr. Butler refused to be drawn, but promised to 'take up the right hon. Gentleman's invitation and see whether, at a later date, we could carry this further'. In response to Mr. F. Noel-Baker's allegation that it was extremely difficult to extract information of general public interest either from the Minister of Transport or the Transport Commission, he stated that his colleagues desired 'to approach Questions put by hon. Members in the House in as sympathetic a manner as possible'. That was why he had suggested that 'we should give this matter a trial run'.[33]

There, for the present, the controversy rests.

During the last ten years, one of the features of the development of parliamentary questioning about the affairs of nationalized industries is the increasing skill which Members have shown in phrasing Questions in such a way as to get them past the Table and to compel the Minister to put up some kind of answer. The Table itself, in fact, has helped them to do this by suggesting forms of words. Nowadays, the favourite 'gimmick' is to ask the Minister what general direction he has issued, whether he has issued a general direction, or whether he will issue one. As we have seen, it was Mr. Gaitskell who, as Minister of Fuel and Power, first invited Members to make use of this ploy. They have responded most satisfactorily. In the majority of cases, of course, they do not really wish the Minister to use this power and almost invariably they would be exceedingly surprised if he did so. This was overtly recognized in an interchange, during the course of the Adjournment Debate of 19th November 1959, between Mr. F. Noel-Baker and the Parliamentary Secretary to the Ministry of Transport, Mr. Hay. After Mr. Hay had painstakingly explained that it would be inappropriate for him to use a general direction to deal with the matter on which Mr. Noel-Baker had requested ministerial action, the latter admitted that he had asked for a general direction only for the purpose of getting his Question past the Table and that the actual issue of a general direction was 'not the intention behind it'. To this, Mr. Hay replied: 'I was so recently on the back benches myself that I can remember that that is the drill one must adopt in these cases.'

During the Session 1957–8 a very high proportion of the Questions about nationalized industries were of this kind. Ministers were asked to issue directions for the following purposes: (a) to instruct the electricity boards to 'dispose of electrical appliances of all kinds'; (b) to order the British Electricity Authority 'not to refuse applications for employment on the sole ground that applicants are members of trade unions not affiliated to the T.U.C.'; (c) to accelerate the introduction by the British Transport Com-

[33] H.C. Deb., Vol. 618, cols. 577–83.

mission of automatic train control; (d) to regulate the 'allocation of contracts and sub-contracts to firms whose personnel are associated with the Central Electricity Authority and the area boards'; (e) to instruct the National Coal Board 'to give guarantees of coal tonnage for export to the continental market'; (f) to compel the mining industry to 'revert to the hours worked per shift before the 1926 lock-out'; (g) to deal with the closure of the less remunerative collieries; (h) to regulate the carrying out by the Electricity Boards of Section 29 of the Electricity Act, 1957, which required them to fix maximum charges for the resale of electricity to sub-tenants and other persons; (i) to instruct the North of Scotland Hydro-Electric Board 'not to defer connecting applicants for electricity for the sole reason that the necessary cables have to be laid underground'; (j) to instruct the National Coal Board to reduce its prices so as to encourage domestic sales of stocked coal; (k) to order the Gas and Electricity Boards to reduce expenditure on the modernization of their showrooms; (l) to effect the co-ordination of the National Coal Board's 'charges for coal to the publicly owned electricity and gas industries with those of similar grades of fuel sold to other industries generally'; (m) to bring about an increase in the export of coal and coke by the N.C.B. 'in view of the very large stocks in the country'; (n) to order the N.C.B. to reduce the price of small coal to the electricity supply industry; (o) to cause the Transport Commission 'to institute a general revision of all schedules in the light of existing traffic conditions'; (p) to regulate the fares charged by the Transport Commission in the London area; (q) to order the Commission to 'place all parts in the United Kingdom on the same footing in the matter of all charges within its control'; (r) to order it to consult the Transport Users Consultative Committees about the London Transport Executive's proposals to discontinue certain omnibus services; and (s) to order it to include among the members of its Boards of Management persons with experience in the organization of workers.

As might be expected, the kinds of answers given to these types of Questions varied considerably in accordance with the extent, if any, to which the Minister was prepared to take responsibility or to provide information. Sometimes, asked whether he would issue a general direction, he simply replied 'No'; asked what general directions he had issued or intended to issue, he replied

'None'. Rather more often, he supplemented this negative with a formal explanation to the effect that the matter was one of 'management' or for the 'commercial judgement' of the corporation concerned. Occasionally, when pressed by supplementaries, he encouraged the questioner to make direct representations to the Board or promised that he himself would see what he could do to draw the matter complained of to the Board's attention. Frequently, while disclaiming responsibility, he briefly indicated what the Board's policy was and stated, or implied, that it met with his approval. The Minister of Fuel and Power, for instance, after saying that the N.C.B. had to take 'its own decisions' about the closure of unremunerative pits, assured his interlocutor that all the closures had been 'carried out very smoothly indeed'. In refusing to issue a general direction to ensure that the N.C.B. would reduce its prices to encourage the domestic sales of its stocked coal, he explained that the increase in stocks had been 'almost entirely in coal in sizes too small for domestic use'. To justify his refusal to direct the Electricity Boards to reduce expenditure on modernizing their showrooms, he explained that the boards were 'already fully aware of the need to reduce all forms of capital expenditure to the minimum consistent with good commercial practice'. Asked to issue a direction to bring various coal prices into line with one another, he expressed the opinion that these prices were not in fact 'out of balance'. To supplement his 'None, Sir', to a questioner who wanted him to make a general direction about coal exports, he stated that the Board was 'already making every effort to increase exports'. To a questioner who wanted a direction for the revision of train schedules, the Minister of Transport explained that the British Transport Commission, whose responsibility this was, was 'already giving it special attention'. After stating, in response to another Question, that no general direction was necessary regarding passenger fares in the London area, he embarked upon a fairly lengthy justification of his refusal to issue one, using such expressions as 'The Chairman of the British Transport Commission told me . . .', 'The Commission intend . . .', 'They do not propose . . .', etc. Refusing to direct the Transport Commission to include on its Boards of Management people with experience of organizing workers, on the grounds that this was a matter within the responsibility of the

Commission, he added: 'It is clear from the appointments which it has made in recent years that it fully appreciates the value of a Trade Union background among other forms of experience'.

It would be useless to search for any principle governing ministerial replies to 'general direction' Questions. Only the form in which they are asked—which, in almost every case, is chosen simply for the purpose of getting them across the Table—differentiates them from Questions of a more normal kind. One cannot doubt that the Minister and his Civil Service advisers bear in mind the extent of his ill-defined statutory responsibility; but it is realistic and not unfair to suppose that the main consideration is what the Minister can get away with, in the light of a given political situation.

It is much the same with other Questions about nationalized industries. Those that simply asked for information (Session 1957–) received answers that can be divided into the following categories:

1. Refusal of information, accompanied by denial of responsibility, e.g., date of completion of railway workshop repairs; salaries of members of the B.T.C.'s Area Boards.

2. Refusal of information, accompanied by statements suggesting some degree of ambiguity about responsibility, e.g. N.C.B. recruitment policy, on which the Parliamentary Secretary said (a) that such policy was for the Board itself to formulate and (b) that he and his noble friend were 'in constant touch with the Board on all major questions of policy'.

3. Provision of information, unaccompanied by any statement about responsibility, e.g., the electrification of the Euston–Glasgow and Fenchurch St.–Tilbury railway lines.

4. Provision of information, preceded by the phrase 'I am informed that . . .' or 'I understand that . . .', e.g., amount of redundancy consequential upon the implementation of the 'Fleck' Report; percentages of home-grown and imported timber used in the mines; cost of distribution faciltes for the electricity produced by a North of Scotland Hydro-Electric Board project.

Those that asked the Minister to do something received the following treatment:

1. Straightforward refusal, e.g., many of the Questions asking the Minister to issue a general direction (see above).

2. Denial of responsibility, accompanied by an explanation of the Board's policies, e.g. treatment of railway superannuitants.

3. Denial of responsibility, accompanied by an explanation and justification of the Board's policies, e.g. effect of mechanization on the coal industry.

4. Denial of responsibility, accompanied by a promise to 'draw the Board's attention to' or to 'look into' the matter, e.g. alleged inadequacy of railway pensions; alleged failure of B.E.A. officials to change currency at the current rate; alleged discrimination by B.T.C. against South Wales Ports; alleged failure of B.T.C. to appoint to Boards of Management sufficient people with experience of organization of workers.

5. Statement that 'assurances' have been received from the board or that the 'Board is convinced' that its course of action is the right one, e.g., allegation of excessively remote control arising from structure of B.O.A.C.'s subsidiary companies; alleged excessive cost of North of Scotland hydro-electric schemes in comparison with alternative nuclear power schemes.

All the above examples have been taken from the Session 1957–8. Other recent Sessions, similarly analysed, yield almost precisely the same results. It is reasonable to conclude, therefore, that although there is by no means such a fuss about Questions as there was when the nationalized industries were new, the prospect then held out that clearly-defined conventions would gradually establish themselves has not materialized. Admittedly, a Member can easily discover, by consulting the Table, whether the Question he wishes to ask will be accepted. Once his Question has been refused, however, he knows that for the remainder of the Session he will be unable to obtain information on the subject that has stimulated his curiosity, no matter how urgent it may appear to him to have become—except in the rather unlikely event of the Speaker's ruling that it may be regarded as of major public importance. Furthermore—and it is this that most clearly emerges from the analysis—he has very little idea of what *kind* of answer he will receive to an accepted Question, for the extent to which a Minister

will provide information or admit responsibility, being subject to
no clear rules, cannot be predicted. Much would seem to depend
on how hard the Minister is pressed and on his views about what
is politically expedient. This, on any reckoning, is an unsatisfactory
situation, and it is not likely to be much improved by Mr. Butler's
recent ambiguous 'concessions'. But whether, although unsatisfactory, it is nevertheless inevitable, in view of the need to protect
the nationalized industries from over-detailed parliamentary inquisition, is a question that must be deferred to a later stage in this
discussion.

V

Debates

THE occasions when the House can debate the affairs of the nationalized industries have already been specified (see above, Chapter III, pp. 42-4). The purpose of the present chapter is to examine what use it makes of these opportunities.

It will be convenient to begin with Adjournment Debates—not because these are the most important, but because many of them arise directly out of Questions. As is well known, a Member who considers that the Minister has answered his Question unsatisfactorily sometimes announces that he will raise the matter again on the Half-hour Adjournment Motion. Members successful in the ballot or selected by the Speaker may also use this occasion to ventilate matters on which their Questions have been refused.

One of the first to use this opportunity to discuss the 'day-to-day' affairs of a nationalized industry was Mr. Boyd-Carpenter, who, in November 1946, raised the question of the salaries of the members of the Divisional Coal Boards, on which the Minister of Fuel and Power, Mr. Shinwell, had refused him information.[1] The Minister was anything but happy under this form of attack. He denied that there was 'jobbery' but repudiated responsibility for it even if it did exist. While justifying an admitted lack of uniformity between salaries for analogous posts in different Divisions by saying that there was 'great variety in local conditions and hence in the selection and remuneration of personnel', he proclaimed his determination not to interfere in any way with the Board's administration.

Mr. Boyd-Carpenter's subject was undoubtedly one of public importance. That was more than could be said of the subject chosen by the next adjournment-mover, Mr. Teeling, who on April 6th 1948, dealt with the requisitioning by the British Electricity

[1] H.C. Deb., Vol. 430, cols. 475–86.

Authority of the Princes Hotel, Brighton, a matter on which a Question of his had been refused. On this occasion, the House spent 42 minutes discussing allegations which could have been disposed of in less than two at Question Time, had the Minister received Mr. Teeling's Question and chosen to answer it.[2]

Since then, the nationalized industries have been the subject of a great many Adjournment Motions,[3] many of them dealing with matters which—at least in the opinion of the Minister or Parliamentary Secretary—fall clearly within the day-to-day category. Some protection is afforded by the fact that competition for the Adjournment is fierce and only a few of the successful Members choose to raise matters relating to nationalized industries. Nevertheless, it is clear that the determined Member whose Question on a day-to-day matter has been rejected by the Table or stone-walled by the Minister can, with luck, ensure that at least half an hour of the House's time shall be devoted to its discussion. Moreover, if he is intelligent in both his choice and presentation of subject, he can also ensure that the Minister or Parliamentary Secretary suffers a certain amount of embarrassment. The attitude that the latter normally adopts is Mr. Shinwell's original one—of denying responsibility yet offering explanations and justifications of the Board's decisions. Such an attitude, which might be illustrated by reference to almost any one of these Adjournment Debates, is not easy to maintain, and perhaps it is fortunate for the ministerial spokesman that he rarely has need to keep it up for more than ten minutes or a quarter of an hour. By the end of that time the contortions involved begin to be distinctly uncomfortable.

Of the many examples of this embarrassing situation, perhaps the best is provided by the already mentioned Adjournment Debate of November 10th 1959,[4] which was used by Mr. Francis Noel-Baker to raise the subject of the British Transport Commission's policy for its railway workshops. As Member for Swindon, a railway constituency, he had raised it on many previous occasions, the most recent being Question Time on November 4th 1959,[5] when he asked the Minister of Transport, Mr. Ernest Marples, '. . . what

[2] H.C. Deb., Vol. 449, cols. 115-27.
[3] See list, Appendix, p. 239.
[4] See above, pp. 71-2.
[5] H.C. Deb., Vol. 612, cols. 1027-30.

general direction he has given to the British Transport Commission regarding the proportions of carriage, wagon and locomotive building to be allocated to British Railways factories and to private firms, respectively'.

The Minister had simply replied 'None, Sir', and in response to a lengthy supplementary, alleging 'great anxiety' in the railway towns about the sending out of work to private firms, had maintained that 'the construction and repair of locomotives and rolling stock' was 'entirely a matter for the Commission'. Further supplementaries had drawn from him no more than a promise to discuss the question with the Chairman of the Transport Commission at their next meeting. Mr. Noel-Baker then announced his intention of raising it on the Adjournment, which he was fortunate enough to secure six days later.

On November 10th, therefore, he was able to dilate at some length on the grievances of the railway shopmen.[6] The Parliamentary Secretary, Mr. Hay, in his reply, reaffirmed that the matter was entirely one for the Commission, 'a commercial undertaking engaged in a competitive enterprise'. But he could hardly leave the matter there. First, he chose to treat literally Mr. Noel-Baker's request for a general direction, and contrived to suggest that although the Minister *might* intervene in a matter of this sort, a general direction, which was 'a kind of sledgehammer kept in some dark cupboard in Berkeley Square', was not the instrument he would use for the purpose. Hence the question of what the Minister could do became confused with that of what the Minister *ought* to do. He followed this with a justification of the policy that the Commission was actually pursuing, thus implying that the real reason for the inappropriateness of a general direction was not so much the Commission's need for autonomy as the Minister's satisfaction with its performance.

Three factors, he said, were responsible for the policy of which Mr. Noel-Baker had complained. First, British Railways had more workshop capacity than they needed. Secondly, the whole railway system was engaged in a process of contraction. Thirdly, the decline in freight traffic and the more efficient utilization of

---

[6] As we have seen (above, pp.71-2) Mr. Noel-Baker also used this occasion to criticize the existing rules and conventions about Parliamentary Questions on the nationalized industries.

equipment made inevitable a reduction in the size of the wagon fleet. In spite of these things, however, there would be no whole-sale closing of railway workshops, which were very busy, and no serious problem of redundancy, as the demand for skilled engineers remained high. 'I am sure that there is plenty of work ahead for a rather more healthy and more economic system of railway work-shops,' he concluded, 'and it will be the Government's policy to support and help the British Transport Commisssion in any way we can to achieve that end'.

Identification of Government policy with the 'commercial judgement' of the Transport Commission could hardly have been carried further, and Members may well have been left wondering where, after all, the real responsibility was situated.

The pattern of this reply was simply a rather elaborate repetition of a pattern already made familiar by the extremely numerous Adjournment Debates about the closing down of branch lines and about delays in rural electrification. Some of these show with even greater clarity the extreme difficulty experienced in distinguishing general policy from day-to-day administration. On 12th June 1953, for instance, Mr. Nabarro complained, with some justification, that the government was 'passing the buck' on rural electrification.[7]

> 'The area boards and the Electricity Authority', he said, 'are blaming the government for the restriction on capital investment specifically for rural supplies—not a global re-striction but specifically for rural supplies—whereas my hon. Friend says that it is nothing at all to do with him and that this question is settled within the autonomy enjoyed by the area boards and the British Electricity Authority.'[8]

The Parliamentary Secretary who answered his complaint

[7] H.C. Deb., Vol. 516, cols. 684–704.

[8] This statement was supported by two quotations, viz. (a) from the B.E.A.'s Fourth Annual Report: 'In August 1951 the Government decided that no new rural electrification schemes should be started . . . In fixing the 1952 civil investment programme the Government decided to restore £1 million . . . to enable the area boards to start some new rural schemes of an urgent character' (para. 223); (b) from a statement in the House by the Parliamentary Secretary: 'The investment programme approved each year contains a global sum for the electricity industry and the Government does not make specific allocations for rural supplies'. (H.C. Deb., Vol. 515, Written Answers, col. 60.)

succeeded neither in defining who was responsible for what, nor in indicating how far the Minister was prepared to answer for decisions which, while not actually taken by himself, were clearly the consequence of policies that he had laid down.

In a previous Adjournment Debate on the same subject, Mr. C. J. M. Alport had asked who took the decision on priorities.[9] 'Is it the Ministry', he inquired, 'or is it in some body which is representative of industry and agriculture, or is the power vested solely in the hands of the various electricity boards themselves?'

The Parliamentary Secretary admitted that it was the Government 'in the long run', but held that in the shorter run the area boards were responsible.

> 'There are great difficulties in deciding upon the necessary priority', he said, 'but that is a job which is primarily one for the area boards . . . The boards have to take into account the national interest, particularly defence requirements for electricity and the requirements of increased productivity. They have to look at the matter from the broadest national aspect and also from the point of view of capital investment, and to consider whether or not they can afford to link up an isolated place, which will consume a lot of capital . . . or whether they can do a more satisfactory job by linking up consumers where connections can be made to existing mains and feeders.'

That such a mixture of national and commercial considerations should have been regarded as falling within the area of a Board's autonomy must have shocked the Herbert Committee, if it ever considered this statement. Clearly, the decision on priorities as thus defined was one of public policy, in which strictly commercial factors of a kind highly important to the board itself played only a subordinate part. Yet such was the reluctance of the Government to regard it in this light that Mr. Alport, as he himself explained, had had to use the Adjournment to raise the matter because there seemed to him no other way of doing so.

The pattern of denial of responsibility *plus* explanation *plus* justification has been repeated most consistently in the debates on

[9] H.C. Deb., Vol. 501, cols. 1787–98, 30th May 1952.

the closure of railway branch lines, which account for nine of the thirty-five Adjournment Debates, held between Session 1951–2 and 1957–8, on matters concerning the nationalized industries. In these debates and others, however, it often happens that the ministerial spokesman endeavours to give the adjournment-movers and their supporters the impression that something will be done as a result of the representations they have made. Thus, for instance, the Minister of Transport (Mr. Lennox-Boyd), assured Major Sydney Markham, Mr. Edward Davies, Captain Robert Ryder and Mr. Geoffrey Wilson, who had taken up the cause of railway pensioners, that 'this debate and its implications' would be 'noted not only by himself and his right hon. Friends but by the employers in this case'. He even encouraged the Members concerned to continue to bring pressure to bear on the Transport Commission.[10] Similar encouragement was given by the Parliamentary Secretary to the Ministry of Fuel and Power (Mr. Joynson-Hicks) to Mr. William Hamilton, who used the Adjournment to take up a case of an alleged wrongful dismissal of an employee by the National Coal Board.[11] When Mr. Roy Mason expressed his uneasiness about the implementation of the 'Fleck' Report by the National Coal Board, the Parliamentary Secretary (Mr. Renton), while disclaiming on the Minister's behalf any responsibility for the Board's 'day-to-day administration', said: 'I am sure that the Board will take due note of what has been said. Indeed, I propose to ask the Chairman if he will be good enough to write to the hon. Member for Barnsley about several points which were raised'.[12]

On the future of Bo'ness Dock, Mr. John Taylor was assured that the Government would 'view the problem sympathetically'.[13] After explaining the difficulties confronting the North of Scotland Hydro-Electricity Board, the Joint Under-Secretary of State for Scotland (Mr. Niall Macpherson) told Mr. John Macleod, who had complained about the deficiency of electricity supplies to the Torridon area, that the Board would 'keep this matter under review'.[14]

Mr. George Thomas, who was uneasy about the future of the

[10] H.C. Deb., Vol. 502, cols. 1704–12.
[11] H.C. Deb., Vol. 526, cols. 322–30.
[12] H.C. Deb., Vol. 568, cols. 914–34.
[13] H.C. Deb., Vol. 580, cols. 379–88.
[14] H.C. Deb., Vol. 575, cols. 355–64.

Port of Cardiff, was assured by the Joint Parliamentary Secretary to the Ministry of Transport and Civil Aviation (Mr. Airey Neave) that what he had said would be 'drawn to the attention' of the B.T.C., and that the 'assistance of hon. Members in this very difficult matter' was welcome.[15]

Only very occasionally is the ministerial spokesman prepared to go further than this in the acceptance of responsibility, as when the Parliamentary Secretary to the Ministry of Transport, in answer to a complaint from Mr. Arthur Palmer about the replacement of trolley buses in London, said:

> 'I should like to state briefly the reasons why the London Passenger Transport Executive is proposing to make this change and why my right hon. Friend is supporting it, and will continue to support it, in doing so.'[16]

And only very occasionally indeed, it is fair to add, does the spokesman talk nonsense of the kind exemplified by this gem from the lips of Mr. Profumo:

> "I certainly cannot accept the suggestion that British civil airline pilots are working under unsatisfactory terms and conditions of service, that is, if their terms and conditions of service were a matter of determination by Her Majesty's Government, which, of course, . . . is not the case.'[17]

It is reasonable to conclude, from a consideration of Adjournment Debates alone, that the degree to which the present régime protects the nationalized industries from the attentions of over-inquisitive parliamentarians is somewhat problematical. One must immediately add, for better measure, that such debates by no means provide the only occasion upon which 'day-to-day' matters can be tossed across the benches. Sometimes a Private Member's Motion is used for this purpose, as when Mr. Hector Hughes raised the question of freight charges by British Railways,[18] Sir Wavell Wakefield that of securing an 'adequate supply of men

[15] H.C. Deb., Vol. 591, cols. 1404–14.
[16] H.C. Deb., Vol. 560, cols. 1896–904. It is possible that, in this case, the existence of post-Suez petrol rationing affected the nature of the reply.
[17] H.C. Deb., Vol. 529, cols. 2485–96.
[18] H.C. Deb., Vol. 497, cols. 2739–834.

of the highest quality and qualifications for aircrew duties',[19] and Mr. Anthony Hurd that of developing 'the supply of electricity in rural areas as much and as fast as possible'.[20] Criticisms of board policy and administration may also be found scattered about in debates on subjects that have no immediate relevance to the affairs of the nationalized industries. Debates on Scottish and on Welsh Affairs, for instance, provide Members with yet another opportunity to grumble about the closing down of branch lines and about the slow progress in the supply of electricity to rural areas. On 4th February 1952, for instance, in the Debate on Welsh Affairs, Mr. T. W. Jones (Merioneth) appealed to the Merseyside and North Wales Electricity Board not to 'in any way retard the progress of rural electrification . . . whatever economies (were) contemplated by the Government', while Mr. Roderic Bowen (Cardigan) accused the South Wales Electricity Board of wasting money on hire-purchase equipment and on advertising, and complained that there was no uniform principle, applying throughout rural Wales, for determining the charges made for connecting farmers to the electricity mains. Both he and other Members asked the Minister to 'take steps' to improve the South Wales Electricity Board's performance. Even debates on the Address or on the Economic and Financial Situation have occasionally been used to take up matters of considerable detail.

Far better opportunities than these, however, are provided by the three annual 'Reports and Accounts' debates, by the fairly frequent debates on the capital requirements of the nationalized industries and on Bills (Public and Private) to modify their statutory powers or to change their organization, by the somewhat less frequent debates on government plans for the future of transport or coal, and by the occasional Supply debate when the Opposition chooses Estimates (or proposes a Resolution) to enable the House to discuss a nationalized industry. For it must always be remembered that the rules of Order are not interpreted in such a way as to prevent a Member, on these occasions, from raising matters for which the Minister claims that he is not responsible.

The 'Reports and Accounts' debates, in particular, are frequently employed by Members to raise 'constituency' points on

[19] H.C. Deb., Vol. 537, cols. 1585–625.
[20] H.C. Deb., Vol. 516, cols. 1359–442.

which Questions would never get past the Table. This is at least partly responsible for the well-known and much-criticized 'incoherence' of these debates.

The debate on the gas and electricity industries of 26th November 1957 may well serve as an example. As it generated little political heat—for both industries were giving reasonable satisfaction and neither was in a state of crisis—Members felt free to range at large over the Reports and Accounts and to dwell, sometimes at considerable length, on issues affecting their constituencies or areas. Thus Mr. H. R. Spence (Aberdeenshire West) seized the opportunity to talk again about the supply of electricity to the rural areas of the Highlands, Mrs. Braddock to complain about smoke emission from a Manchester power station, Mr. Sidney Silverman to take up the case of a poor consumer in his constituency who, as a result of being robbed, had been unable to pay his electricity bill and was consequently deprived of supplies, Mr. William Hamilton to allege that certain employees of his Area Electricity Board were 'going around getting private business for themselves', and Messrs. J. C. George, F. H. Hayman, Raymond Gower and Tudor Watkins to reinforce Mr. Spence's warnings against complacency about rural electrification. In addition to these constituency points, a large number of detailed technical matters were introduced into the discussion, particularly by the leading Opposition spokesman, Mr. Robens. He was followed by Mr. Maurice Macmillan, who talked of raw materials and the utilization of waste products, by Mr. Nabarro, who included thermal insulation and selling arrangements among the many subjects he covered, by Mr. W. A. Wilkins, who wanted standardized tariffs, by Mr. J. C. George, on thermal efficiency, and by Vice-Admiral John Hughes Hallett, who expressed approval of these discussions of 'the details of the practical side of the workings of the nationalized industries'. Well might the Parliamentary Secretary to the Ministry of Power (Mr. David Renton) make the following complaint at the beginning of his winding-up speech:

'One of the most serious defects of nationalisation is that, at the end of a six-hour debate on the Annual Report and Accounts of at least one industry . . . an unfortunate Parliamentary Secretary has to stand up and answer a mass of detailed points, some of them on very technical matters, at the same time trying to pretend to the House that he has shown an intelligent appreciation of all the general trends displayed in the debate. One should place on record, as has been done before, that it is an almost impossible task to give satisfaction.'

It would be unfair to Members, however, to suggest that they use their debating opportunities exclusively, or even mainly, for such purposes. It would also be unfair to claim that, when they do so, they are necessarily wasting Parliament's time. For, after all, Members *do* represent constituencies and *are* connected with various pressure and interest groups, and must be expected to find what opportunities they can to give expression to the views and grievances of these collectivities. What is obvious, however, is that a great many matters of minor importance are dragged into the debates simply because Members have been unable to get them dealt with at Question Time or through private correspondence with the Minister or the Board. Hence the 'protection' of the nationalized industries from certain kinds of Questions has its counterpart in their exposure to all kinds of criticisms when debate frees Members' tongues.

This makes debates less valuable and less coherent than they might otherwise be. But it does not make them useless, as some critics, whose contempt for parliamentary institutions is stronger than their respect for the evidence provided by Hansard, have from time to time alleged. There was a time, admittedly, when every debate on a nationalized industry tended to degenerate into a futile slanging-match between the Labour nationalizers and the Conservative anti-nationalizers. This could hardly have been avoided during the period of the Third Labour Government, when nationalization was regarded by many Socialists as a means of ushering in the millenium and by many Conservatives as an affront to the British way of life. But with the acceptance by the Conservatives of all Labour's nationalizations except iron and steel and road haulage, and with the advent of Conservative administrations which were compelled, by the nature of the political situation, to defend the nationalized industries which they now supervised, these days came to an end. Today, such exchanges as take place on the principle of nationalization are comparatively mild and gentlemanly. Only when there is strong disagreement from the Opposition about the kind of policy which the Government is pursuing vis-à-vis the nationalized industry (as with transport at the time of writing) do debates become at all acrimonious. Discussions of a nationalized industry, such as electricity or gas or civil airways, which is producing satisfactory financial results and not currently subject to any reorganization plan, take place in an atmosphere of political calm. On these occasions, Members on either side of the House vie with one another in making constructive suggestions, and even the most virulent erstwhile opponents of nationalization sometimes congratulate the Board on its performance. The beginning of this new spirit may be traced back to the Debate on the Address in 1951, when the Conservative Government had just assumed office. The Minister of Fuel and Power, Mr. Geoffrey Lloyd, replying to complaints from Mr. Gaitskell of 'unfair criticisms' of members of the National Coal Board, said:

> 'Once you have accepted the nationalized coal industry, you cannot sit around looking at it with neutral or even semi-hostile eyes, much less "mess around with it", to use a phrase of the right hon. Gentleman's. Once you accept it, then in the national interest you have got to back it and do your level best to make it a success.'[21]

This drew from Mr. Noel-Baker the promise that if the Minister would persuade his 'friends' to 'stop sniping', Labour would not 'play politics with coal'.

With both political parties agreed on the wisdom of having certain industries in the public sector and both committed, according to their different lights, to making these industries a 'success', playing politics with them became a more difficult exercise than it had previously been. Its skilful performance, moreover, was no longer likely to enhance parliamentary reputations.

Indeed, by 1957 some of the 'Report and Accounts' debates had become so sedate that they attracted very few Members to the Chamber. In the Gas and Electricity Debate already mentioned,

[21] As Minister, Mr. Lloyd certainly did his best to live up to the spirit of this declaration.

Mr. Cyril Osborne, after recalling the bitter nationalization debates of former years, said:

> 'Let us see how that atmosphere has changed. Earlier this evening there were present only four hon. Gentlemen opposite, and there were six Members on this side of the House. At 6.35 there were only three hon. Gentlemen opposite, and there were five only on this side . . . Compared with the enthusiasm of ten years ago, the debate on these accounts shows that nationalisation is a dead issue.'

'We have not had an exciting debate', said Mr. George Thomas, '. . . for success does not make for exciting debates here', while Mr. Raymond Gower, from the other side of the House, expressed the opinion that one of its 'most attractive features' was 'its non-partisan, non-political character'. Another Conservative found Members' lack of enthusiasm actually disturbing, and expressed the belief that it was due to the fact that there was no Minister 'directly responsible for the matters under discussion'.

Even reorganization plans do not necessarily produce political acrimony nowadays. The Transport Bill of 1953, of course, was fought tooth and nail by the Labour Opposition, because it involved the denationalization of road haulage, a 'folly' for which Labour has never ceased to reproach the Conservatives. It was the same, *a fortiori*, with the bill to denationalize iron and steel. But the Opposition did not even divide the House against the Electricity Bill of 1956, which most Members succeeded in discussing in the quiet, thoughtful and constructive way that it clearly deserved.

But it would be wrong to give the impression, particularly at the present juncture, that parliamentary excitement about the nationalized industries has ceased to exist. What has already been said about Questions indicates, to say the least, that there is considerable uneasiness, on all sides of the House, about the nature of the board-minister-parliament relationship. More importantly in the present context, it is inevitable that the Opposition should vigorously blame the Government when a nationalized industry is not doing well. This is particularly so when Conservatism is in office and Labour in opposition, for Labour cannot but continue to take a paternal interest in its own creations and is therefore much inclined to attribute their failures not to any organizational or administrative defects on their part, but to unwarranted and hampering 'government interference'. According to some Labour spokesmen, the British Transport Commission would not have had to face a whole series of crises if the Conservatives had not denationalized road haulage and interfered with the Commission's charging policy. This accusation has been made many times, but never more fiercely than on the first occasion when the Minister suspended fare increases endorsed by the Transport Tribunal. This suspension, which was effected by the issue of a general direction —a unique method—took place at the height of the controversy about road haulage denationalization. Hence it produced a series of acrimonious discussions which, because of the light that they shed on the attitudes both of Ministers and of private Members, deserve some detailed attention.

The controversy began on 10th March 1952, when there was a series of Questions on the Order Paper asking the Minister either to refer the recently-announced increased transport charges to the Central Transport Consultative Committee or to remit them, under Section 80 of the Transport Act, to the Transport Tribunal, which had just sanctioned them. The Minister, Mr. Maclay, replied as follows:

'I am advised that it would be inconsistent with the intentions of the Transport Act in regard to the control of the Commission's charges for the Consultative Committee to review the Tribunal's decisions, or for me to invoke Section 80 to require the Tribunal to review the operation of a scheme which they have just confirmed.

'The scheme, however, laid down maxima within which the Commission have discretion to fix actual fares and this discretion covers alteration of fare stages which appears to me to be the main cause of complaint. Alterations of fare stages and fares in relation to them are matters which can properly be referred forthwith to the Consultative Committee and I am so referring them.

'I must make it clear that under the Transport Act, 1947, no action other than reference to the Consultative Committee is open to me.'

This answer related to two separate classes of increased fares, viz. those for the London area, which had actually come into force on 2nd March, and those for the rest of the country, which were not due to come into force until 1st May. It was the first class of increase that the Minister was referring to the Consultative Committee. It was about the second that he claimed that he could do notoing.

In answer to further Questions on 17th March he reasserted his powerlessness. Pressed by Mr. Ernest Davies to ask the Consultative Committee 'to consider the manner in which the British Transport Commission proposes to exercise the discretion allowed by the passenger charges scheme in relation to railways outside London, in view of its declared intention to increase railway fares thereon on 1st May', he repeated his previous refusal and asked Members to remember that he was 'working under the structure of the 1947 Act', which tied his hands. Asked by Capt. Robert Ryder whether he could issue a direction under Section 4, 'to ensure that this burden is evenly shared in all sections of the country', he replied:

'The scheme was confirmed by the Transport Tribunal after a public inquiry. This is the procedure laid down by the Transport Act and I am advised that it would not be proper for me to issue directions such as those to which my hon. and gallant friend refers.'

A month later, on 15th April, the Minister gave a direction to the Transport Commission suspending the fares increases which were due to come into operation on 1st May.

This *volte-face* naturally provoked a barrage of parliamentary Questions. On 21st April Mr. Ernest Davies asked him to explain his reasons and the grounds on which the 'advice' as to his powerlessness had been found defective. Mr. Douglas Jay wanted to know how he proposed to enable the Commission to meet its financial obligations, and Lt.-Col. Lipton whether he had decided to amend the Transport Act so as to make himself responsible for fares. Mr. Maclay replied by asking Members to wait for the statement that the Prime Minister was to make at the end of Questions. Several Members then protested at the Minister's refusal to accept responsibility, e.g.:

Mr. Callaghan: 'On a point of order, I must give notice that we intend to pursue this matter. It is surely without precedent for a Minister to come to the House, and on a whole series of Questions . . . to tell us that he is not going to answer them, and is going to pass the matter on to the Prime Minister. This is really a complete derogation of his own responsibilities, and if he cannot carry out his duties better than this, he should resign.'

The Prime Minister, Mr. Winston Churchill, rose at the end of Questions to explain and justify the action taken. The fare changes for London, he said, had come into operation almost immediately. Hence it was only after the increases had been made that the Government could 'measure the full effects of the use which the British Transport Commission had made of its discretionary powers under the scheme'. To do this the Minister had made reference to the Consultative Committee, which had submitted a report accepting the need for the increases. The Government was now considering 'whether any action should be taken in respect of the disproportionate increases in sub-standard fares'.

Outside London, the scheme was to come into force on 1st May. Hence the Government was able to inform itself, in advance, 'more precisely of the effect of these proposed increases'. In the light of this information, it had decided that 'some further delay' ought to be imposed, for it was concerned at 'certain exceptionally severe changes in the cost of workmen's tickets and season tickets' and also felt that 'some of the proposed changes ought not to be imposed upon the public without Parliamentary discussion'. Hence the Minister of Transport had 'felt it his duty' to issue the suspensory directive. He now proposed 'to seek the views of the Consultative Committee on the question of railway fares outside London', and must await the Committee's report before 'reaching a full and final decision'. The whole question required 'the urgent attention of Parliament' and there would be a full debate on 28th April.

Questioned by Mr. Morrison 'why what was proper now was not proper on 17th March', he refused to be drawn.

The promised debate began with a series of Points of Order, during the course of which Mr. Fitzroy Maclean asked the Speaker to rule whether it was now in Order to ask Questions about fares. The Speaker cautiously replied:

> 'The matter of Questions is still under examination by a Select Committee. I undertook earlier to operate a provisional procedure until the Committee has reported and the House has come to some decision on its report. In the meantime each Question must be judged on its merits.'

In the absence of the Minister of Transport, who was ill, the Home Secretary, Sir David Maxwell-Fyfe, then moved as follows:

> 'That this House approves the action by the Minister of Transport to suspend the introduction outside the London area of new rail charges which would have increased disproportionately the cost of season tickets, workmen's fares and concessionary rates for special classes of passenger; upholds the decision that these disproportionate increases should not be applied to railway charges outside the London area; and agrees that means should be sought of applying the same principle, so far as practicable, to rail and omnibus fares already introduced within the London area.'

As might have been expected, a major part of his speech was devoted to justifying the ministerial action in terms of the prevention of hardship. This was comparatively plain sailing. When he came, however, to employ his legal skill to justify the intervention in terms of the powers accorded to the Minister by the Transport Act, he was much less happy. Section 4 of the Act, of course, provided him with his *locus standi*.

> 'I realise very well', he said, 'that different views may exist as to when the point is reached at which the Minister should intervene. I say that the point is reached when for a large section of our countrymen the basis of choice of place of residence in relation to the earning of their daily bread is suddenly and unexpectedly upset. In the last resort, the Government and Parliament are the shield of these classes of individuals against injustice. It is certainly in the national interest in the highest sense that the Government should fulfil its duty in this respect.'

To explain why the Minister of Transport had formerly considered himself powerless to act in this sense, Sir David had recourse to what can only be described as a piece of legal sophistry, saying that 'on 10th March my hon. Friend was dealing with the normal functioning of the Act and not with the overriding provisions'. Feeling, no doubt, that this did not carry much conviction, he filled out his brief with an attack on nationalization and a defence of the denationalization of road haulage (a subject which the Opposition had included in the Amendment that they were to move at the end of the debate). 'The fact is', he said, 'that Socialist legislation has given rise to a difficult situation for the people of this country'.

Mr. Morrison, opening for the Opposition, claimed that the Government had been influenced by party interest rather than by the national interest, and had been put in a condition of 'panic' by the adverse results of the County Council elections, which had intervened between the announcement and the suspension of the fares increases. What the Minister had done, at the instigation of the Prime Minister and against his own 'honest judgement', was to exercise 'quasi-judicial' powers in a partisan fashion, thereby placing a vital constitutional convention in jeopardy.

> 'We dislike profoundly', said Mr. Morrison, 'the methods employed, and we expect a considered reply. I do not want the House to degenerate into a situation where the fares and charges for publicly-owned industries are subject to a political Dutch auction, where Members are competing with each other to be able to go to their constituents and say, "I got this, that and the other for you". With respect, I do not believe that this great House of Commons is an appropriate body to deal like that with detailed charges of this sort. If it tries to settle detailed charges of this sort the next thing it will be driven to do is to try to settle the details of the wages and salaries of the people employed. That will not do.'

During the course of a debate which covered railway economics and road haulage denationalization as well as the proper constitutional method of fixing fares, and which was consequently notable neither for its clarity nor its cohesion, Mr. Alfred Barnes, the former Labour Minister of Transport, suggested that relations between the Government and the Commission had been very much better when Labour was in office and that the Conservatives were making a muddle of them.

> 'I never experienced any difficulty', he said, 'in my discussions with Lord Hurcomb and the Transport Commission on matters of this kind. Everyone knows that people who hold such positions are prepared to meet, accommodate and agree on matters of this sort.'

In other words, he was complaining, not so much that the Government was interfering with the discretion of the Commission, as that the 'old boy' method of interference, which he had used so successfully, had come to pieces in the unskilled hands of his successor.

For the Government, Mr. David Renton suggested that the arguments that the Labour Party was employing were inconsistent with its own proclaimed political philosophy. In the former debates about nationalization, he said:

> 'The strongest argument against us was that it would put the whole thing on a democratic basis and that we should at least have the opportunity of exercising some kind of control over a basic public industry ... All the Government have done has been to use the democratic opportunity, which is provided by the Transport Act, for considering the matter. The Transport Tribunal, within its limits, and the Consultative Committee have considered the matter; but Parliament must be the final arbiter; and, if hon. Gentlemen had had the same experience as I have had in recent weeks, they would find that it is no use whatever saying to the travelling public, 'Parliament have no power and the Minister has no power'. The people just will not accept that as a policy. Why should they? Parliament passes laws, Parliament can amend laws, and Parliament should take notice of public opinion.'

Taking this line of reasoning to its logical conclusion, Mr. Norman Cole said:

'We cannot continue to tie the hands of a representative and constitutional body such as the House of Commons in dealing with these basic industries and, whenever any intervention is made, to have a fuss about it.'

Perhaps it was Mr. Reader Harris, however, who really got to the heart of the matter when he said:

'This British Transport Commission and the Transport Tribunal are bodies with strictly limited powers, and they are not able to see the whole economic position in the country. They have to act solely in relation to their own particular problems without relation to the problems of any other parts of the national economy, and that is why the Government have had to step in, and that is why there will always be this liability on the Government to take action to protect the consumers against these great monopolies.'

By the inconsistency of its behaviour, the Conservative Government had certainly placed itself in an awkward position, from which Labour was attempting to derive the maximum party advantage. But the Labour Party itself was by no means sitting pretty. It was bound to respect the force of Mr. Harris's argument, could hardly deny that, under Clause 4 of the Transport Act, the Minister possessed interventionary powers, and was certainly not prepared to forfeit political popularity, for the sake of the Transport Commission and Transport Tribunal, by straightforwardly condemning a ministerial action which, on its own admission, had been taken in response to popular pressure. It therefore chose not to reject the Government resolution, but to move an amendment which added the following:

'. . . but regrets the vacillation and lack of co-ordination between Ministers which have caused the present confused position and further regrets that in coming to its present decision, the Government has made no proposals for making up the deficit in the Commission's revenue which would be further adversely affected if road haulage were denationalized; and accordingly calls for a review of the financial basis of the

British Transport Commission, reaffirming the view that the interests of the travelling public and commercial users will be best served by the integration under public ownership of road and rail transport as provided in the Transport Act, 1947.'

Pressed to a Division, this Amendment was lost by 256 votes to 300. The original Question was then put and agreed to without a Division.

The main thread of argument running through the Labour contributions to this debate may be summarized as follows: 'The Transport Commission is doing its best, but the Government, far from helping it, is hindering it at every step. Not only do the Conservatives propose to destroy the integrated road-rail structure created in 1947; they will not even allow the Commission to charge fares, already approved by the Transport Commission, which will enable it to perform its statutory duty of breaking even one year with another. Furthermore, by intervening in the pursuit of scarcely-disguised party political purposes, and by using a general direction to this end, they have undermined both the autonomy of the Commission and the relationship of confidence and co-operation which ought to exist, and formerly did exist, between the Commission and the Government.'

Defence of the Commission's autonomy and condemnation of the Government's use of its powers improperly and for improper purposes were again prominent in Labour speeches when the 'fares and freights' issue was debated once more, in April 1956, after a further suspension by the Minister of Transport of proposed increased charges. On this second occasion the *casus belli* was in some respects even more complicated, as the Minister simultaneously used both his formal powers (but not by way of general direction) and his informal influence.

On 19th March 1956, Mr. Watkinson made a statement in the House about the British Transport Commission's charges. The immediate circumstances were the Commission's application to the Minister, under one of the transitional provisions of the Transport Act, 1947 (Section 82, sub-section 1) for the issue of a regulation authorizing it to increase its freight charges.[22]

[22] 'The Minister may at any time, if he thinks it expedient to do so with a view to ensuring a sufficient revenue to the Commission . . ., by regulations
[*footnote continued on page 100*]

Mr. Watkinson indicated that, as a result of the previous year's railway strike and of continued increases in costs and wages, £30 million had been added to the Commission's deficit. For the current year there might be a further addition of £55 million, making a total deficit of £100 million. The Commission, therefore, was justified in its application. Nevertheless, he did not propose to grant it in full, because he was of the opinion that the Commission's 'renewed and strenuous efforts' to cut costs, together with the better labour relations which now appeared to prevail, would bring about an improvement in the financial situation of the railways. He therefore considered it 'expedient' to make regulations authorizing increases smaller than those requested, and was accordingly consulting the Transport Tribunal. On passenger fares, he announced that the Commission had informed him that it would defer certain increases for which it had made application to the Tribunal under Section 23 of the Transport Act, 1953. The Chairman of the Commission, he said, had stated the Commission's desire 'to co-operate fully in this policy'. In view of the Commission's statutory obligations, however, the position would have to be reviewed in six months' time, and it was 'on this clear understanding' that the Commission had 'agreed to the course of action proposed'.

For the Opposition, Mr. Strauss asked the Minister whether he seriously believed that there would be any dramatic, spectacular change within the next six months, and whether, in view of his interference with the Commission's commercial judgement, he was prepared to give it a subsidy. Mr. Watkinson replied that the six months referred to was a period in which he trusted that the Commission, 'working in close collaboration with the unions concerned', would 'come forward with the necessary proposals' for

---

[footnote continued from page 99]

authorise the Commission . . . to make, in respect of any services or facilities provided by them the charges for which are regulated by statutory provision, charges additional to those in operation under that statutory provision: Provided that before making any regulations under this subsection, the Minister shall consult with, and consider the advice of, the permanent members of the Transport Tribunal, acting as a consultative committee.'

The following subsection specifies that the above provision shall not apply 'to any service or facilities in respect to which a charges scheme is in force'. In 1956, therefore, it applied to freights but not to passenger fares.

putting its business on a sounder basis. These, he suggested, might 'well include much more drastic closure of branch lines' and 'many more drastic economies'. There had been no interference, for everything had been 'done with the willing co-operation of the British Transport Commission'; and there was no question of a subsidy.

'Are not the Government being quite inconsistent in this policy?' asked Mr. Ernest Davies. 'Does not the right hon. Gentleman recall that under the 1953 Act the Commission was given full authority to go ahead, and to act with flexibility on a commercial basis? Is not this policy a departure from that? Therefore, is not the Minister being quite unfair to the Commission in that he is preventing it from operating commercially and at the same time giving it no assistance?'

On the following day, 20th March, the Minister referred the Commission's application to the Tribunal by means of an official letter which requested its advice and also contained the following statement:

'The Minister is impressed with the importance of authorising some immediate increases in these charges. He is, however, of the opinion that, in determining what those charges should be, account should be taken of the signs which exist that strenuous efforts will improve the financial outlook of the railways through more efficient working arising from better relations in the industry, and it would be in the national interest that a reasonable opportunity should be given for the measures necessary to this end to be put in train. The Minister has consulted with the Commission, who have expressed their desire to co-operate fully in this policy, and have informed him that they will defer those increases in certain fares on London Transport services and British Railways for which they have made application to the Transport Tribunal under Section 23 of the Transport Act, 1953.

The Minister considers, therefore, that while regulations should be made under Section 82 with a view to ensuring a sufficient revenue for the Commission, it would be expedient

that the increases which these regulations authorise should
for the next six months be limited to one half of those proposed
by the Commission, except in the case of the dock and canal
charges where the increase should in his view be limited to
one of 5 per cent instead of being $7\frac{1}{2}$ per cent as proposed.'[23]

In its reply, sent to the Minister on 3rd April, the Tribunal rejected this attempt to influence its judgement and declared itself
in favour of the full increases requested by the Commission.

'We regret that we are unable to agree with the provisional
decisions which you have reached', it wrote. 'It may be that
there are considerations not expressed in your statement to
the House of Commons or in (your) letter which are thought
to make it necessary to disregard at all events for the time
being the obligations and interests of the Commission. It is
no part of our duty to discuss this possibility even if we considered ourselves competent to do so. We are expressly prohibited by s.85 of the 1947 Act from doing anything which
would in our opinion prevent the Commission from discharging
their general duty to secure that their revenue is not less than
sufficient for making provision for the meeting of charges
properly chargeable to revenue account taking one year with
another.'

On 11th April, the Minister announced to the House that he
had rejected the Tribunal's advice and was making Regulations of
the kind he had originally proposed. The cost to the Transport
Commission, he said in reply to a Question, was only £8 million
'as against a total turnover of . . . £700 million'. Asked by Mr.
Davies why he had consulted the Tribunal and then ignored its
advice, he very reasonably replied that his responsibility was to
the House and not to the Tribunal. But he also used the occasion
to clear up certain 'misconceptions' arising from the Tribunal's
letter. The latter had referred to the Minister's opinion that it was
'expedient' that the proposed increases in passenger fares should
be deferred. To this the Minister replied by emphasizing that the

[23] This letter, together with the Transport Tribunal's reply to it, is reproduced in H.C. Deb., Vol. 551, cols. 183–191.

decision was the Commission's own, taken 'as an earnest of their desire to co-operate fully in this matter'. He also asserted, with reference to the Tribunal's remarks about the Commission's obligations under the Transport Act to 'break even', that his 19th March statement had been made 'with a full consciousness of the statutory duties imposed on the Commission' and involved 'no disregard of their duties', since it was proposed 'only that, in present conditions and for a period limited to six months, the increases in charges should be on the lines indicated in that statement'.

The House had an opportunity to debate the whole matter when the Regulations were made and laid. On 7th May, Mr. Ernest Davies moved for the presentation of a humble address that they should be annulled. Labour's line of attack was a fairly obvious one. There had been 'unwarranted interference' by the Minister in the affairs of the Transport Commission. Not only had he 'brushed aside the advice of the Tribunal'; he had made up his mind even before consulting it. This was 'most extraordinary and irresponsible'. With regard to the standstill on passenger fares, it was obvious that the Minister was pusillanimously sheltering behind an alleged 'decision' of the Commission which had in fact been imposed upon it. Why had not the Minister had the courage to issue a general direction, asked Mr. David Jones, seconding the 'prayer'.

> 'After all, we know about those convivial afternoons after lunch when the Minister tries to shake off his responsibility and place it on the Commission . . . He does that deliberately in order to avoid making it look like a political move.'

In his reply, Mr. Watkinson reverted to the point that had been made in the 1952 debate, about the narrowness of the Tribunal's terms of reference.

> 'I do not disagree with the Tribunal in its advice to me', he said, 'because it was advice which, as it said, it felt bound to give . . . The Tribunal cannot take account of the wider matters of policy which I have been discussing . . . and it would not be proper for it to do so.'

Allegations of 'interference' he rebutted, by asserting the need for continuous, intimate and informal relationships between Minister and Commission. After specifying 'some of the things on which the Commission and I are working very hard', he said:

'I must add that I am not interfering . . ., but merely saying to the Commission, "This is how I believe you can best help me to show the country that you mean to put yourself into a more efficient and greatly improved state. This is how you can help me to justify the immense sums which you are rightly asking the country to devote to your modernisation plan".'

Does the House, he asked, 'really think that it is not right for me, as Minister, to apply all the fair pressure I can on everyone in the railways to make them feel that they must get on with the task?'

These arguments, one may imagine, carried little weight with the Opposition. Nevertheless, it chose not to divide the House on the 'prayer', for the obvious reason that it did not wish to present itself to the public as champion of the unpopular cause of increased transport charges. Its dilemma of 1952 remained unresolved.

Both of these cases present certain complexities, of a kind that do not arise in connection with other nationalized industries, as a result of the specific terms of the two Transport Acts and of the powers conferred on the Transport Tribunal. Nevertheless, the basic problems that confronted both Government and Opposition were essentially simple. The Government had to decide whether to intervene or to abstain from intervention in matters which, from the standpoint of the Commission, were, if not of a day-to-day kind, certainly commercial in character. If it decided on intervention, it had to make up its mind whether to proceed by formal or by informal methods. In this respect, its hand was forced twice. The issue of a general direction in 1952 was necessary, one presumes, because the Commission refused to be persuaded temporarily to forego the increases which the Tribunal had granted it. The reference to the Tribunal and the publication of Regulations in 1956 were statutorily prescribed, once the Commission had taken the step of making formal application to the Minister. On both occasions there appears to have been a temporary breakdown of that 'co-operation' which is the normal method by which the

Minister ultimately gets his way. The 1956 passenger fares standstill, on the other hand, was successfully presented as a decision of
the Commission itself.

The Opposition, for its part, had to decide how, consistently
with its principles, it might best use the situation for the purpose
of defending its own creation, the Transport Commission, and
discrediting the Government. Simply to say that fares increases
ought to be left to the commercial judgement of the Commission,
as approved by the Tribunal, was impossible, for political reasons.
Labour therefore had to concentrate on criticizing (a) the Government's general transport policy—and particularly the denationalization of road haulage—which could be presented as making
inevitable a type of intervention which was both undesirable in
itself and contrary to the spirit, if not to the letter, of the nationalization acts, and (b) the manner in which that intervention was
accomplished. It is the latter which is the more interesting from
our standpoint, for it shows the Opposition as involved in contra-
dictions hardly less serious than those affecting the Government
itself. In 1952, Labour's concentration was on the inappropriateness of issuing a general direction, partly because it represented
an interference with the judgement of a quasi-judicial body, but
also because it gave evidence of the breakdown of those informal,
co-operative relations between Minister and Commission which
were essential to the success of a great public enterprise. In 1956,
on the other hand, it was precisely this informal co-operation that
met with severe criticism. If the Minister wanted to prevent the
Commission from raising passenger fares, it was argued, he ought
to do so by issuing a General Direction for which he could be held
responsible to the House.

In general, it is the latter type of criticism that has tended, of
recent years, to be made most frequently by Labour's official
spokesmen.[24] It is, of course, natural for an Opposition to demand
that ministerial responsibilities shall be more clearly defined and
openly admitted, just as it is natural for a Government to find what
shelter it can. Moreover, this line of attack fits in well with Labour's
desire to present the nationalized industries as attempting to
'serve the country well', but persistently hampered in their efforts

[24] See, for instance, Mr. Robens' comments on the 'gentlemen's agreement'
between the Ministry of Power and the National Coal Board, below, pp. 152-3.

H   105

by the 'unwarranted interference' of politically-prejudiced Conservative ministers.

In no field have debates about ministerial responsibility been simultaneously more bitter and more confused than that of wage negotiations between the nationalized industries and their employees. Here again the Transport Commission has been the storm centre, for the simple reason that the Commission, permanently 'in the red', does not possess the financial resources to meet the reasonable claims of the unions. As the Commission must therefore rely on government financial backing to satisfy wage demands and thereby prevent crippling strikes, and as the Government, in its turn, cannot wash its hands of responsibility for the maintenance of essential services or indeed for a financial situation at least partly created by its own policy on fares and freights, 'interference' in the field of collective bargaining has become almost continuous. Yet it is precisely in this field that the autonomy of the Commission is supposed to be most carefully safeguarded, and it is for this reason that the Government has here made the most strenuous efforts to keep its intervention behind the scenes and, by using the Commission as a screen, to avoid direct responsibility to the House.

A well-known instance is the debate of 3rd February 1955, on a Government motion:

> 'That this House welcomes the settlement of the recent wages dispute and believes that the steps proposed by the British Transport Commission will, with the co-operation of all concerned, lead to the establishment of a modern and economic railway system for the benefit of both industry and of the travelling public.'

The 'wages dispute' referred to was of long standing. By the end of 1954 the Unions had been in negotiation with the British Transport Commission for eighteen months, and the patience of the N.U.R. had become exhausted. After an appeal to the Minister of Labour, who advised it to return to negotiations, it announced that it would call a national strike. Immediately, the Government called the Commission and the N.U.R. together and persuaded them to agree to the appointment of a Court of Inquiry. Working very swiftly, the Court produced an interim report favourable to the union's claims and containing the famous phrase about 'willing the ends' and 'willing the means'. On the basis of this Report the Commission and the union resumed negotiations.

'What', asked Mr. Callaghan in the debate, 'made the Transport Commission decide after the Court of Inquiry that it had money to pay the wage claims?'

Sir Brian Robertson, he pointed out, had remarked that where the money was coming from was 'not his concern'.

'I am absolutely certain', said Mr. Morrison in reply to government disclaimers of responsibility, 'that the Government were in this business from start to finish. I do not think the Chancellor would deny it. I have no doubt they handled it in a long-distance manner and were careful of not becoming politically involved. That I understand, but in matters of this magnitude it is inevitable that the Government would be in it.'

Equally well known, and in many respects more enlightening, are the debates which accompanied the London Omnibus Dispute of May 1958. In this case, the Minister of Labour, Mr. MacLeod, refused to take action to bring the two sides together. When the strike broke out on 4th May, he washed his hands of it with the words:

'Whether the London Transport Executive will put forward new proposals to the Unions, I, of course, do not know. That is a matter for the Executive.'

In debate on 8th May, when the strike was still in progress, Mr. Robens gave a history of the dispute in which he drew attention to a letter sent to the British Transport Commission by the Minister on 22nd October 1957, in which he had said that the Government was not prepared to find money to cover any further increase in the Commission's deficit caused by increased costs. This, said Mr. Robens 'was a clear indication that the Minister of Transport was being used to prevent proper negotiations on the busmen's claims'. Again, in March, the Minister had announced that he had told the London Passenger Transport Executive that 'they would get no support for increased fares'. Even a Committee of Inquiry had been rejected by the Government, acting under the influence of Tory back-benchers, who wanted a 'show-down' with the unions. It was not surprising that the busmen had, under these circumstances, refused arbitration, for they had 'lost confidence in any arbitration award'. The real dispute, Mr. Robens suggested, was not between the unions and the L.P.T.E. or the B.T.C., but between the unions and the Government. Generalizing, he said:

> 'In my view, the whole procedure of negotiations under the Government concerning the railways and the buses is a farce, because those who are managing these two industries are not free agents. The Government have tied their hands. They cannot move in any direction; they have no flexibility. We cannot have negotiations on that basis. If the negotiations are with the Government, let the Minister tell the Unions to go and see the Government and negotiate with them.'

By the evasiveness of a reply he gave to a question from Mr. Walter Monslow, the Minister of Labour lent support to Mr. Robens's charges. Mr. Monslow asked 'whether Sir John Elliott and Sir Brian Robertson had the authority to effect a settlement without prior consultation with Her Majesty's Government', to which Mr. MacLeod replied: 'I answered that last week. As far as I am concerned, entirely, yes. If the hon. Gentleman wants to question any other Minister he must, of course, ask him.'

For the Liberals, Mr. Mark Bonham-Carter distinguished between the two criteria for the settlement of wage claims: the 'competitive' and the 'public service'. 'The present position', he said, 'is an unhappy compromise between the two extremes.'

> 'Is it the case, or is it not,' asked Mr. Gaitskell, 'that Sir Brian Robertson and Sir John Elliott are free to make whatever settlement they think fit with the unions in both the bus and the rail dispute, or do they have first to refer any question of that kind to the Minister of Transport or to other Ministers?'[25]

[25] A railwaymen's claim, on which a strike had been threatened, was in the course of being settled through government intervention.

He did not think that there was very much doubt about the answer to this question, and 'begged' the Government 'to come out into the open and admit it fully, instead of trying to shelter behind the Chairman of the Commission and members of nationalized boards'.

To this Mr. Macmillan answered, very reasonably:

'The answer is . . . that they are completely free to act within their own resources, but quite apart from the responsibility that lies in all the Acts upon the Minister . . ., when the Government have not only, as it were, to be the equity holder and also the banker, I say quite frankly that they have not a free right to draw on unlimited overdrafts. That seems to be a sensible situation.'

He was less frank, however, in dealing with the objection immediately raised by Mr. David Jones:

'. . . but the Minister of Transport denies the Commission the right to raise the price of its product when the cost of producing it goes up.'

'Not at all', said Mr. Macmillan, 'I had some valuable . . . discussions on this matter with the Chairman of the Transport Commission and three of the railway unions. I think there was general agreement that simply to put up the fares and the freights would be going too far and that returns would be diminished . . . Everybody feels that that method must come to an end.'

In the end, Mr. Macmillan admitted that the situation was 'difficult and new', arising from a problem 'inherent in the policy of nationalized industries'. That was one of the main reasons why he hoped that nationalized industries would 'not be extended'.

A week later, in reply to a supplementary Question by Mr. Mellish, Mr. MacLeod agreed that the dispute was 'not between an outside employer and the trades unions concerned having an argument about salaries and conditions', and added:

'After all these matters are settled, perhaps we should try to define more closely the position of the nationalised industries and the Government in relation to industrial disputes. It is a position of great flexibility and it causes great difficulty and embarrassment to the Government and, I dare say, to the corporations as well.'

Mr. MacLeod's hopes have not been fulfilled, and 'these matters' continue to cause difficulty and embarrassment to both corporations and Government. The latest example, at the time of writing, is the threatened railway strike of February 1960. Although the Government was, *de facto* if not *de jure*, closely involved in negotiations which led to the calling off of the strike, in return for concessions, at the eleventh hour, the House never received the opportunity to give the matter any sustained attention until 12th February, when the negotiations had reached a most critical stage. The leaders of the Parliamentary Labour Party seem to have been satisfied with this situation; otherwise they would have made some of 'their own' time available. Mr. Robens, in fact, specifically said that a debate in the House, while discussions were taking place 'would not help towards a settlement'.[26] Other Members, however, were less happy about Parliament's exclusion from the scene. Mr. Grimond, for instance, thought that it would be 'very strange if the negotiations broke down and the House of Commons could not discuss this very important public matter'. Later in the day he expressed himself thus:

'I am sure everyone hopes that there will be no strike, but how can it be maintained, when these are nationalised industries over which the House of Commons has deliberately taken some control, and placed that control in the hands of the Government, that the House of Commons should not discuss this matter at all? It is freely discussed on the air and in the newspapers, and yet in the House, where we are responsible for these industries, apparently we cannot discuss it.

Why is it thought that any discussion here will necessarily make the situation worse? It is only a few days since we embarked on a discussion about Cyprus while negotiations, presumably of a delicate nature, were going on . . . As far as I know, no harm was done by that. I think it will be difficult

[26] See also the remarks of Mr. Ernest Popplewell.

110

for the public to understand why we can debate that issue but cannot debate the strike which, if it comes about, will have a devastating effect on the country.'

On similar grounds, Mr. Shinwell criticized his own front bench.

'Every one of us have constituents who are railwaymen, and they will ask us what we have done to try to avert this stoppage', he said. 'What is our answer to be? That we waited until the last minute of the eleventh hour before asking the Government what they proposed to do. I do not think that that is a satisfactory position for the Opposition to take. It certainly cannot be maintained. But apparently there is no redress. All I can do is to make my protest, which I hope is supported at any rate by a number of my hon. Friends.'

He was supported by Mr. Marcus Lipton, who said that the public would consider that Members of the House had not faced their responsibility.

However, as Mr. Butler pointed out, these representations ought to have been made earlier if the Members advancing them were to have convinced the House of their urgency, and it appears that there was general support for this view that the 'best help' that the House could give was to exercise 'restraint'.

Even when the dispute had been settled, no opportunity for debate was provided. By way of protest against this, Mr. Shinwell, Mr. Donnelly and other Labour Members tabled an Amendment to a back-bench Conservative Motion on the railways which had appeared upon the Order Paper. This Amendment called upon the Government:

'to recognise the rights of all Members of Parliament to receive full information about a dispute gravely affecting the interests of the travelling public and the employees of the British Transport Commission and to make a full statement to Parliament on the recent dispute and the negotiations which brought about a settlement.'

When this was drawn to Mr. Butler's attention in a 'Business of the House' discussion on 18th February, he replied that it was the

Government's wish in due course, to make a statement about the railways and the plans for the future, which were 'subjects in everyone's mind'.

It may be argued that we have made too much of these parliamentary disputes about ministerial responsibility for matters of fares, freights, wages and conditions; that the case of the British Transport Commission is an exceptional one; and that controversies of this kind are merely evidence of 'growing pains' and not of any fundamental *malaise* in board-minister-parliament relationships. Such a view would be superficial. The fact is that the Government cannot divest itself of responsibility for any aspect of the performance of a nationalized industry, whether it be categorized as one of 'general policy' or 'commercial judgement' or 'day-to-day administration'.

Even the idea that the Minister could—and in some circumstances should—express public disagreement with board policy has now faded into oblivion. It was first suggested by Mr. Morrison in his *Socialisation and Transport*, and restated by Mr. Molson in his evidence before the 1953 Select Committee, where he quoted the case of Mr. Callaghan's defence of the British Railways' 'bogus Gothic restaurant cars'[27]. But the only occasion, as far as we can discover, when a ministerial spokesman engaged in 'courteous but frank criticisms' of a nationalized industry, was in the 1953 Debate on the Report and Accounts of the British Transport Commission.[28] These criticisms, which were stimulated by what the spokesman called 'somewhat querulous references to the matter of consultation' contained in the Report, gave pleasure to Mr. Morrison himself, who said:

> 'It is legitimate that Ministers should be free to say so if they do not agree with something in a Report. They should never be the slaves of the public corporations. They have a right to their own point of view.'

At the same time he impressed on the Parliamentary Secretary that it was also 'competent and legitimate for public corporations publicly to disagree with Ministers about certain elements of their own policy affecting the work of public corporations.'

[27] See H.C. 235 of 1952–3, Minutes of Evidence, Q. 369.
[28] H.C. Deb., Vol. 518, 1980–2108.

Despite Mr. Morrison's encouragement, however, no subsequent ministerial spokesman has had the courage to grasp this nettle. The reason is obvious. If the subject of disagreement between Minister and Board is trivial, it is not worth mentioning. If it is important, it is bound to be regarded as a matter of ministerial responsibility. No Minister who values his political reputation can afford to say that his respect for the autonomy of the Board precluded him from correcting a serious mistake.

What the debates and Questions we have examined clearly indicate is that at any point matters which engage the 'public interest' can arise, and that consequently it is impossible to place precise limits on ministerial responsibility. Obviously, when things are going well, the ministerial hand will rest lightly on the helm, and most Members will be quite content that it should do so. But things never do go well for all of the nationalized industries all the time. So far, at least one of the industries has always been at the centre of a political storm. In these circumstances, ministerial intervention becomes continuous and virtually unlimited, and Members are naturally anxious to know what is going on and how the Ministers concerned are exercising their *de facto* powers. Yet convention enables the Government, if it so desires, to shelter behind the Board, to pretend that its own decisions have been taken by the industry itself, and to reply to parliamentary criticism with bromides and even with hypocrisies. No one can pretend that, from a democratic point of view, this is a desirable situation. Yet few are prepared to advocate the obvious remedy, full ministerial responsibility, for fear of hamstringing the nationalized industries and destroying the very concept of the public corporation. It is not our intention, in the present chapter, to suggest any solution to this problem, but simply to explain and to illustrate it. The lines along which, in our view, a solution might be sought will be the subject of the last chapter.

As we have seen, the causes of parliamentary frustration vary from time to time. For the most part, Members have concentrated on areas where the degree of ministerial responsibility is ambiguous, such as prices, industrial relations and the closing down of branch lines, However, in the Spring of 1960 the most publicized *casus belli* was a matter for which ministerial responsibility is in no doubt, viz. the capital financing of the nationalized industries. Here the

113

complaint was not that powers of control were inadequate, but that the procedure adopted by the House did not permit them to be brought fully into play.

From 1956, when the Government decided that the industries should be financed from the Budget, 'below the line', there were periodical complaints, voiced by Mr. Nabarro and his friends during debates on the Finance Bills, that the House had little opportunity to hold full and effective discussions of capital investment programmes, for which it was called upon to supply vast sums of money. But not until the present year did they bring their concentrated fire-power to bear on this subject. These Conservatives, thorns in the sides of their ministerial friends, then advanced specific demands for the better parliamentary supervision of the industries' financial requirements as part of a general campaign (which they pursued at every stage of the debates on the Estimates and the Finance Bill) for the curbing of 'excessive' government expenditure.

The first shot in this exercise was fired by the indefatigable Mr. Nabarro himself, towards the end of a lengthy speech directed against 'an appallingly bad Budget, the worst Budget brought in by a Conservative Chancellor since we returned in 1951'.[29]

While proclaiming himself reconciled to the principle of 'below the line' financing, which he had previously criticized, he said that what he and his friends wanted was 'annual accountability for capital sums before the money is spent, and not in retrospection'. An attempt in Consolidated Fund debate to question a particular item of capital expenditure had been ruled out of Order. The only remaining opportunity to raise such matters was now on the Finance Bill; but the Chancellor, in the Bill shortly to be introduced, had 'flouted the wishes of a majority of Members' on the Conservative side by bringing in a three-year provision, in accordance with the recommendations of the Radcliffe Committee, instead of a one-year provision. This decision, incompatible with annual accountability, was 'provocative', and the Chancellor would 'reap his due reward'.

'He wants a debate on the National Coal Board, the electricity boards, the gas boards, the Airways Corporations and

[29] H.C. Deb., Vol. 621, cols. 300–14, 5th April 1960.

the British Transport Commission on the appropriate Clauses of the Finance Bill. He will have it. I will see to it that he has the necessary Amendents.'

By the use of these tactics, Mr. Nabarro and his friends would 'drive him to a position whereby he will take this Clause for financing nationalized industries out of the Finance Bill and have instead an annual Bill called "Nationalized Industries (Capital Investment) Bill", with a separate Clause for the annual investment required for each of these State boards'. This, the ultimate object of the campaign, was intended to put an end to the situation in which Members could be told by the Parliamentary Secretary to the Ministry of Power that they 'had no statutory right whatever to challenge any item of capital investment by a State board'. The case was an unanswerable one, and would have to be met if there was to be 'appropriate accountability to Parliament and proper control over the expenditure of taxpayers' money'.

During the remainder of the Budget debate this demand remained undiscussed, apart from a passing reference to it by a Labour Member, Mr. George Darling, who questioned the honesty of the motives behind it. Nor did the Chancellor, in a winding-up speech which totally disregarded Mr. Nabarro's important contribution to the debate, choose to give his views on the subject. In response to an interruption from Mr. Nabarro which reiterated the demand, he merely replied that he would take note of his hon. Friend's observations.

The persistent Member for Kidderminster, however, found another opportunity immediately after the conclusion of the Budget debate, when the normal procedural resolution was introduced, authorizing 'provision . . . in any Finance Bill . . . for giving effect to any resolution which may be passed by a Committee of the whole House and agreed to by the House for the purpose of continuing the power to make advances under section 42 of the Finance Act, 1956 . . . and repealing the limit contained in that section on the total of the advances which may be so made.'

On this rather narrow basis he succeeded, without more than occasionally putting himself out of Order, in once again expressing his 'dissent from the continuing practice of financing nationalized industries within a section of the Finance Act'. Referring to the already-announced intentions of his group, he asked the Chancellor whether he thought it wise 'that, in the later stages of the Finance Bill, a group of my hon. Friends and I should be placed in the position, if we are to safeguard capital investment moneys in the State boards, of having only a single opportunity on that occasion of challenging any one of hundreds of different capital investment projects in these seven boards.'

Was it right, for instance, that 'on the appropriate Clauses of the Finance Bill . . ., there should be a debate about the wisdom, or otherwise, of the Secretary of State for Scotland vesting £15 million in the North of Scotland Hydro-Electricity Board, and the advisability or otherwise of a particular project being built at Loch Shin'?

Was it a good thing 'that we should debate, in the appropriate capital investment provision for British Overseas Airways Corporation, the type of aircraft it is to buy in the next five years? Does the Chancellor really think that it is sound parliamentary practice that the wisdom, or otherwise, of employing certain kinds of jet aircraft on a trans-Atlantic route should be debated in the later stages of a Finance Bill? Does he think that the provision of a North Midlands gas grid and the investment programme for it should appropriately be discussed in one of the later stages of the Finance Bill'?

If the Chancellor really wanted proper accountability, as he had claimed he did, then he would not press this procedural motion. But if he persisted, he would put Mr. Nabarro and his friends in a 'rigid position'.

> 'He will cause us . . . when the appropriate Clause of the Bill is reached . . . to move a reduction in the aggregate sum under that Clause, and then move for alteration of each of the constituent parts in capital sums for each nationalised industry. The effect of that in the later stages of a Finance Bill might be to cause a debate on capital investment in nationalised industries to go on for days on end.'

In reply, the Economic Secretary to the Treasury, Mr. Anthony Barber, asked Mr. Nabarro to agree that 'the way in which we finance nationalized industries—especially if we do so by direct means from the Exchequer—has a considerable bearing on the financial and economic policy of the Government'. It was because of this that the Government thought the subject 'should be included in the Finance Bill'.

The procedural resolution was passed without a division, and was immediately followed by a Finance (Exchequer Advances) Resolution, to provide the basis for the Clause in the Finance Bill authorizing the necessary capital advances. This gave Lord Hinchingbrooke the opportunity to continue the struggle. He strongly objected to the proposed 'three year' powers, and invited the Committee to reject the Motion, in order to oblige the Government 'to produce the sort of Bill that we can debate on Second Reading and in Committee and take some time over to see exactly what the plans of the nationalized industries are and approve them point by point'. Mr. Barber, in a reply which dealt only peripherally with the substance of Lord Hinchingbrooke's case, pointed out that the Motion itself did not specify any period of time, and suggested that his hon. Friend should table an Amendment in Committee 'to the effect that he would prefer that it should be one year'. Mr. Chuter Ede, speaking individually and not on behalf of the Labour Party, then expressed his uneasiness at the current method of handling this 'very important part of the national financing' and suggested that conversations should take place through the usual channels 'to ensure that reasonable arrangements are made'. Sir Toby Low, on the other hand, thought that the job was already being done by the Select Committee on Nationalized Industries (of which he was Chairman) and could not see that further opportunities were needed on the floor of the House.

> 'The nationalisation Acts make the specific Ministers responsible for approving the investment programmes of each nationalised industry. In their various different ways they make various Ministers responsible for approving borrowings. If the House wants at any time to raise a question whether a proposed investment programme is right or wrong, it has the opportunity in the ordinary course of business—Supply days and so on.'

Mr. Roy Jenkins (Labour) agreed with Mr. Nabarro and Lord Hinchingbrooke that the Finance Bill was an unsuitable occasion.

117

'The Finance Bill is, broadly speaking, a revenue-raising Bill, not a Bill for authorising expenditure. As the Chancellor knows and as the Committee knows, we on this side do not share the view of the hon. Member for Kidderminster and the noble Lord about the desirability of providing these funds for nationalised industries. We are in favour of doing this, but this is not the same as not being able to apply one's mind to the separate issue of how the House can best maintain control over this desirable objective.'

He hoped, therefore, that the Government 'would not close their mind to the possibility of having a separate Bill'. Mr. Houghton, another Labour speaker, shared this opinion, saying that he could not follow the Economic Secretary's argument that 'because this provides a method of financing the nationalized industries and prescribes a limit of finances to be provided, it is necessarily part of the Finance Bill'.

'It is only a few moments ago that the Chancellor was saying that it was not customary to deal with pensions at the time of the Budget and that pensions were always dealt with in separate legislation. However, considerable sums of money are always involved in National Insurance legislation. Do I not remember that we have hived off post-war credits into a separate Bill, which provides for extensions of the repayments of post-war credits to be made by regulations with which the House will deal on Tuesday? There is not over much consistency in the arguments of the Economic Secretary about the appropriate places in the Finance Bill.'

Further discussion did not throw much extra light on the subject, nor produce any concession from the Government. Mr. Nabarro therefore divided the House, mustering in his support a slightly odd-looking assortment of twenty Members from all three parties.

All this was on 7th April. It was not until 31st May that the relevant Clause of the Finance Bill—Clause 72 (Exchequer Advances to Nationalized Industries and Undertakings)—was reached. Mr. Nabarro then moved an Amendment to 'substitute

118

£2,007 million for £2,050 million, a net reduction of £43 million in the aggregation of sums to be voted for these seven nationalized industries in respect of their capital investments programmes for the year ending 31st August, 1961.'

This, he announced, was the 'master Amendment'. It would be followed by ten others, three of them consequential, and seven 'dealing respectively with each of the seven nationalized industries which are covered by this particular method of Exchequer financing'.

Part of Mr. Nabarro's case had already been conceded by the Chancellor, for when the Finance Bill had been published it was seen to contain no provision for the much-criticized 'three year period'. Mr. Nabarro was therefore able to concentrate on the main demand of his group: the need for a Nationalized Industries (Capital Investment) Bill. The purpose of his Amendments, he said, was a 'transitional' one—to enable the House to discuss the capital requirements of the industries until the passing of such a Bill provided a more suitable opportunity.

> 'In the past we have been able to debate the Reports and Accounts of these industries and the large sums of money expended only after the money has been committed and expended. If we agree to the Amendments today, we should have some sort of opportunity on later stages of this (Finance) Bill and, if the precedent were created and followed, in ensuing years on every Finance Bill, to debate the individual investment programmes of each of these seven industries. We have none of these facilities at present.'

Opposition spokesmen again expressed some sympathy for Mr. Nabarro's demand, while casting suspicion on the motives behind it, and strongly suggesting that Government subsidies to private industry should be vetted by the House with equal thoroughness. Thus Mr. Harold Wilson:

> 'What we complain about is that we have all this partisan "binding" by hon. Members opposite about the nationalised industries but not one of them suggest that similar powers be given in relation to private industries. We are voting very considerable sums of money to private industry . . . Do hon.

119

Members propose that we should go into the same detail
about them? Is there to be a Select Committee on privately-
owned industry comparable with the Select Committee on
Nationalised Industries? Are three days to be regularly allotted
every year by the Leader of the House for the purposes of debating these industries? No one would suggest doing that, and
yet Government money is going into those industries under
conditions about which we know very little.'

He agreed, however, that there was 'something inappropriate'
about including in a Finance Bill, which dealt mainly with the
raising of money, a Clause authorizing or at least regulating its
disbursement—a point which had already been made by Viscount
Hinchingbrooke.

When Mr. Wilson had concluded, the Chancellor rose to 'make
a few comments on what the hon. Gentlemen have said so far in the
debate'. The first part of his remarks was devoted to the rather
complicated techniques of authorizing capital advances to the
nationalized industries, with the object of showing that the belief
that Clause 72 of the Finance Bill actually controlled the borrowings of the industries was a mistaken one. He then admitted
sympathy with Members who found 'all this' confusing and who
wondered whether it constituted the best method 'of providing
Parliament with information about the amounts which the nationalized industries will be borrowing from the Exchequer in the
coming year and of authorizing the Exchequer to advance that
money'.

'Parliament', he said, 'is interested and entitled to be interested in the investment programmes of those industries, to be
informed of the broad lines of those programmes, and to be
able, if it wishes, to examine and debate them before they are
put into execution.'

It was also rightly concerned with 'the financial implications to
the Exchequer of those investment programmes', and ought to be
informed 'if during the course of the year the financial implications
for the Exchequer of the activities of the nationalized industries
turn out to be very different from those which they were expected

to be at the beginning of the year, namely the expectations on which the Budget was based'.

Having thus virtually conceded the case of the 'Nabarro group', he concluded with the following announcement, which received considerable publicity in the following day's papers:

'The Government now are examining these questions urgently in view of the representations which have been made from the House of Commons. It is our expectation that by the autumn we shall be able to make new proposals—agreeable, we hope, to the House of Commons—for the handling of these matters in the future on a more satisfactory basis, including supplying to the House of Commons information which hon. Members can examine and debate, both on the annual investment programme of each industry and, at a later stage, the estimated amounts which each industry will require to borrow from the Exchequer in the coming year.'

Well might Mr. Nabarro have felt satisfaction in begging leave to withdraw his Amendment. But it need not be supposed that the satisfaction was confined to him and his group. For once he was expressing a frustration experienced, to various degrees, on all sides of the House.

Mr. Butler produced the 'new proposals' with commendable speed shortly before the Summer Recess. These took into account a whole series of suggestions, many of them emanating from the Nabarro-Hinchingbrooke group, for strengthening parliamentary control of expenditure, a subject which had been frequently debated, in a context wider than that of the nationalized industries, during the Spring and Summer of 1960. With the proposals that concerned reforms in the methods of debating Supply and changes in the constitution and functions of the Estimates Committee we are not here concerned. The part of Mr. Butler's statement germane to our present subject ran as follows:

'There will be published in the autumn a White Paper on the investment programmes in the public sector including, of course, the nationalised industries.

'In the Government's view, this White Paper and any Reports which may be received from the Select Committee on the nationalised industries would provide suitable subjects for debate on the three days which are customarily allotted out of Government time for debates on the Reports from the various boards themselves.

'One day will definitely be allocated before Christmas, when it would presumably be the wish of the House to debate the investment programmes set out in the White Paper.'

The statement as a whole was well received, and the only Member who—rather 'ungallantly' according to Mr. Butler—looked at this particular gift horse in the mouth was Mr. Nabarro himself, who, referring to the demands he had previously made, asked:

'Does my right hon. Friend's reference to a White Paper on public expenditure, which is a sort of compendium of all public expenditure, give those precise facilities to my hon. Friends and myself to examine the individual capital allocations of nationalised industries and not in a single comprehensive form on a sort of innocuous Motion to take note of a White Paper, which would be useless to my hon. Friends and myself?'

To this Mr. Butler replied that the Chancellor had shown even more generosity than had been asked of him; for the White Paper would deal with all 'below the line' investment, and not merely with investment in the nationalized industries. Moreover, the Chancellor had also told the House 'that he would publish another White Paper in February or March on the estimated figures of borrowings to meet the programmes of the nationalized industries during the ensuing financial year.'[30]

The latest step towards the implementation of these promises that we can here record is Mr. Butler's announcement, on 25th October 1960, that the Chancellor would be presenting the White Paper on 1st November and that 'the Government would be

[30] H.C. Deb., Vol. 152, cols. 1292–1302, 26th July 1960.

submitting in due course a type of broad motion upon which they thought a two-day debate could be held.'[31]

While the usefulness of these procedural changes cannot be assessed until the House has begun to operate them, it is clear that their intention is entirely sensible: to strengthen parliamentary control precisely at the point where it may be most intelligently and effectively exercised.

Although this last dispute has been amicably and constructively settled, most of the proceedings on which we have concentrated in this chapter show the House in a frustrated rather than in a euphoric mood. This may easily give a wrong impression: for there are many occasions, even under the present dispensation, when debates on nationalized industries are of a kind that ought to give reasonable satisfaction to even the most embittered critic of the 'talking-shop'. Some of these have already been mentioned, but the best of them have been deliberately left to the last. They are the debates when Parliament is engaged in discussing resolutions based on certain carefully-formulated, fully-documented, concrete proposals. Of the several examples which might be quoted, perhaps the best is the 'Fuel and Power' debate of 28th October, 1952. On this occasion the House had before it not only the latest Annual Reports of the nationalized Fuel and Power Industries but the Report of the ('Ridley') Committee on National Policy for the Use of Fuel and Power Resources. No one reading the debate can doubt that its concentration on the 'Ridley' proposals was responsible for its exceptionally useful, sensible and well-informed character. For once, the Parliamentary Secretary, in winding up the debate, was being more than conventionally complimentary when he said:

> 'We are exceedingly grateful for the expression of (Members') views and for the way in which they have been made, helpfully, constructively and sympathetically, by hon. Members who know many aspects of the problems which lie behind the recommendations of the Report.'

Another example, already quoted, is the series of debates on

[31] *The Times*, 26th October 1906.

the Government's Electricity Bill of 1957, when Members took full advantage of the mass of information and reasoned criticism contained in the 'Herbert' Report.

It may be surmised that experience of debates of this kind caused many Members to look with favour upon suggestions designed to enable Parliament to become more *regularly* briefed, by a non-party or inter-party information-gathering and proposal-formulating agency, on the affairs of the nationalized industries.[32] At any rate, it is certain that dissatisfaction with the character of the more usual type of debate gave powerful support to those who, since the late 1940s, had been advocating the establishment of a Select Committee on the Nationalized Industries. As is well known, such a Committee has now been in operation for several years, and it represents the only important innovation in respect of parliamentary control since the introduction of the 'general direction' clauses into the post-war nationalization acts. The next chapter, therefore will be mainly devoted to an examination of the origins, constitution and functions of this body, and to a discussion of how far it has succeeded in bringing about any improvement in the board-minister-parliament relationship.

[32] Such views about debates were certainly held by Mr. Hugh Molson, one of the earliest advocates of the establishment of a Select Committee on Nationalized Industries (see below, p. 132).

VI

Select Committees

Up to the time of the appointment of the first of the Select Committees on Nationalized Industries (Reports and Accounts), the only specialized parliamentary body with any authority to inquire into the performance of the nationalized industries was the Public-Accounts Committee. As the nationalization acts required the Minister to lay before each House of Parliament the Annual Report and Statement of Accounts of each industry, these automatically came within the scope of the Public Accounts Committee's jurisdiction, in so far as it was empowered to examine not only the Appropriation Accounts but 'such other accounts laid before Parliament' as it might 'think fit'.

There have been several occasions on which the Public Accounts committee *did* think it fit to exercise this right, but its examinations of the nationalized industries were always rather cursory and never particularly enlightening. The reason for this is not far to seek; for the Committee's expert watch-dog, the Comptroller and Auditor-General, has never been given the right to investigate the nationalized industries' accounts—nor, indeed would he be in a position to investigate them at all profitably, unless his existing staff were to be enlarged by new personnel skilled in the techniques of commercial accountancy. The Committee, therefore, is deprived of technical advice in respect of the very accounts which cannot be examined and criticized along the lines of its traditional procedures.

It was realized that this would be so as early as 1946. Then, in the debate of the Coal Industry Nationalization Act, Captain Crookshank, for the Opposition, moved an amendment which would have made the Coal Board's accounts subject to audit by the Comptroller and Auditor-General.[1] It was rejected, albeit with

---

[1] H.C. Deb., Vol. 422, col. 1938. See also *Official Report of Debates in Standing Committee C*, 2nd April 1946, col. 683.

some slight misgiving, for the same reason that Questions about 'day-to-day' matters were to be rejected. While admitting that this was 'really a border line case', Mr. Gaitskell gave the following reason for the Government's obduracy:

> 'Sometimes we think it is a good thing that civil servants should be frightened off, and that they should have at the back of their mind the fear that they have to account to the Comptroller and Auditor-General for everything they do, but in this case we think that that would be undesirable, because we do not want the National Coal Board to be unenterprising, and to have the feeling all the time, on every detail of their work, that around the corner is this representative of Parliament, who is likely to pull them up on the slightest thing and worry and restrict them.[2]

Even if the Government had accepted the amendment, however, certain easily foreseeable difficulties would have arisen. Two of these are pointed out by Dr. Chubb in his treatise on the control of expenditure.

> 'First, the time difficulties of the Accounts Committee would inevitably grow worse, for the amount of time which it would almost certainly wish to give to the examination of these accounts, especially in the first years, would further complicate the already complicated time-table. Second, examination by the Accounts Committee would raise the question "whether the Accounting Officer of the sponsoring Ministry will be the witness who appears before the Public Accounts Committee to answer on the accounts, or whether the officers of the corporation concerned who have first-hand knowledge of the accounts will do so". The Accounting Officer has neither the knowledge nor the direct responsibility necessary to answer. He does not sign the accounts, nor is it desirable that he should interfere in the corporation's affairs. Moreover, the Treasury could hardly write Minutes on the Committee's views of these accounts.'[3]

[2] H.C. Deb., Vol. 423, cols. 49–50.
[3] Basil Chubb: *The Control of Public Expenditure*, Oxford 1952, p. 146.

A third—mentioned by Dr. Chubb as applying to the Estimates Committee as well as to the Public Accounts Committee—is that the Committee 'would almost inevitably apply to the boards the criteria used in the case of government departments', instead of the commercial criteria which were the only appropriate ones.[4]

It is not surprising, therefore, that the Committee spent very little of its valuable time looking at the Reports and Accounts of the nationalized industries. Nevertheless, it did make some attempt to discharge its responsibilities. In the session 1948–9, for instance, it examined Sir D. Ferguson, Permanent Secretary of the Ministry of Fuel and Power, on the National Coal Board, extracting from him a fairly important statement on the relative responsibilities of the Minister and the Board for the fixing of prices, and asking him about the adequacy of the Board's provisions for depreciation and obsolescence.[5] In the following year it conducted a rather more detailed inquiry into the same industry, asking questions on (a) the size of reserves for the satisfaction of workmen's compensation claims; (b) the reasons for the unprofitability of the Northumberland and Durham coalfield; (c) the desirability of establishing a contingency fund against successfully-pursued supplementary claims by former owners; (d) the closing down of uneconomic pits; (e) the reasons for certain increases in administrative staff; (f) the production policy of the Board with reference to the quality of coal; (g) export policy; (h) items entering into the cost of production; (i) the economic value and profitability of different kinds of briquetting plants; and (j) certain aspects of the Board's financial relationships with the Ministry.[6] The miscellaneous nature of these inquiries, which occupied no more than thirteen pages in the Minutes of Evidence, indicates that the Committee was casting about for things to ask without much sense of purpose or direction. It did, however, produce a rather interesting statement from Sir Donald Ferguson about 'general directions'.

Following an expression of opinion by Sir Donald that the amount of coal to go to the export market and the home market was 'in a sense a matter of Government policy rather than the National Coal Board's policy', Sir John Mellor asked him whether

[4] *Ibid*. p. 258.
[5] *3rd Report*, H.C., 233–1, pp. 369–73, Qs. 3979–4023.
[6] H.C. 37–1, 78–1, 138–1, pp. 241–54, Qs. 3569–3674.

the Government had given directions to the Board on this subject. On being told that it had not, Sir John asked whether it had the power to do so, to which Sir Donald replied that he 'thought' that 'in this matter the Minister could give directions to the National Coal Board'. Evidently, even the permanent officials of the Ministry were a little vague on this tricky subject—or perhaps they had become so used to 'old boy' methods that they regarded the issue as one of theoretical interest only.

In 1951–2 the Committee made a new departure. During the course of its investigation of the Report and Accounts of the Transport Commission, it heard evidence from the joint statutory auditors of the Commission's accounts, Sir Alan Rae-Smith (of Deloitte, Plender, Griffiths & Co.) and Sir Harold Barton (of Barton, Mayhew & Co.). The reason for this rather surprising move, apparently, was that these auditors had appended 'qualifying remarks' to their formal certificates. To answer on behalf of the Commission, Lord Hurcomb, its Chairman, was summoned.

A full analysis of the Committee's examination of these witnesses, and of Sir Gilmour Jenkins, who represented the Ministry of Transport, has been provided by Miss Gweneth Gutch.[7] The issue that it raised which is of main interest to us was the extent to which the Committee had the right to 'go behind' the statutory auditors' reports and to examine the reports of the Transport Commission's 130 internal auditors. On being requested to provide the Committee with a copy of the internal auditor's report to which the statutory auditors had referred in their certificate, Lord Hurcomb asked for time 'to consider that question', as he felt that to accede to the request would create a dangerous precedent. He was supported by Sir Gilmour Jenkins, who suggested, very respectfully, that the Committee was 'going rather further than Parliament intended'. There followed some discussion about the extent to which the internal auditors' reports could be regarded as matters of 'day-to-day' administration, which revealed 'how precarious' was 'the . . . tightrope traversed by the public corporation'.

'I think we are bound to give to Parliament all the detail

[7] Gweneth Gutch: *Nationalised Industries and the Public Accounts Committee*, 1951–2, in *Public Administration*, Vol. 31, Autumn 1953.

and the information that can be reasonably afforded', said Lord Hurcomb. 'It is a question as to how far points of detail of purely commercial or business character are pursued and made public'.

Although the extract from the internal auditors' report requested by the Committee was eventually produced, the question of principle remained unsettled—as, indeed, it remains to this day. For the Public Accounts Committee did not choose to repeat its experiment, and no similar type of investigation was subsequently attempted by the Select Committee on Nationalized Industries (Reports and Accounts). Whether the powers of the latter body, would extend so far is a matter of some doubt. As we shall see, it is empowered to examine only the Reports and Accounts of the nationalized industries, but the tendency is always to give a liberal rather than a restrictive interpretation to any Select Committee's terms of reference.

Subsequent Reports of the Public Accounts Committee contain comparatively little material of interest to the student of the nationalized industries, unless we extend the meaning of this term to include the B.B.C. and the Colonial Development Corporation. To both of these bodies special circumstances apply, in so far as they are financed by Exchequer grants. Inevitably, the Public Accounts Committee has fewer inhibitions about going into matters of 'day-to-day' administration when public money, specifically made available from budgetary sources, is involved. Both in 1953–4 and in 1955–6 it took fairly extensive evidence on the affairs of the Colonial Development Corporation,[8] and in the latter year it subjected Sir Ian Jacob, the B.B.C.'s Director-General, and Mr. J. G. L. Francis, its Chief Accountant, to a rather severe and wide-ranging examination.[9] Civil Airways were also very much its concern, so long as they were in receipt of annual Exchequer grants.[10] But since its investigation of the Transport Commission it has almost entirely neglected the nationalized

[8] *Third Report of* 1953–4 (H.C.231), pp. 41, 427–9; *First, Second and Third Reports of* 1955–6 (H.C. 15–1, 22–I, 124–I), pp. 40–6.

[9] *Fourth, Fifth and Sixth Reports of* 1955–6 (H.C. 204–I, 238–I, 282–I, 348–I), pp. 63–74.

[10] See, for instance, *First, Second and Third Reports of* 1952–3 (H.C. 48–I, 106–I, 203–I).

enterprises with which we are here concerned. The main reason for this is quite simple. In 1955, Parliament established the first of its Select Committees with the specific responsibility of examining the Reports and Accounts of the nationalized industries. This did not deprive the Public Accounts Committee of its rights of examination, but it did make the further exercise of these rights superfluous, in view of the fact that the new Committee was supposed to be better adapted to the task.

The train of circumstances that led up to the appointment of the first Select Committee on Nationalized Industries (Reports and Accounts) is somewhat complex, but the reason for its appointment was straightforward. Members on both sides of the House were discontented with what they considered to be the inadequacy of parliamentary information about the nationalized industries and of the House's capacity to make constructive criticisms of the manner in which they were administered. A Select Committee appeared to be the best method of overcoming both deficiencies. While a Labour Government was in office, there was little possibility of such a Committee being set up, owing to Mr. Morrison's opinion that 'this would result in taking chairmen and principal members of Boards away from their business, and would make them always nervous of the prospect of appearing at any time before a half-circle of Members of Parliament, all having their pet views and putting them through a certain amount of cross-examination'.[11] The Conservative Government which took office in 1951 was, however, much more sympathetic to the Select Committee device and, after a number of delays and hesitations and one false start, eventually appointed the body whose work will subsequently be examined.

In doing this, it was well in line with recent developments in parliamentary procedure, for the general tendency is to make increasing use of Select Committees. A Select Committee on Statutory Instruments was first appointed in 1944, and the Estimates Committee, re-established in 1946 after a war-time interregnum during which a National Expenditure Committee conducted vigorous and often unwelcome investigations, proved far more effective than its somewhat effete predecessor of the period between

[11] See *Report from the Select Committee on Nationalised Industries* (H.C. 332–I of 1951–2), Appendix A, p. 133.

the wars. In general, Select Committees to investigate the behaviour of government departments were not exactly popular with Ministers of the Crown or with civil servants, but they did seem to offer a useful method of supplementing Parliament's more normal and traditional methods of bringing 'the bureaucracy' to account. New Select Committees tended to acquire something of the prestige already won by the formidable Public Accounts Committee, and also to reproduce the 'non-political' atmosphere which surrounded that body. The process of hearing, sifting and weighing evidence, by a small number of Members in a committee room where parliamentary reporters had no right of entry, made for 'responsibility'; and the necessity of producing a Report which had to be unanimous or near-unanimous if it were to carry much weight discouraged the pushing of mere party arguments to the point of a division. These factors tended to prevent a Select Committee from getting too deeply involved in matters of policy and thereby, as the opponents of constitutional innovation feared, undermining ministerial responsibility. They were also responsible for the growing habit, on the part of Members, the Press and the public, of treating Select Committee Reports as weighty, if not completely authoritative documents, whose criticisms and proposals deserved serious consideration. Many, therefore, regarded Select Committees as offering a way out of the *impasse* in which Parliament appeared to be involved as a result of the growing size and complexity of the administrative apparatus. Some believed, and continue to believe, that the House of Commons ought to equip itself with a positive network of specialized committees, each attached, in an advisory and critical capacity, to a department or group of departments.[12]

The idea of a Select Committee on the Nationalized Industries, however, had its special difficulties. If the Committee was not to be concerned with policy, because this was ultimately a matter of ministerial responsibility, and if it was simultaneously to be excluded from day-to-day administration, on the grounds that it would be looking over the shoulders of the Boards, just what could it do? Moreover, was a body of parliamentarians, relatively ignorant of industrial management and very busy with other

[12] See A. H. Hanson and H. V. Wiseman: *The Use of Committees by the House of Commons*, in *Public Law*, Autumn 1959.

matters, really the right one for this purpose? If the nationalized industries needed periodical outside investigation, would it not be better to give the job to acknowledged experts? And would it not hamper the managers of these industries far less seriously if the investigatory body were appointed by and responsible to the industries themselves, forming something in the nature of a common efficiency unit? These were some of the questions vigorously canvasssed during the five years or so preceding the establishment of the first Select Committee on Nationalised Industries (Reports and Accounts). Some description of this controversy will therefore help to clarify both the advantages and the limitations of this body and of its present-day successor.

It is difficult to say who first suggested the idea, but among Members of Parliament, Mr. Baird (Labour), who drew it to the attention of the House of Commons in the Autumn of 1948, would appear to have pride of place.[13] In the Socialized Industries (Questions to Ministers) Debate, Mr. Hugh Molson (Conservative) amplified Mr. Baird's views, adding to them the suggestion that Parliament should appoint an 'Efficiency Auditor-General', to provide the proposed Select Committee with expert assistance.[14] He found opportunity in the Second Reading of the Coal Industry Bill to return to the theme,[15] and on September 8th 1949, produced a careful and considered version of his proposals in a *Times* article. In this, he criticized current debates on the nationalized industries as 'rambling and discursive . . . with many speeches delivered primarily for constituency consumption'. The House, he thought, was at its best when debating a Bill or other document which offered for discussion a limited number of fairly precisely-defined issues. Such a document, he held, could periodically emerge from the labours of a Select Committee on nationalized industries, which could conduct investigations similar in scope and kind to those of the war-time Committee on National Expenditure and the post-war Select Committee on Estimates. These had done valuable work in 'exposing blunders, inefficiency and waste'. The methods of investigation that they had employed, however, were unsuitable for the new task, in so far as they might have the effect of

[13] H.C. Deb., Vol. 435, col. 2305.
[14] H.C. Deb., Vol. 448, cols. 423–32.
[15] H.C. Deb., Vol. 458, cols. 1731–2.

'destroying the flexibility of the Board method of administration'. A new body was therefore required, 'serviced by an appropriate staff'. Its reports 'should focus attention on the more important issues', and should be debated by the House on the basis of substantive motions.

In the Socialized Industries debate, Mr. Morrison, for the Government, had expressed interest in these views. By the time of the Coal Industry Bill debate, however, he had decided against them. Later, he expressed the opinion that a periodical investigation of each nationalized industry by a Royal Commission offered a preferable alternative. There the matter rested until the Conservatives came into office, when, as we have seen, Captain Crookshank announced the appointment of a Select Committee to inquire into the relationships between the nationalized industries and the House of Commons. The First Report of this Committee, which dealt with Questions to Ministers, has been examined.[16] It followed this by taking voluminous evidence about the proposed Select Committee, and by producing a second and final Report in which it set the seal of its approval on the idea.[17]

This recommendation was rather surprising, for it by no means corresponded with the weight of the evidence that the Committee had received. Mr. Morrison expressed the view that the proposed Select Committee would lack authority 'on matters of managerial or industrial efficiency', and tend to create, among the 'ordinary business men who are running, in the main, the publicly-owned industries . . . a rather red-tapish, unadventurous and conventionally civil service frame of mind'. He reiterated his preference for the periodical, *ad hoc* Committee of Inquiry, composed of 'competent business people who know the ropes of business organization and management, and of ordinary good citizens, with a certain number of Parliamentarians'. He also suggested the formation of a 'common efficiency unit'—'a common product of the Boards collectively', which could look at 'obvious economic problems, costing problems, managerial problems, which had arisen and which the Board could not solve itself'. Of the Corporation representatives examined, Lord Reith was most vehemently opposed to the Select Committee idea. 'Institutionalizing in terrifying form

[16] See above, pp. 62-6.
[17] H.C. 235 of 1952–3.

the Parliamentary Question' was the way he described it. Sir
Geoffrey Heyworth, then a part-time member of the National Coal
Board, although far less categorical and prepared to admit that
he did not 'know the answers', was also, to say the least, unen-
thusiastic. Speaking from his experience as Chairman of Unilever,
he said:

'If people came to looking at everything I did in a year,
after the event, the shareholders would be horrified because
they would see that some of those decisions were quite wrong
in the light of after events. The mere fact therefore that I felt
someone was looking over my shoulder all the time and was
going to examine these things at any time later, the less I would
be inclined to take a decision and the less decisive I would
become.'

The more that nationalized industries could be made into 'autonomous units', he considered, 'the better chance there is for
success'.

Lord Hurcomb, however, thought that some kind of Committee
would be useful. In his view, indeed, there ought to be more than
one Committee, as different nationalized industries presented
different kinds of problems. His conception of what a Committee
might do was expounded in some detail and is worth quoting *in
extenso*:

'If there was some sort of relationship, not of investigation
or probing into financial detail, or in which challenge to its
efficiency were the main object, but designed to get to know
what the undertaking was doing, . . . if one could establish
that sort of relationship so that the organization did not feel
itself perpetually under the harrow, but was having an opportunity of explaining its policy and endeavours, and answering
any challenge there might be put to what it had done, including its financial results, I think in a broad way that would be
extremely helpful to the organization, and ought to go a long
way towards informing the mind of Parliament . . . One of the
very greatest handicaps under which anyone in my position
suffers is that he gets no opportunity of stating his own case

or of explaining what his difficulties are direct to Members of Parliament. It is true I meet a great many individually, or I may dine with some group or other from time to time, but one does not have the opportunity of putting before a Committee of Parliament, or a group of Members of Parliament, even the bare facts. It has been borne upon me, if I may say so, without causing offence in any quarter . . . that a great many misapprehensions do exist, and perhaps decisions are taken on some supposition of fact which is not correct. A Committee of this sort would, or ought to mean . . . that a large number of Members of Parliament would have the opportunity of satisfying themselves and conveying, not by way of attack and of public speech, but by way of suggestion to the organization, the points where they thought something might be going wrong, or, at any rate, would be worth looking into. That would be of great value. There is a particular direction in which I feel that a committee of that sort might help to make the way in which Parliament uses its time more economical. I think everyone who has listened to debates on annual reports, and so on, comes away with the impression that a great part of the evening has gone on comparatively trivial details, or just an interchange of pleasantries between the two sides. If there were a committee of this sort which could examine the annual report of the Commission, or any other report they might make about special matters, and could report to the House and say, "Here are major matters which we have considered, and which we think deserve the attention of the House" it might guide discussion into a more useful channel.'

Sir Edward Bridges, Permanent Secretary to the Treasury, envisaged a similar role for the Select Committee, and also suggested that it might sometimes propose the appointment of a special, expert commission of inquiry into matters which appeared to demand investigation but which it was not competent itself to investigate. He was not 'awfully happy', however, about the Morrisonian proposal for 'a periodic review on a grand scale', considering that this would indeed keep the corporation 'under the harrow' as the time between successive reviews was likely to be too short.

Apart from Lord Hurcomb, the only two witnesses who gave

definite support to the Select Committee idea were Mr. Molson and Captain Crookshank, both Members of Parliament. One of these, of course, had for many years been a strong advocate of the device, and his evidence consisted of a repetition of the views for which he was already well known. The other, however, being a prominent member of the Government and a politician who, up to that time, had not clearly committed himself on the issue, must have been regarded by the Committee as a witness whose evidence carried considerable weight.

In spite of the conflict of evidence, the Committee's main recommendations were clear and definite, viz.

(a) There should be appointed a Committee of the House of Commons by Standing Order, to examine the Nationalized Industries, with power to send for persons, papers and records, power to set up sub-committees, and to report from time to time;

(b) The Committee should direct their attention to the published Reports and Accounts, and to obtaining further information as to the general policy and practice of the Nationalized Industries established by Statute, whose controlling Boards are wholly nominated by Ministers of the Crown, and whose annual receipts are not wholly derived from moneys provided by Parliament or advanced from the Exchequer;

(c) The object of the Committee should be that of informing Parliament about the aims, activities and problems of the Corporations and not of controlling their work;

(d) The staff of the Committee should include an officer of the status of the Comptroller and Auditor-General who should be an officer of the House of Commons, with high administrative experience; at least one professional accountant, and such other staff as required:

(e) The statutory auditors of the corporations shall, in preparing their annual reports, give such information in addition to that now provided by them as may be of use to the Committee and of interest to Parliament.

On the proposed Committee's sphere of investigation and methods of work, however, the Report was rather vague, and one or two of the suggestions that it made were quite evidently 'non-starters'. One of these was that the Committee should receive from the Board, each year, a statement of anticipated expenditure and revenue, with the aid of which it could 'satisfy itself that the corporation was genuinely trying to comply with its statutory requirements of breaking even, taking one year with another'. Precisely what use such a crude criterion would be the Report made no attempt to explain. Even less eligible was the suggestion that each Board 'should publish with its annual report to Parliament the best estimate it can make of the percentage increase or decrease since the date of its establishment in the average cost to the consumer of its products or service, taken as a whole', so as to 'enable the Committee to form some opinion, though not a conclusive one, on the efficiency of the industry', by comparing this estimate with the general cost of living index. Mr. D. N. Chester moderately described this proposal as 'startling'.[18] It certainly showed that its authors had distinctly elementary ideas about the techniques of efficiency-measurement.

The Report clearly envisaged that the new Committee should have wider powers than the Public Accounts Committee. 'It should have a regard, not merely to present and past financial policy and stability, but to future plans and programmes'. But the question of just what it should investigate and how it should organize itself for the task were met with studiously vague answers. It should avoid investigating, said the Report, (a) decisions which resulted from a direction given by the Minister, under his statutory powers; (b) matters normally decided by the established machinery of collective bargaining; and (c) 'matters which fall into the category of detailed administration'. But how far could it go into those informal contacts between Minister and Board through which his supervisory powers were in fact exercised? And how could any serious and penetrating inquiry into the organization of a Board keep on the right side of that vague and fluctuating line that divided matters of 'detailed administration' from those of a more general character? The first question was not considered at all, while on the second the members of the Committee seem to have had some difficulty in making up their minds. The Report, in its

[18] *Select Committee on Nationalised Industries*, in *Public Administration*, Vol. 31, Autumn 1953, p. 274.

commendable anxiety to avoid exasperating the Boards, rejected a suggestion made to it by the President of the Institute of Chartered Accountants, to the effect that the statutory auditors of the corporations might make, for the investigating body's benefit, supplementary reports drawing attention to 'any matter of a material or substantial character which may have arisen' under the various headings of their main reports. It nevertheless recommended that the statutory auditors should be asked to provide the new Committee with certain 'additional information'.

There is also evidence of some unclarity about the precise functions of the proposed 'officer of the status of the Comptroller and Auditor-General' and his professional staff. What powers of investigation were they to possess? To what extent could *they* be expected to exercise their functions without looking over the shoulders of the Boards and getting deeply involved in day-to-day matters? What qualifications would they require for the performance of their difficult task? The Report had very little to say in reply to these rather obvious queries. Nor did it have anything to say about the *frequency* of investigations, except the very considerable understatement 'that the proposed Committee may not have time each year to conduct a detailed examination of each of the Nationalized Industries'.

For the rest, it seemed to assume that the procedure of the new Committee would not differ substantially from that of the Estimates Committee. In respect of its relationship with the whole House, the Estimates Committee also provided the model to be followed. There was no suggestion that every report should be debated, and Mr. Molson's demand 'that the proposed Committee should have the task of directing the debates which are held in the House on Nationalized Industries, and of suggesting the allocation of time to each subject of debate' was definitely rejected, on the grounds 'that such direction of the work of the House might not appeal to the House and that it conflicts in some degree with the principle of free debates which has so far prevailed in the House of Commons'.

Several months went by before the Government, having tentatively defined its attitude towards this challenging Report, offered it to the House for debate. Even then, the Leader of the House produced no substantive motion, but used an Adjournment motion for the purpose of initiating a discussion in which Members, by freely expressing their reactions, could help the Government finally to make up its mind.[19] Captain Crookshank, opening, was neither convincing nor impressive. He made much of Lord Hurcomb's evidence, and produced a rather curious argument, which many Members found puzzling, to justify the 'constitutionality' of the proposed Select Committee.

> 'It would be a constitutional innovation', he said, with complete disregard of the Estimates Committee, 'to set up a Select Committee working with existing Departments, but I cannot see that it is so in the case of the nationalised industries, because we have gone out of our way not to consider them as State Departments. We have made them something different.'

While expressing general agreement with the Committee's proposals, he suggested their modification in four respects. The proposed Committee should have no concern with *future* plans and programmes of the nationalized industries; it should not be permitted to divide itself into sub-committees, for fear that it might get involved in 'detail and excessive investigations'; it should not be equipped with an Efficiency Auditor-General, but only with a Clerk and a Treasury liaison officer; and it should not necessarily publish all the evidence it received.[20]

Captain Crookshank was followed by Mr. Morrison, who claimed to speak not only for the Opposition but for the General Council of the Trade Union Congress and the National Executive Committee of the Labour Party. Morrison, and presumably those for whom he spoke, had not been convinced by the Report. He suggested that Crookshank himself was in a 'dilemma', as evidenced by his desire to impose restrictive terms of reference on the proposed Committee.

> 'He wants to go so far in order to further what he conceives to be a Parliamentary right, but he does not want to go so far that he becomes a commercial menace to the well-being of the undertaking.'

[19] H.C. Deb., Vol. 523, cols. 833–962, 8th February 1954.
[20] 'If it were to be found that an independent officer was required, it would be a question then for Parliament to consider.'

Mr. Morrison underlined the evidence given by the hostile witnesses, particularly Sir Geoffrey Heyworth, and dwelt upon the alleged evils of the committee systems of the French and United States legislatures. Of Lord Hurcomb, he said: 'I thought that he wanted a nice little body of Members of Parliament to whom he could come and tell his troubles now and again. I doubt if he wanted the formality of a Select Committee.'

His general theme was that the proposed Committee would be 'either . . . so limited, so circumscribed, by its sphere of activities' that it would become a 'farce' or so 'wide as to imperil the reasonable freedom of the commercial management of the undertakings'. Existing parliamentary opportunities of supervising the nationalized industries, had, he suggested, been underestimated. If five, instead of three days were in future 'allocated to debates on corporations', there should be no further cause for complaint.

In the remainder of the debate, all Conservative and some Labour Speakers supported the establishment of a Select Committee. The strongest support, on the Labour side, came from those who had been members of the Committee that produced the Report, which was a unanimous one. Of these, Mr. Ernest Davies made the most interesting contribution, stressing the value of a Select Committee as a means of bringing home to ministers their responsibility to Parliament for the manner in which they conducted their *informal* relationships with the Boards. He said:

> 'If those Ministers influence the nationalised industries and have close contact, quite rightly, with the chairman and members of the boards, and if they then do not accept responsibility to this House, cannot answer questions on detail—with which we all agree—and do not inform this House of the influence, pressure, persuasion, or whatever it might be, that they exert on those boards, there must be some other channel through which the House can be better informed.'

For him, the menace of interference in 'day-to-day' matters, so strongly stressed by Mr. Morrison, was little more than a bogey. If Parliament was better informed, he considered, it would be far less anxious to interfere. 'It would not harbour suspicions and doubts', said Mr. Davies, 'but would realize that it would be more helpful to assist the nationalized industries in the ways suggested in our Report.'

Two Labour Members, however, backed Mr. Morrison in such a way as to make the question of establishing a Select Committee into a political issue. Mr. Holmes saw the proposal as a covert attack on nationalization itself. He was supported, at greater length and with some display of synthetic fire, by Mr. Douglas Houghton. Two others, Mr. W. Griffiths and Mr. Eric Fletcher, while taking opposite views about the desirability of a Select Committee, chose to challenge the assumed need, which everyone else had accepted, of limitations on ministerial responsibility. Mr. Griffiths asked why the nationalized industries should be regarded as fundamentally different, in this respect, from the National Health Service.

'The National Health Service', he said, 'employs 300,000 people. The Minister of Health, every Thursday in the House, has to answer in detail, if so requested, for every aspect of the administration of the Service. The Service was introduced in an atmosphere of violent political controversy at least as violent as the nationalisation measures . . .'

Yet, 'six years after the opening of the Service, we do not find trivial Questions placed on the Order Paper to the Minister of Health'. Mr. Fletcher used the rather over-worked example of parliamentary Questions to the Postmaster-General.

On the Conservative side, the most constructive contribution came from Mr. Spencer Summers, who attempted to illustrate the value of the proposed Select Committee by reference to his experience as a member of the Estimates Committee.

'To start with', he said, 'I wondered whether we were really competent to render any service to this House in tackling very highly technical subjects, knowing very well that, technically, we were not qualified, and that the experts who answered the questions were better qualified to answer them than we were to ask them . . . However, as time has gone on I have become convinced that the time is not wasted and that the very fact that we are not technical experts is the source of the benefit, if any, that our Select Committee, and other of our Select Committees, can render.'

As an example of an innocent inquiry that had led to useful action he quoted the question, 'What are you going to do about Woolwich Arsenal?' In the Department, he said, they had 'not asked themselves that question for a very long time. It was of the utmost possible value that somebody should have said: "What are you going to do about it?" . . . The Minister took notice of the question, and began doing something about it'.

There was no ministerial reply to the debate, which was cut off, in the manner of Adjournment debates, by the clock; and Members apparently remained satisfied with this six hours' ventilation of the subject until 13th April 1954, when Mr. Nabarro asked the Prime Minister what the Government was going to do, and received the reply that a further statement would be made as soon as possible.

On 13th July, Captain Crookshank announced that the Government would appoint 'a Select Committee of this House on the general basis recommended in the Select Committee's Report,' and circulated a note, 'commenting in detail on certain points'. This laid down (a) that the terms of reference should empower the Committee to inquire into the '*current* policy and practice' of the nationalized industries, and not the '*general* policy and practice', as the Report had recommended; (b) that it should not concern itself with matters engaging ministerial responsibility, with matters normally decided by collective bargaining, with matters dealt with by the formal machinery established by the relevant statutes, and with matters of day-to-day administration; (c) that it should consist of 14 members, not 21, as recommended by the Report; (d) that it should not be empowered to divide into sub-committees; (e) that it should normally take evidence from the Chairman of the Board or a representative nominated by him, and that 'Ministers should not normally be invited to appear' before it; (f) that it should publish its evidence 'except when such publication might be held to be contrary to the public interest'; and (g) that its staff assistance should consist only of liaison officers from the Treasury and from the Department concerned.

Clearly, the Government had been impressed by those, such as

Mr. Austin Albu, who believed it essential that the Select Committee should have 'exceedingly narrow terms of reference', and by those who feared to equip it with too elaborate an investigatory apparatus. Even so, it delayed the actual appointment of the Committee until 16th March 1955. As a General Election took place almost immediately afterwards, the Committee had no opportunity to do any work, and a new one had to be appointed by the new Parliament (7th July 1955). Both of these committees were given terms of reference which closely followed the note that Captain Crookshank had circulated.

The Government now reaped the meagre fruits of its fears and hesitations, for in November the Committee, after a few meetings, issued a Special Report to the effect that the restrictions imposed upon it were so severe that there was nothing it could usefully do.[21] There is some doubt as to whether it was justified in thus throwing up the sponge,[22] but one can sympathize with its difficulty in discovering something of importance which was not one of ministerial responsibility, of collective bargaining, of relevance to formal statutory machinery, or of day-to-day administration, particularly as any such matter had to be one of *current* policy and practice. The Committee had the alternative of virtually disregarding its terms of reference—as Select Committees have been known to do— or of telling the Government that it was demanding the impossible. Rightly or wrongly, it chose the latter course.

Immediately, there were Questions in the House, to which the Government replied that it was considering the Special Report and would issue a statement 'in due course'.[23] By 24th April, however, the promised statement had still not been issued, and Members began to complain about the delay, particularly as it had now become the policy of the Government to finance the nationalized industries directly from the Treasury. On 10th May, the Prime Minister announced that the Government intended to establish a new Select Committee with new terms of reference, which he specified. The necessary motion would be placed upon the Order Paper and an opportunity for debate provided.

[21] H.C. 120 of 1955–6.
[22] See D. N. Chester: *The Select Committee on Nationalised Industries*, in *Public Administration*, Vol. 34, Spring, 1956, p. 95.
[23] H.C. Deb., Vol. 546, cols. 2118–9; Vol. 547, cols. 556–7.

The new terms of reference were as wide as the previous ones had been restricted, viz.

> 'That a Select Committee be appointed to examine the Reports and Accounts of the Nationalised Industries established by Statute whose controlling Boards are appointed by Ministers of the Crown and whose annual receipts are not wholly or mainly derived from moneys provided by Parliament or advanced by the Exchequer.'

This Motion was introduced to the House by its Leader, Mr. R. A. Butler, on 30th November 1956, in a carefully-phrased, conciliatory and studiedly non-political speech. In justification of the Government's apparent *volte-face*, he said:

> 'We have come to the conclusion . . . that it is wiser not to try to debar the Committee from discussing certain questions by a series of specific prohibitions—and therefore we have learned something from experience—but simply to trust to the good sense and good will of the Committee itself.'

The Committee would need to have regard to the 'general state of opinion in the House at the time of its appointment'. That opinion, said Mr. Butler, indicated that there were 'two extremes' which it ought to avoid, namely, 'where the issues involved are purely matters of day-to-day administration', and 'where they are matters of major Government, as distinct from commercial, policy'. In addition, it should steer clear of 'the type of question which is dealt with by machinery established by statute' such as 'the fares and charges dealt with by the Transport Tribunal', and of matters 'affecting wages, conditions of employment, and so forth, . . . which are normally decided by collective bargaining arrangements'.

From this it appeared as though Mr. Butler was attempting to take away with one hand what he had given with the other. In advocating more general terms of reference, he simultaneously expressed the view that most of the former restrictions should, *de facto*, continue to apply. He did, however, pluck up the courage to suggest, as no previous government spokesman had done, what specific matters the Committee should regard itself as empowered to investigate.

'One would be the financial outcome of operations. That is a fairly broad subject. Secondly, the working of the industry with reference to the devolution of authority within it. Thirdly, the working of the industry with reference to the techniques of managerial efficiency. Fourthly, recruitment and training of technical and managerial staff. Fifthly, relations with consumer councils and the public. Sixthly, relations with outside industries. Seventhly, the unremunerative responsibilities of the boards.'

In respect of the expert assistance available to the Committee, Mr. Butler proposed 'an improvement', viz., that it should have the 'advice and assistance of those senior Treasury officers who are in charge of the Treasury divisions concerned with the industries in question.' He rejected, once again, the Report's recommendation that there should be 'a whole-time officer with the status of Comptroller and Auditor-General', on the grounds that this would not only involve legislation but 'tend to fix the pattern of the Select Committee's work too definitely and too finally'.

The appointment of the Committee, under the new terms of reference, was, he said, 'an act of faith'. It might be that the scheme would not work, in which case other solutions to the problems would have to be attempted. 'But', he went on, 'if the new Select Committee works, as I have a hunch it may, perhaps just for this Session at any rate, we may be able to build upon that and find the right method of associating Parliament with the industries which have been nationalized in this sector'.

Mr. James Callaghan, for the Opposition, then moved a negative amendment to the effect that 'this House, while recognizing the need for improving arrangements for Parliamentary discussion of the affairs of the Nationalized Industries, does not consider that the appointment of the proposed Select Committee is the appropriate way of dealing with the problem'.

The main burden of his song was that the proposal was a 'slipshod' one, evading 'the major issues', and failing to 'give a clear reply to the questions of responsibility or, indeed, to the principles which should be followed in this matter'.

'This proposal', he said, 'will blur the chain of responsibility from the Boards to the Ministers and, through the Ministers, to Parliament. It will interfere with that chain which, in any command, must be kept clear, by poking in this Parliamentary Committee half way up. It will, in fact, create the very bureaucracy and the fear that the right hon. Gentleman always wants to get rid of.'

The Labour Party, he admitted, had no alternative proposals to make, as it was 'in the middle of considering these problems'. He nevertheless suggested three possibilities, viz. (1) that Ministers should make greater use, for the benefit of the House, of their statutory powers to secure information from the nationalized industries; (2) that there should be 'a much closer direct relationship between the consultative committees and the local communities which they are supposed to represent'; (3) that there should be 'some sort of audit team which would roam over the whole field of the nationalized industries'.

The remainder of this short debate, which was wound up by Mr. Harold Watkinson, the Minister of Transport and Civil Aviation, produced nothing new in the way of argument. The Opposition divided the House, which rejected its amendment by 292 votes to 225.

The new Committee was appointed on 20th December 1956, and held its first meeting on 12th February 1957, when, after 'deliberation', it ordered:

'That the Chairman do write to the Chairmen of the Boards of the Nationalised Industries, informing them of the terms of reference of this Committee, and assuring them that this Committee will always be ready, so far as their terms of reference allow, to help them in their relations with the House of Commons.'

Thus, four years and six months after the presentation to Parliament of the Report recommending its establishment, a Select Committee on Nationalized Industries got down to business.

What is to be learnt from this necessarily rather lengthy account of its period of gestation? It shows, firstly, how reluctant are Members, on both sides of the House, to embark upon something that can be regarded as a constitutional innovation. Although it was very generally admitted that parliamentary supervision of the nationalized industries needed to be improved, the opinion was widely held that this ought to be achieved, if possible, by changes in existing procedures and institutions rather than by the creation of new ones. Except in an emergency, the British House of Commons, bowed down under the weight of its own traditions, is slow to innovate. Secondly, it shows how deeply what I have described as the 'Morrisonian' view of the relationship between the House and the nationalized industries had penetrated. On all sides, it was taken for granted that if there was any contradiction between efficiency and parliamentary control, it was the latter that would have to suffer. Those who wanted more parliamentary control had to try to prove either that it would not decrease or that it would actually increase the efficiency with which the industries were conducted; no one, to our knowledge, had the temerity to suggest that it might conceivably have some deleterious effect, but that, on democratic grounds, the sacrifice would be worthwhile. Even a unanimous all-party Report failed to produce general conviction that the establishment of a Select Committee would not result in harm to the nationalized industries, by making their managements excessively cautious and circumspect. The Government itself, although much more sympathetic towards the idea than the Opposition, felt the need to move slowly and warily, and not even the most convinced advocates of the Select Committee device made much effort to hurry it up; and when the Government finally made up its mind, it hedged in the new body with so many restrictions designed to prevent invasions of ministerial responsibility and commercial autonomy, that the Members to whom the assignment had been given decided that they were virtually powerless. Only after it had made the decision to finance the nationalized industries, at least temporarily, from Exchequer sources, did the Government come to the conclusion that it ought to take the risk of appointing a Committee with practicable terms of reference.

Thirdly, the story of the origins of the Select Committee shows that, to some extent, party political factors were inhibiting a fully rational approach to the question of parliamentary control. Many Labour Members, particularly those with trade union connections, could not convince themselves that the Select Committee proposal was anything but a Tory plot, foolishly aided and abetted by a few innocents on their own side of the House, to bring discredit on Labour-initiated nationalized industries which, after going through rather severe teething troubles, were establishing themselves as successful examples of practical socialism. Admittedly, most of the overt expressions of this view came from the back benches— one Member actually used the expression, 'industrial McCarthyism'—but one does not need to read too closely between the lines of Mr. Morrison's and Mr. Callaghan's contributions to the debates to realize that the front-benchers, too, were inclined to hold it. These fears were reinforced by suspicion on the part of trade unionists—which appeared to receive confirmation from certain suggestions made by Mr. Molson in his evidence[24]—that the proposed Select Committee would develop an ambition to trespass on the field of labour relations. In general, there was still a strong feeling on the Labour side that the nationalized industries ought to be 'kept out of politics'. The fact that the Conservatives, who had once been equally insistent on this score, were now, apparently, trying to play politics with them, strongly suggested that the Government, urged on by its back-benchers, was up to no good. Only a minority of Labour Members, who believed that the Conservatives were now, according to their lights, just as anxious as the Labour Party to make the nationalized industries work well, and that these industries were beginning to pass outside the sphere of party-political controversy, regarded such fears as entirely groundless. One of them, indeed, specifically stated that it was only the cooling off of political passions about nationalization that would now permit a Select Committee to act 'in a sympathetic, helpful and businesslike way, without having to divide along party lines'. Previously, under the Labour Government, it would have been like a 'bear-garden'.[25] Most of his fellow-socialists, by contrast, were not convinced that the necessary measure of inter-party agreement had yet been achieved. It is even possible that some of them—although we fully admit that there is no evidence to support the suggestion—felt that Select Committees themselves, with their all-party membership and striving for unanimous recommendations, were examples of an undesirable form of 'class-collaboration'.

[24] H.C. 235 of 1952–3, Minutes of Evidence, Q. 352.
[25] Mr. Ronald Williams; H.C. Deb., Vol. 523, cols. 891–2.

These three factors fully explain the hesitancy of the Government about establishing an effective Select Committee, and its insistence that the device should, in any case, be regarded as experimental.

As yet, it is too early to pass judgement on the success of this experiment, but there can be no doubt that, from many points of view, the début of the new Select Committee has been promising.

Its first Report,[26] issued on 29th October 1957, fully justified Mr. Butler's confidence in its 'good sense'. Wisely, it confined its attention to two subjects of reasonably manageable size, viz. (1) Ministerial control over nationalized industries, with special reference to 'the extent to which the Treasury is in a position to make its influence felt'; and (2) the Report and Accounts of the North of Scotland Hydro-Electricity Board. The latter subject also had the advantage for an initial and experimental investigation that while not being highly controversial, it did offer a number of issues of genuine public importance some of which Parliament had already discussed in a rather unsystematic way.

Within these two fields, the topics chosen for inquiry were all of the kind to which Mr. Butler had suggested the Committee might devote its attention, and there can be no doubt that—with one possible exception—the recommendations that it made were based upon a judicial weighing of the evidence it received. Where it felt that the evidence was too slight or too ambiguous to support a firm conclusion, it did not hesitate to say so. Thus it left open the question whether there were 'any grounds for thinking that the influence of the Treasury had in any way unduly hampered . . . the initiative of the Boards'. It also carefully avoided giving its recommendations a carpingly critical tone, and showed a commendable readiness to give praise where praise was due. It recognized, in fact, that to be complimented by an all-party Select Committee constitutes one of the best possible defences of a public agency against unjustified and politically-inspired attack. Thus it went out of its way to state that the achievements of the North of Scotland Board 'themselves rebut the criticism of the Board's present personnel which was made by one witness'.

On specific aspects of the Board's policy and administration, it put forward the following opinions and recommendations: (a)

[26] H.C. 304 of 1956–7.

that there was some uncertainty whether the Board was concentrating too much on hydro-electric as distinct from thermal-electric stations; (b) that, as a matter of general practice, it should submit contracts to competitive tender; (c) that its accounts should specify the basis adopted for the calculation of depreciation costs; (d) that it should take steps to rectify considerable inaccuracies in its estimates of the costs of its schemes; (e) that it ought to use more fully the services of its Consultative Council, which were insufficiently publicized; and (f) that its policy of subsidizing rural electrification was justified.

Of these, only the last could be regarded as highly controversial or insufficiently supported by the evidence received. One has the impression that, instead of trying to get to the bottom of the rural electrification controversy, it preferred to hold some kind of balance between the economic 'purists' and the representatives of the Scottish rural constituencies. This indicates a possible weakness in Select Committee reports, even when their recommendations are unanimous. Dog does not eat dog, and when Members of Parliament, belonging to all three parties, appear as witnesses to press a deeply-felt constituency need, it may be difficult to tell them that they are wrong. This suggestion as to the influences behind the particular recommendation, however, is pure guesswork, and it may well have been that the Committee, feeling itself out of its depth in the waters of economic theory, simply decided that safety lay in approving the *status quo*.

The North of Scotland Hydro-Electricity Board investigation appears to have been regarded by the Committee as a kind of pilot project. As such, it was successful, for the response to the Report made by the House of Commons was distinctly encouraging. The Government quickly found time for a debate, in which the work of the Committee received commendation from both sides of the House. Most of the participants had obviously read the Report and considered its recommendations, and the general tone of the discussion was moderate and constructive. It would be going too far, however, to say that the character of the debate was determined by the quality of the Report, for the affairs of the North of Scotland Hydro-Electricity Board were not productive of political passion. That they had never received parliamentary discussion during the previous fifteen years of the Board's existence is evidence enough of the fact that the work of this nationalized industry was giving general satisfaction (except, perhaps, to a handful of Highland crofters who felt that they were not getting their electricity supplies as quickly or as cheaply as they should). For its first Report, in fact, the Committee had chosen a particularly successful public enterprise in which members of all parties were able to take legitimate pride, particularly as its establishment had been the work of the war-time Coalition Government.

Emboldened by the favourable reception of its initial effort, the Committee went ahead with the second of its investigations, which was already under way. This time it was after bigger game: the National Coal Board. Oral evidence was provided by Mr. A. T. K. Grant, of the Treasury, Sir John Maude and Mr. R. J. Ayres, of the Ministry of Power, and Sir James Bowman and Mr. J. Latham, respectively Chairman and Deputy Chairman of the Board. Memoranda were submitted by the National Industrial Fuel Efficiency Service, the British Coal Utilisation Research Association, and the Coal Utilisation Council. The collection of evidence was completed by 13th March 1958, and after four meetings for deliberation, the Committee presented its second Report to the House of Commons on 29th April.[27]

Recognizing the 'vast scope' of the subject of its inquiry, it wisely decided that it could 'best serve the interests of the House' by 'concentrating on a number of specific major topics, rather than trying to range over the whole field'. These major topics, according to its own account, were 'investment, manpower, prices, and the problem of the balance between the amounts of large and small coal produced'. Such matters fell well inside the informal terms of reference that Mr. Butler had given to the Committee, but in examining them it was almost inevitably led to consider and make recommendations on other matters, of a more politically-contentious kind, which Mr. Butler and his colleagues had perhaps hoped it would try to avoid (although some of them had already been broached, in a preliminary and tentative way, in its first Report). These related to the role of the Minister of Power. The first recommendation directed towards the Ministry, rather than towards the Board, was that the former 'should be able to make a greater financial check on the Board's investment schemes' than it was

[27] H.C. 187–I of 1957–8.

actually making. This, perhaps, could be regarded as having a predominantly 'technical' character. The second, however, struck right at the heart of the prevailing relationship between the Ministry and the Board. It concerned the so-called 'gentlemen's agreement' whereby the Minister exercised *de facto* control over coal prices, although he possessed no statutory authority to do so. While approving the purpose of this arrangement, the Committee expressed dislike of its informality.

'The Board', it said, 'when proposing alterations in coal prices, should consult the Minister as to the public interest and having done so, should then take full responsibility for their price determinations. The Minister should have the power to give the Board specific directions in relation to prices in the national interest, but this power should be statutory and its use disclosed to Parliament.'

In this way, 'Parliament and the public would be fully informed about the respective responsibilities of the Minister and the Board in a particular case.'

This recommendation naturally received particular attention when the Report came up for debate, on 14th July, on the motion 'That this House takes note of the Report from the Select Committee . . . and of the Annual Report and Statement of Accounts of the National Coal Board for 1957'. For the Opposition, Mr. Robens gave it his support, thereby condemning a practice of which the existing Government and the former Government of which he had been a member were equally guilty.

'We in this House and the public outside', he said, 'do not know exactly what fight is going on between the Government and the National Coal Board. We do not know whom to blame for what takes place. When, as a consequence, we examine the accounts and are critical about the losses made . . . whom are we to blame? Should we blame the Government for preventing the Board obtaining proper prices or should we blame the Board for its inefficiency in not having its prices properly attuned?'

But already Sir Ian Horobin, for the Minister of Power, had rejected the recommendation in words which showed how far the Conservative Party had departed from its original conceptions of the correct relationship between a minister and a nationalized industry.

> 'The Government', he said, 'do not believe that it is possible to conduct great industries like the coal industry except on the basis of constant and confidential consultation between the Board and the Minister. There is a joint responsibility, especially for prices. It is not realistic to suppose that any Government could completely dissociate themselves from the general level of coal prices. It is equally a statutory obligation on the Board so to arrange its affairs that, taking one year with another, it makes ends meet. The Government therefore feel that it is inescapable in this matter that responsibility should be shared, and they feel that to introduce a formal direction would be a very grave step and would hinder the proper relations between the two.'

General directions, he considered, should be 'avoided at all costs'.

Very pertinently, Sir Toby Low, the Chairman of the Select Committee, asked why the price-fixing machinery in the coal industry should be any different from that in the iron and steel industry. Under the Act of 1953, the Iron and Steel Board normally laid down prices 'without ministerial interference', but elsewhere in the Act the Minister was given the power to give to the Board a direction on prices which had to be laid before the House.

No government spokesman, however, chose to offer any explanation or justification of this apparent discrepancy.

The alleged desirability of informal Board-Minister relations was also the reason for the rejection of a suggestion, supported by Sir Toby Low, that the Coal Board should lay before the House its reply to the Report of the Select Committee. Sir Ian considered that this was a matter on which it was 'too early to be dogmatic'. The Government was still considering it, but 'as at present advised' they thought that it 'would be a mistake'.

In general, however, the Report of the Committee was very favourably received, and one of its more important recommendations, to the effect that 'the Ministry of Power should make a greater financial check upon the Board's investment schemes, particularly the marginal ones', was specifically accepted by the Government. On the whole, the debate was a sensible and constructive one, ranging less widely than most previous debates on the coal industry and keeping fairly closely to the issues that the Select Committee's Report had raised. How far this was due to the existence of the Report is again doubtful, but in this case it seems very probable that the copious and carefully-sifted information that the Committee had provided compelled Members to be more careful in their statements than they might otherwise have been, and it is almost certain that the quality of the debate was improved by the House having at its disposal what Mr. Robens justly described as the 'best evidence' he had 'ever seen in relation to the coal industry of this country'. Congratulations to the Select Committee and its Chairman were copious, and Mr. Robens announced that his views about the Select Committee device—at first he had not been 'happy about it'—were 'entirely changed'. Only Mr. Shinwell, representing the Labour Party's 'old guard', sounded a dissonant note. While welcoming the fact, as he saw it, that the Select Committee had given the Coal Board 'a clean bill of health', he expressed the hope that there would 'not be too many Select Committees'. There were no Select Committees, he said, for Imperial Chemical Industries or General Electric 'or the many concerns with which the right hon. Member for Blackpool North (Sir Toby Low) is associated'. Like private industries, the nationalized industries 'should be empowered to conduct their administration without unnecessary interference'. The system, inaugurated by the Labour Party, whereby 'the only possible interference . . . was by way of general direction from the Minister' had 'worked very well'. Perhaps it was out of respect for Mr. Shinwell's elder statesman status that no one chose to point out that it had not worked at all. Or perhaps no one was listening.

The next Select Committee Report, on the Air Corporations, was more voluminous, informative and ambitious than either of the previous two. It broke new ground in two respects, viz. (1) that it attempted a comprehensive survey of the affairs of the industry under examination; (2) that, in assessing the performance of that industry, it made extensive use of comparative statistics.

In both respects it was brilliantly successful. The greater part of the Report, which occupies fifty-nine pages, is factual, containing an abundance of succinct information, never before gathered together, about 'the conditions under which the airlines have been operating'. Members of the House who take the trouble to read it can bring to the test of accurately ascertained fact their preconceived ideas, so often based on hearsay or 'hunch'. It seems 'obvious', for instance, that the two aircraft corporations could effect considerable economies by co-operating to a much greater extent than they do at present in providing common coach services, joint advertising, a joint medical service, a joint organization for the disposal of surplus aircraft, and a common central organization for overhaul of aircraft or for the repair and maintenance of aircraft parts. Perhaps some of these alleged needs were obvious to certain members of the Select Committee when they started their inquiry. If so, these members would certainly not have been satisfied by a ministerial assurance in the House, or even a corporation chairman's assurance, conveyed by letter, that their ideas on the subject were impracticable. The extent to which they *are* impracticable—which is something like ninety per cent—was carefully elicited by memorandum and by question and answer. As a result, any Member of the House who cares to read the Report can obtain a very clear idea, supported by factual evidence and expert opinion, as to which paths are still worth exploring. Members need no longer rely on gossip and contacts, and have had their attention directed away from those questions to which the experts have given a definitive answer and towards those on which there is still room for reasonable differences of opinion. This is exactly what the advocates of the Select Committee said that it *could* do, and what its opponents claimed was beyond the capacity of a mere bunch of laymen. In this respect, therefore, the Select Committee has justified the hopes that were placed in it.

Still more encouraging is the intelligent way in which it has employed comparative statistics of airline performance. In its previous Report, on the National Coal Board, it said:

'Your Committee have been conscious of the absence of a yardstick by which to judge the performance of the Board. Some comparisons were attempted with the performance of the coal industry before nationalisation; but often it was found that circumstances had changed so much that such comparisons were of doubtful value. To have sought independent evidence on the performance of previously privately-owned mines in the United Kingdom, or on the progress and conditions in coal industries in other countries would, in Your Committee's opinion, have taken them far beyond their proper function.'

Apparently the Committee has now decided—with the increasing courage and self-confidence that successful Select Committees normally display—that its 'proper function' does, after all, include statistical comparisons with corresponding nationalized industries in other countries. It was encouraged to do so in this case, no doubt, by the ready availability of such statistics in the offices of the Corporations and in the Ministry of Transport, and by the fact that, if used with care and with due allowance for the different conditions under which the foreign competitors of B.E.A. and B.O.A.C. operate, they can yield significant comparisons.

What the Committee has done is to concentrate attention on those figures that suggest, *prima facie*, that the corporation concerned is considerably less efficient in certain respects than its major foreign competitors. It has carefully inquired whether there are any factors outside the control of the Corporation to account for the discrepancy. If it has found that there are none, or that those discoverable are insufficient to account for a comparatively poor performance, it has said to the Corporation, in effect, 'There is apparently no adequate reason for your failure in this respect, and therefore it is high time that you did something about it'.

In one of the statistical comparisons, B.O.A.C.'s performance appeared strikingly inferior to that of the American 'long-haul' airlines, Pan-American Airways and Trans-World Airways. Whereas these two lines had a c.t.m. per employee (the quotient of the airline's capacity and the number of its employees) of 37,700 and 44,100 respectively, B.O.A.C. had one of 16,400. The Committee recognized that there were certain 'contributory reasons' for this discrepancy, largely outside B.O.A.C.'s control, viz. that the Corporation did more things for itself and fewer by outside contract than its competitors, that it had been undergoing a period of re-equipment, that its more widespread operations and more stringent safety regulations compelled it to employ larger flight crews. But when all these things had been allowed for, the fact remained that B.O.A.C. was over-staffed, particularly in its workshops. The Corporation itself had been concerned with this problem 'for some years'—since 1952, in fact—but had apparently done little about it until the June of 1957. Several explanations were offered for this failure, viz. the difficulties of obtaining trade union agreement for new staffing arrangements, and the delay in undertaking the 'major investigation' that was necessary, owing first to the preoccupation of the Chief Engineer with the Britannia's icing troubles and secondly to the illness of the Managing Director. Rejecting these explanations as inadequate, the Committee went on to consider 'whether any of the blame . . . could rest on the shoulders of the Air Registration Board, which lays down the standards of airworthiness and safety to which the Corporations must conform'. Having satisfied itself that this was 'far from being the case', it concluded that 'the responsibility for what has happened in the past must reside inside the Corporation'.

'A state of affairs', says the Report, 'which was believed to be unhealthy in 1952, and which was proved to be unhealthy in 1956, may not be healed until the middle of 1960. It is clear that, however rigid the negotiating procedure may have become, it is the responsibility of the management of B.O.A.C. to achieve at a very early date a drastic improvement in the productivity of their aircraft maintenance department. Until this has been done, B.O.A.C. cannot expect to compete on even terms with the other airlines of the world.'

This investigation, starting with a statistical comparison and proceeding by way of a rigorous examination of the evidence to an almost unchallengeable conclusion, seems to us a model of its kind.

As we are here concerned with the Select Committee, and not with the economics of the civil airlines, it would be redundant to give an account of all the other suggestions and conclusions to be found in the Report. Some of them, however, merit more than a passing mention in this context, because they show a tendency on the part of the Committee to become involved in matters of government policy. This tendency has already been noted in the Coal

PARLIAMENT AND PUBLIC OWNERSHIP

Board Report, but the Air Corporations Report seems to take it a stage further. The committee is clearly aware that it may thus be exposing itself to attack, and hence, from time to time, attempts concealment through what can only be regarded as a form of words. On the question of the petrol tax, for instance, it carefully refrains from making any explicit recommendation, but nevertheless indicates quite unmistakably that its opinion is that B.E.A. should be accorded some relief from this imposition.

> 'It is a matter of Government policy that B.E.A. should have to carry the weight of this tax, and Your Committee appreciate that, however competently the Ministry presented their case to the Treasury, the Chancellor's decision was not going to be taken specifically to please B.E.A. Yet the decision has had unexpectedly heavy repercussions on the airline. Not only has it persuaded them to withdraw the Elizabethans, but also—since they have not been able to sell many of these aircraft in the second-hand market—it has had a deleterious effect on their balance sheet.'

Elsewhere, with slightly greater boldness, it expresses the 'hope' that the Minister will take certain facts into account. For instance, after stating that 'an arbitrary division of traffic between B.O.A.C. and the independent companies, based on a definite percentage of traffic, will hinder the efforts of B.O.A.C. to improve the efficiency' of the West African service and 'to expand their activities', it 'hopes' that 'the Minister of Transport and Civil Aviation will take this into account in any review of this aspect of his policy'. A similar hope is expressed, rather more indirectly, in respect of the distribution of the cost of aircraft development. This cost, the Committee considers, falls too heavily on the Corporations, thereby placing them 'at a disadvantage compared with their foreign competitors who use American aircraft'. Hence, although 'whatever arrangements are made' must be 'left to the Government', it is 'not surprising' that B.O.A.C. 'suggest that a direct subsidy should be given to cover their high development costs'. Occasionally, taking its stand on the generally accepted belief that a corporation should be allowed and encouraged to behave as far as possible as a straightforward commercial organization, the Committee makes a completely overt 'policy' recommendation. After recording 'the fact that the airlines are in effective competition with other forms of transport over their domestic routes', it 'questions' whether the Minister 'needs to control the fares charged on them'. In view of the fact that the unprofitable Highlands, Islands and Isle of Man routes have been undertaken at the direct behest of the Government, it recommends that provision should be made in the Annual Estimates of the appropriate government departments to cover the losses incurred by B.E.A. in operating them. On similar grounds, it recommends that B.O.A.C.'s unremunerative subsidiary, Kuwait Airlines, should be subsidized.

> 'If a nationalised industry, which is statutorily required to pay its way, is to be used as an instrument of foreign policy, it should not be required to bear substantial losses as a result.'

Finally, the Committee criticizes, with even greater vigour than it did in the Coal Board Report, the informality of the relationship between Board and Minister. The Minister's 'unofficial powers', it says, 'comprise a formidable collection'.

> 'Thus, although the Minister has no express statutory control over the Corporation's capital expenditure, they always seek his approval (and that of the Treasury) for orders of aircraft, and these amount to 80 per cent of their total capital expenditure. They have agreed not to open new routes without the Minister's consent. They fly on various routes, domestic and international, because he asks them to, and they lose money in the process. They seek his approval for all fares and rates on non-international routes. They refrain, at his wish, from keeping aircraft specifically available for charter work. They come to him for permission before creating or investing in a subsidiary company, and, in effect, get his authority before they dispose of such an investment.'

The Committee admits that there are 'powerful arguments' for the exercise of these non-statutory powers, and it records that the Corporations, whose relations with the Ministry are good, 'have accepted the assumption of these powers by the Minister, generally without protest'. Nevertheless, it feels 'bound to ask if these do not add up to a degree of control far in excess of that envisaged by the statutes under which B.O.A.C. and B.E.A. were created, and so lead to an undesirable diminution in the authority of the Chairmen and Boards of the Corporations, and in their feeling of responsibility'.[28] It concludes:

> 'Your Committee consider it essential to the efficient running on commercial lines of the Air Corporations that there should be a clear cut division of responsibility between the Chairmen on the one hand and the Minister on the other. When the Minister wishes, on grounds of national interest, to override the commercial judgement of a Chairman, he should do so by a directive, which should be published.'

As yet this remarkable Report has failed to secure the measure of parliamentary discussion that it undoubtedly deserves. It was mentioned only very occasionally—and almost parenthetically—during the course of the Supply Debate on Aircraft Production.[29] In the following week's Supply Debate on Civil Aviation, the Report had to compete for Members' attention with the much more exciting Report on the Civil Aircraft Accident at Southall which provided the subject matter for most of their contributions.[30] Mr. Frank Beswick, who opened for the Opposition, and Mr. Harold Watkinson, the Minister of Transport and Civil Aviation, who followed him, agreed that the Report deserved a full day's debate, instead of the smaller portion of half a day's debate that it was actually receiving. Nevertheless, Mr. Watkinson used the occasion to make policy announcements of some importance on certain matters reported on by the Select Committee. Perhaps

[28] The prevailing 'paternal' attitude of the Ministry towards the Corporations was well brought out by a witness, Mr. M. M. V. Custance, Deputy Secretary, who, during the course of his answers, made the following statement: 'I would very much like to emphasise the general point here that the Ministry regard themselves very much as "fathers in God", so to speak, of the Corporations. We expect them to come to us if they are in trouble. And if we think they are in trouble we will go to them.' (*Report*, Minutes of Evidence, p. 232, Q. 2030.)

[29] H.C. Deb., Vol. 608, cols. 595–722 (16th July 1959).

[30] *Ibid.* Vol. 609, cols. 949–1014. The Motion was as follows: 'That a further sum, not exceeding £35, be granted to Her Majesty, towards defraying the charges for the year ending on the 31st day of March, 1960, for the following Services relating to the Report from the Select Committee on Nationalised Industries (Reports and Accounts) on the Air Corporations and the Report on the Civil Aircraft Accident at Southall, namely . . .'

rather unexpectedly, he stated that he 'accepted one of its main contentions, that the Ministry was, on the whole, rather too mixed up with the Air Corporations', thereby distinguishing himself from his colleague, Sir Ian Horobin, who, as we have seen, considered the 'mixing-up' of the Minister of Power and the National Coal Board both inevitable and desirable. Mr. Watkinson, however, hastened to explain that the criticized peculiarities of the minister-corporation relationship flowed 'from the, I will not say unworkable, but most difficult circumstances under which we have had to work due to the 1949 Air Corporations Act'. This Act was not working well and ought to be amended. He did not give Members much idea of how extensive were the amendments he had in mind, but, in response to an interjection by Mr. Beswick, did provide the following foretaste of things to come:

'The hon. Member may like to know that in the Department we have put much painstaking work into this concept, which he appears to dislike, of a new central licensing body that will license both operations and the organisations themselves. That will have two advantages. One is that it will get the minister a bit more out of this business of trying to sort out routes and services . . . and, secondly, it will give the Ministry . . . the power, which it now has on the roads, of withdrawing the licence of an unsatisfactory operator; in other words, a clear mandate to control the situation more satisfactorily than we can under the present Acts.'

In the remainder of his speech, the Minister justified his vetting of the Corporations' capital investments (which the Committee had not, in fact, criticized), agreed with the Committee's view that 'when a Minister over-rides the commercial judgement of the Corporations the fact should be clearly recorded', and announced that he had appointed Sir George Cribbett (Deputy Chairman, B.O.A.C.) to 'go into the whole matter' of the 'extremely grave' financial situation in Middle East Airlines.[31]

[31] The Committee had reported a 'substantial loss' on Middle East Airlines, and had predicted that the loss for the current year was likely to be £900,000. It nevertheless thought that, if political conditions in the area settled down, the line had 'good commercial prospects'. But if it lost heavily again, B.O.A.C. would have to consider whether it was worth their while to continue to participate in it.

Once again, the Committee received congratulations from all sides of the House on an excellent Report. No one criticized it for trespassing too far into the field of 'policy'. Its shrewd Chairman, Sir Toby Low, had evidently not been mistaken in his judgement of what the House would tolerate.

There is another respect in which the Air Corporations Report forms a landmark in the life of the Select Committee: it is the first Report on which the 'comments' of the industry under investigation have been published. The Government evidently had had second thoughts about the advisability of such publication, for on 18th September 1959, the responsible minister, Mr. Sandys, in reply to a Question from Sir Toby Low, agreed to lay B.E.A.'s and B.O.A.C.'s comments before the House, and on 16th November they were published in the 'Written Answers' columns of Hansard. The Corporations' reactions followed much the same pattern as those of a government department confronted with an Estimates Committee report. They provided further information purporting to show that certain weaknesses diagnosed by the Select Committee were being remedied and that others were irremediable until circumstances changed. They indicated that many of the Committee's recommendations were 'under review', 'being explored', or subject to 'careful consideration'. While B.O.A.C. offered no general comment on the Report, B.E.A. was more forthcoming, stating that it 'welcomed the inquiries by the Select Committee and found them useful in directing attention to important aspects of its business in a way which provides an admirable solution to the problem of public accountability'.

Cautious as most of the comments were, they at least indicated a serious attitude towards the Select Committee's Report, and provided a possible *point d'appui* for further investigation at a later stage.

The latest of the Select Committee's Reports, on British Railways,[32] is not only the longest but the most adventurous and controversial. As at the time this book goes to press it has only just appeared, we cannot subject it to a thorough examination, still less explore the wealth of material contained in its massive Minutes of Evidence. Some of its outstanding features, however, ought to be briefly noted. The most outstanding, undoubtedly, are the boldness

[32] H.C. 254–I of 1959–60.

with which it broaches questions of high policy and the trenchancy with which it criticizes both the Ministry of Transport and the Treasury.

The Committee states its belief that a large-scale British railway system can be profitable, and expresses the following views about the 'size and shape' of the railway system and about the respective responsibilities of the Commission, the Minister and Parliament for its policies and financial arrangements.

'What size and shape should British Railways be? The first consideration must be financial; the size and shape must be such as can enable the Commission to carry out their statutory task of balancing their accounts, taking one year with another. But if the Commission are to know which of their services are justifiable on grounds of direct financial return, they must first have some form of accounts by which the profitability of the Regions and services can be judged.

However, the consideration of direct profitability is not the only one which applies in this case. Because of the cost of the roads, and of the congestion on them, the national interest may require railway services which do not in fact directly pay for themselves, but which may cost the nation less than the alternatives.

In some cases, there may be a third and different consideration—one of social need. A service may be justified on other than economic grounds, because for example the less populous parts of Britain might otherwise be left without a railway service. Account may, in other words, need to be taken of social considerations.

The consideration of profitability, as mentioned above, should be left to the Commission. But if decisions are to be taken on grounds of the national economy or of social needs, then they must be taken by the Minister, and submitted by him for the approval of Parliament.

Furthermore, if Parliament is to specify that certain services should be undertaken, despite the fact that the Commission cannot profitably undertake them, then the additional cost of them should be provided, in advance, out of public funds.

If subsidies of this kind are to be paid to the Commission

163

then they should be paid for specific purposes, and they should be paid openly. They should not be disguised as, for instance, a payment of track costs (which are an integral part of railway operations), nor as the writing-off of the burden of interest; and they should not be hidden away in the Commission's accounts.'

Although critical of the B.T.C.'s administrative record in many respects, the Committee clearly regards the railways as more sinned against than sinning, and reserves its severest strictures for the Ministry and the Treasury. Much publicity was given to its attack on the competence of the financial control exercised by these two authorities over the execution of the railways' modernization programme.

'Your Committee', says the Report, 'are astonished at the way in which the Commission have been able to set in motion great modernisation schemes, without the departments comparing the economics of them with those of the possible alternative schemes: that in giving a banker's sanction to the expenditure on the London Midland electrification, for example, the Ministry did not know what the alternative expenditure in using diesel locomotion would be.

'In saying this, Your Committee are not merely being wise after the event, for their predecessors recommended a closer supervision by the executive over large capital expenditure by the nationalised boards, more than two years ago (H.C. 187 of 1957–8; Q. 1961–3). If that kind of thinking had percolated more quickly through departments, the laxity of financial control in this case would have been checked earlier.'

While making no comment on the 'policies' underlying ministerial intervention to prevent the raising of fares and freights the Committee emphasizes the extent of the losses which the Commission has thereby sustained (which it estimates at between £15 million and £23½ million between 1952 and 1956), and suggests that whatever the amount 'the Commission should be compensated for it by a payment from public funds'.

'Although in present circumstances this would be no more than an accounting transaction, Your Committee wish to recommend the principle that where Government action causes a nationalised industry to incur a specific loss or specific expenditure which it would not otherwise incur, the Government should take steps to compensate the industry'.

Among the Report's other 'radical' recommendations is that the Transport Tribunal should be, if not abolished, at least severely curtailed in its functions, to the extent that it should cease to have jurisdiction 'in all fields where the railways are meeting effective competition'.

The above extracts from the Report necessarily do scant justice to the wealth of information and ideas that it contains. *The Times* called it 'a timely contribution to the wider debate' about the operations of the B.T.C. and the future of British Railways. Timely it certainly is, but it is also likely to be an essential source of knowledge for a long time to come. With this Report and the earlier one on the Civil Airlines—both of which must have cost Sir Toby Low and his colleagues a formidable amount of time and energy— we may perhaps say that the Select Committee has come of age.

For the House of Commons, for the student of nationalized industries, and for the public, the Select Committee has done an excellent job. Of that there can be no doubt. As yet, however, the feelings of the Chairmen and Boards of the nationalized industries towards its investigations have received little public expression. As might be expected, their witnesses have offered— and, as far as one can judge, have actually given—full co-operation; and the Committee has usually treated them with courtesy and tact. This does not mean, however, that they positively like being questioned or regard the Committee's investigations as a welcome opportunity to express their views; and it was perhaps a little unfair of the Committee to imply, in one of its Reports,[33] that this was the case. Referring to the evidence given by the Chairman and Deputy Chairman of the National Coal Board, it underlined Mr. Latham's statement that it was 'desperately important . . . that we should have the opportunity of expressing our point of view'. The reader thereby tends to draw the conclusion that Mr. Latham was

[33] H.C. 187–91 of 1957–8.

165

fully in agreement with Lord Hurcomb, who, in evidence before the Select Committee appointed to consider methods of parliamentary control, had said: 'One of the very greatest handicaps under which anyone in my position suffers is that he gets no opportunity of stating his own case of or explaining what his difficulties are direct to Members of Parliament.'[34] The full context of Mr. Latham's remark, however, suggests a rather different interpretation. The witness was in the course of making a very long statement about capital investment, output, reconstruction and mechanization, when he was interrupted by the Chairman. The dialogue was then as follows:

Chairman: I do not want to stop what you are saying, but we do want to have the opportunity of asking you questions.

Mr. Latham: Yes.

Chairman: And at present you are reinforcing what Mr. Bowman said last time and referring to the Report. What we want is more information from you than just that, and I notice that you appear to be reading from a document?

Mr. Latham: I was referring to it; I was not reading from it.

Chairman: Well, you have got fairly full notes there. You are, of course, perfectly at liberty to put in any memorandum you wish to, but *prima facie* members of the Committee do want to ask you some questions and not just listen to you developing the Report. So, I think if you can bring your remarks to a close, if you can—?

Mr. Latham: But I must deal with prices, if I may.

Chairman: Yes?

Mr. Latham: I think you said to us quite strongly that you wanted us to regard the Committee as something which was helpful to us, enabling us   say things which we believe ought to be known.

Chairman: Yes?

Mr. Latham: And we do feel, on the subject of prices in particular, that it is desperately important that we should have the opportunity of expressing our point of view.[35]

Clearly, at this very early stage in his evidence, Mr. Latham was regarding the Committee as a potentially hostile body, and his anxiety was that the Committee itself would fail to give the Coal Board adequate opportunities for self-justification. Moreover, he was obviously not very familiar—and there was no reason why he should have been—with the techniques of giving evidence before

[34] See above, p. 134.
[35] H.C. 304 of 1956–7. Minutes of Evidence, Qs. 1003–7.

a Select Committee, and not receiving much assistance from the Chairman, Sir Patrick Spens. It should be emphasized, however, that this was an isolated incident, and that nothing comparable has occurred under the suave and skilful chairmanship of Sir Toby Low.

Do the Boards feel that the Committee is constantly 'looking over their shoulders'? Do they agree with Sir John Reith that it represents a method of 'institutionalizing in terrifying form the Parliamentary Question'? If they do, they have not as yet taken advantage of the opportunity to say so. This may be no evidence of satisfaction, as it pays to be polite to parliamentary investigators. For the same reason, the few expressions of approval to which the Boards have given vent need not be taken too literally. But it is unlikely that they have been seriously incommoded.

As the Committee examines only one industry at a time, any crick in the neck is suffered by this industry alone, and for a limited period. It would therefore be somewhat difficult to argue that the effect of the Committee's investigations on the industry's operations is any more severe than would be that of a periodical examination by a Royal Commission or Departmental Committee which those who, like Mr. Morrison, emphasize the importance of autonomy, have suggested as an alternative. The situation, however, might be rather different if the Committee were enlarged and obtained authority, like the Estimates Committee, to divide up into sub-committees for the pursuit of simultaneous investigations. So far, the Government has chosen to deny the Committee this power.

Another interesting question is how much extra work an inquiry by the Committee gives to the officials of the industry under investigation. Quantification is here quite impossible, as, even if an attempt was made to weigh the additional burden—which has not, as far as we are aware, been done—there would be the utmost difficulty in distinguishing between the work performed specifically for the Committee and that which, although perhaps done with the possible requirements of the Committee in mind, was also useful for other purposes. The Committee was evidently thinking of this point when, in its Report on the National Coal Board, it expressed the opinion that 'the substantial amount of time spent in giving evidence and preparing memoranda will prove of value to the Board, and that this kind of inquiry is not prejudicial to the good administration and direction of the affairs of nationalized industries.'

What matters, of course, is not the absolute amount of time and energy involved, which the officials concerned might conceivably have devoted to more directly useful occupations, but the ultimate worthwhileness of this expenditure of human resources, both to Parliament and to the nationalized industry itself. Here quantification is even less possible. How can one measure the 'input' of time and energy as against the 'output' of improved parliamentary and public relations? How can one assess the value to a nationalized industry of a Committee recommendation which it might have already thought of itself or received from some other source? What importance should one attach to the presumably greater authority adhering to a recommendation from a Select Committee of the House of Commons, particularly in view of the fact that the prestige of a parliamentary body confers such extra weight impartially on good, bad and indifferent recommendations? In this field, one is moving among intangibles. As Mr. Butler said, the Committee is an 'act of faith'; and we can only record our general impression, based upon insufficient evidence accumulated over a short period of time, that faith in it has not been misplaced.

There remains to be considered, briefly, the Committee's techniques of investigation. Question and answer, together with the receipt of memoranda, have produced a great deal of high-quality information; but the Committee is obviously worried about its lack of full-time expert assistance. It concluded its Second Report by saying that 'recommendations to the House on how the Committee's work could be made more effective—whether by the use of special staff, or of different terms of reference, or of different powers—would require a Special Report; it is too early in the Committee's life to consider such a Report'. In its Third Report, it said specifically that 'in dealing with the accounts of a vast industry like this (i.e. the Air Corporations)' its task was 'made more difficult by the lack of specialized assistance', and announced that it hoped 'shortly to make a Special Report on this matter to the House'.

This Special Report was published, together with Minutes of Evidence, on 28th July 1959.[36] It began by indicating that the

[36] H.C. 276 of 1959.

production of the Air Corporations Report had strained the Committee's resources to the utmost, and by expressing the view that subsequent investigations might be even more onerous.

'Your Committee make no complaint about the size of the job they have to do; its importance justifies the effort. But they consider that the House should know that, as a result of the considerable work involved and the way in which it was undertaken, more than thirteen months elapsed between the start of the investigation and the publication of their Report (despite the fact that Your Committee met each week while the House was sitting, and thrice a week when they were considering their Report). In addition to the effort that this has required of Your Committee, it should be remembered that the Chairmen and Boards of the industry, too, have been subjected to very long-drawn-out examination.

Yet this particular investigation was comparatively uncomplicated. Had Your Committee dealt, for instance, with the Report and Accounts of the former Central Electricity Authority, they might have had to start with a comparison of the results achieved by the twelve Area Boards, whose Accounts alone amount to more than 400 pages of figures; and the time spent might have been even greater.'

Two forms of assistance might have made the Committee's inquiries 'shorter and more effective', viz. (1) from 'an accountant with experience of industrial and commercial accounts', and (2) from 'a research worker with training in economics'. The case for assistance of these types appeared to be established; 'but a more difficult question is what precise form that assistance should take?'

In its attempts to answer this question, the Committee found itself overwhelmed by the conflicting evidence that had been offered to it by Mr. Butler, Mr. Gaitskell, Sir Edward Fellowes (Clerk of the House), Sir Edmund Compton (Comptroller and Auditor-General), Sir Harold Howitt and Sir Thomas Robson (Chartered Accountants), Sir Thomas Padmore (Treasury), Mr. Strathearn Gordon (Librarian of the House) and Mr. E. C. Thompson (Statistician). Among the proposals it considered were those of the Select Committee of 1953, viz., that it should be given the assistance of:

(i) An officer of the status of the Comptroller and Auditor-General, who should be an officer of the House of Commons, with high administrative experience.

(ii) At least one professional accountant, and such other staff as required.

(iii) Such additional information, as might be of use to the Committee and of interest to Parliament, which could be provided by the statutory auditors of the national corporations.

It also inquired into the following 'other possibilities';

(iv) Should the Committee have assistance from a Treasury official seconded to them for each inquiry?

(v) Or should the Committee be given the assistance . . . from the Comptroller and Auditor-General and his staff?

(vi) Or should the Committee call upon the services of the staff of the Librarian of the House of Commons?

(vii) Or should the Committee be given power to employ an economist from a University or elsewhere and to pay for his services and the necessary staff for him through a small addition to the House of Commons vote?

(viii) Or should the Committee build up a small research staff of their own?

(ix) As an alternative or as an addition to the above possibilities, should an additional Clerk be appointed to the Committee?

To the outsider, none of these possibilities would appear to be particularly revolutionary or subversive of the established principles, but they all seemed to present 'difficulties', and there was a good deal of discussion about their constitutional implications. In particular, the suggestion that the Committee might 'seek advice from outside the House' was treated with great circumspection. 'We are on the edge of an innovation here', said Mr. Butler, 'which we want to watch very carefully'. Indeed, the whole Report and Minutes of Evidence were characterized by what anyone unfamiliar with the extreme conservatism with which the House approaches procedural questions could only regard as ridiculous timidity.

The record of the Proceedings of the Committee provides evidence of considerable disagreement among its members. On two important points, however, they were unanimous. The first was that help from 'an experienced and high-ranking Treasury official', which the Committee had enjoyed since 1956, could not be accepted as an 'idea for the future'. On this the Report says:

'Your Committee are indeed grateful for the help they have received from their liaison officer at the Treasury, whom personally they have held in high regard. The reason why they have not made more use of him, and the reason why they do not think that a Treasury officer can in the future prove to be what they need, is based wholly on principle. Much of Your Committee's work consists in looking at the relationship between the nationalised Boards and the Government; there have been many instances where Your Committee have had to call in question the effect on the Boards of particular aspects of government policy or of departmental administration. It follows that, on many occasions, the Committee might want help from their assistant (whomever he may be) while they were conducting inquiries into the effect of decisions which had been taken in the past by the Treasury. He may find his work being adduced in evidence against his own department, and he may find himself being asked to help in a criticism of decisions taken by his colleagues. Even if he were to be seconded, full-time, to the Committee, it is hardly likely that he would be able to speak objectively on such matters; and it would be unfair to require him to try to do so.

'There is a further point of principle. The Treasury and Government Departments are by statute and convention excluded from a wide area of the activities of nationalised Corporations. It would be quite wrong for the Executives to be brought into closer contact with the operations of the industries through the medium of an official acting on the Committee's behalf.

'For these reasons, Your Committee believe that their help should come from outside the world of Government.'

The second point of agreement was that this help should preferably 'come from within the House', even though it would be 'of a specialized kind which the House has not hitherto provided'.

But as such conclusions did not amount to agreed policy recommendations, the Committee finally decided to pass the ball to the House itself.

> 'They leave it to the House to decide, after further consideration of this small but difficult problem whether more help should be accorded to the Committee from the staff of the House (if necessary, by augmenting it); whether the power should be given to any future Select Committee on Nationalised Industries to appoint an assessor; or whether the best thing would be a combination of both these courses.'

In any case, such assistance should be 'on a moderate scale'.

So far, the House has not considered this Special Report nor has the Government proposed any action to implement its recommendations.

Presumably some assistance will be provided, sooner or later. When this happens, the Committee will be enabled to penetrate much more deeply into the affairs of the nationalized industries. Such penetration will be further facilitated if another suggestion made in the Special Report is adopted: that the Committee should be empowered, like the Estimates Committee, to create sub-committees. These possibilities create alarm in some quarters, where the autonomy and commercial flexibility of the nationalized industries are most closely cherished. They will be further discussed in the last chapter.

The breadth, as well as the intensity, of the Committee's investigations also calls for further consideration. At present, it gives a rather restrictive interpretation to its 'power to send for persons, papers and records'. The Report on the Air Corporations calls attention to this:

> 'It will be noted that Your Committee have not taken evidence from other interested parties—from aircraft manufacturers, for instance, or from the independent airlines or from the Trade Unions. To have done so would, they felt, have taken them outside their proper sphere of action.'

This self-denying ordinance may have been necessary, but it did

172

not have altogether happy results. Lack of evidence from the independent airlines inevitably gave the Committee's conclusions under the heading, 'Competition with the Independent Airlines', a somewhat one-sided appearance, in so far as it was 'not concerned with the reciprocal effects of the competition'. Lack of evidence from the trade unions prevented it from attempting to assess the relative responsibilities of unions and management for the deficiencies in B.O.A.C.'s aircraft maintenance arrangements.

'As the Select Committee states', said the Minister of Transport and Civil Aviation in the House of Commons, 'it was hamstrung by not being able to take evidence from independent air corporations or from the trade unions, and, to this extent, it was not quite able to survey the air field as a whole.'[37]

Its reluctance to enter the field of labour relations is entirely understandable and probably wise; but one cannot so readily see why questioning the independent airline operators would have taken it outside its 'proper sphere of action'. It is hardly likely that the 'independents' would have been reluctant to state their case, and certain that the Committee would have used their evidence with reasonable discretion. The Estimates Committee has no inhibitions about taking evidence from unofficial sources,[38] and there seems no very good reason why the Nationalized Industries Committee should not follow its example, in appropriate circumstances.[39]

In spite of these self-imposed restrictions, the Committee's

[37] H.C. Deb., Vol. 609, col. 970.
[38] This Committee's Report on the Ministry of Power, for instance, contains evidence from representatives of the Coal Merchants' Federation of Great Britain. (See H.C. 198 of 1957–8, p. 114.)
[39] The reason for the Committee's decision to take no evidence from the independent airlines has been given to the author as follows:
'Their terms of reference are that they should examine the Reports and Accounts of the Nationalised Industries; to examine the affairs of other companies would not be immediately relevant to their duties. Although they were bound to consider the degree of competition which exists, they cannot interest themselves in the way that competition affected the independents.'
This is logical enough, but one may still question the desirability of abstaining from any examination of the mutual relations of the public and private sectors within the same industry, which is a subject of great interest to Parliament.

general tendency, as we have seen, is to widen the scope both of its investigations and of its recommendations. Already it has moved a considerable distance into the field of 'policy', and one naturally wonders how much further the advance will go. In a sense, each Report represents a further stretching of the limits of its terms of reference. One has the impression that the Committee is cautiously but determinedly probing, ready at any time to execute a rapid withdrawal if it meets with principled opposition from any significant body of parliamentary opinion. So far, it has not met with such opposition, and possibly it never will. For as with any Select Committee, there is a natural, if vaguely defined, limit beyond which it can hardly attempt to penetrate. Inevitably, there are certain questions which cannot be broached by an all-party committee, if the principle of unanimity in its recommendations is to be preserved. As non-unanimous recommendations, particularly if the division is along party lines, would be of small value and would jeopardize the confidence that Parliament now has in the Select Committee device, there is little likelihood that the Committee will attempt to concern itself with matters of policy on which there are basic political disagreements. It is this factor, rather than inhibitions arising from terms of reference, which guarantees that the Committee will not stretch its functions to the point where angry Members of the House of Commons question its usefulness. There can be no doubt that Mr. Butler had this point in mind when he decided to throw overboard the chains in which the previous Committee was tightly bound and gave the present Committee its charter of freedom.

VII

Foreign Experience

So far, our approach to the constitutional and political problems created by the nationalization of industry has been quite conventional in the sense that, like most other writers on the subject, we have not taken evidence from outside Britain. The time has come, however, when comparative studies in this field are essential, for the problems we have been discussing are not confined to this country, but experienced in every parliamentary democracy where the public sector of the economy has grown to a position of major importance. Some examination of this foreign experience must therefore be made, if only to discover whether it has any lessons to teach us. The dangers of this kind of comparison are well known, but they can be guarded against and do not provide any excuse for failure to undertake the task.

Much of what has already been said would suggest that one could write a history of public enterprise in this country since 1946 under the title of 'The Decline and Fall of the Autonomous Public Corporation'. Although its final chapters are still on the stocks, the general trend is unmistakable. Intractable circumstances have triumphed over pious resolutions. Lip-service to the principle of autonomy is still widely given, but it has been honoured more in the breach than in the observance. We are already in a situation where the dividing line between general policy and day-to-day administration is almost impossible to draw. Continuous and intimate contact between Ministers and corporations has made the assignment of responsibility for all but the lower-level decisions a matter of conjecture, and it is now hardly an exaggeration to regard the corporation as a kind of specialized ministerial agency, whose corporate status is little more than a convenient legal and administrative fiction.

The first question to be asked, therefore, is whether this is a tendency specific to Britain or one that is shared by other parliamentary democracies; and this is the easiest of all questions to answer. The tendency is an almost universal one, particularly in those countries where the public sector plays a key role.

Admittedly, there are some exceptions, of which Western Germany is perhaps the most outstanding. There, according to the principles of the prevalent economic 'philosophy', the state has abstained, to a quite unique degree, from interference in the affairs of its public enterprises, particularly those organized in the form of joint-stock companies (Aktiengesellschaft) and grouped under the three great 'holdings', VIAG (Vereinigte Industrieunternehmen AG), VEBA (Vereinigte Elektrizitats-und-Bergwerks AG), and AG fur Berg-und Huttenbetriebe (formerly Hermann-Göering-Werke). As Professor von Eynern has said, the state 'does not wish, fundamentally, to exercise an influence over the enterprises it owns that goes beyond straightforward financial administration'.[1] So far, this self-denying ordinance has been kept with typical Teutonic consistency. Hostility to 'étatism' has been reinforced by the reaction of public opinion against the methods of economic control characteristic of the Hitlerite dictatorship and by 'general admiration for the activities of the entrepreneurs, which have been particularly successful—both in private and in public industry—during the years of the 'economic miracle'. How much longer this suspicion of state economic intervention will be maintained, however, is open to doubt. Professor von Eynern has tentatively suggested, without giving any specific reasons, that it may not last long.

Superficially, Italy would appear to offer another exception, particularly significant in view of the fact that the extent of the Italian state's 'participations' is such that 'Italy could be transformed overnight, without further legislation, into the most advanced socialist society in western Europe'.[2] The apparently enviable independence enjoyed by these enterprises, however, is due not to any principled anti-statism or reaction against former

[1] Gert von Eynern: *Le Contrôle des Enterprises Publiques par l'Etat dans la République Fédérale Allemande*, a paper presented to the Rome Congress the International Political Science Association, 1958 (mimeographed).

[2] Brian Chapman: *The Profession of Government*, Allen & Unwin, Ltd., London 1959, p. 58.

Fascist practices or admiration for the pioneering entrepreneur, but to administrative muddle reinforced and maintained by the self-interest of a powerful and nepotistic officialdom.

> 'The legal, economic and political position of all the various companies and enterprises in which the state had a direct or indirect interest', writes Dr. Chapman, 'was so complicated that when La Malfa, as minister without portfolio, reported on them in 1951, he described the whole sector as 'una selva infinita'. By that time the minister had arrived at over a thousand different undertakings, not counting provincial or communal ramifications which would have pushed the number into several thousands. Their status, their structure, the forms of control to which they were subject and their place in the machinery of government were utterly incoherent.'[3]

These circumstances gave the officials appointed to run the enterprises the opportunity, of which they were not slow to avail themselves, to build up a series of semi-private economic empires. The Italian situation, therefore, is entirely different from the German one, and does not constitute a genuine exception to the rule that we have enunciated. Moreover, an effort has already been made— with what success still remains to be seen—to clean up the mess by a more clear allocation of political responsibility for the enterprises and a reinforcement of ministerial powers of control. By an Act of 1956, a Ministry of State Holdings was created, in which was vested 'all the powers previously belonging to the Council of Ministers, ministers' committees, and individual ministers, with regard to state holdings, both direct and indirect'. Among these powers is that of issuing 'general directions' to some of the enterprises, including the great holding companies, the IRI (Instituto per la Ricostruzione Industriale) and the ENI (Ento Nazionale Idrocarburi). The process of clearing the jungle would seem, therefore, to be already under way.

The question with which we are here mainly concerned is how far this almost universal process of bringing public enterprise 'under the harrow', as Mr. Herbert Morrison has so often put it, is due to a demand by legislatures that ministers should assume

[3] *Ibid.* p. 58.

responsibilities wider than those originally envisaged by the theorists of public enterprise and, in some cases, by the constituting statutes. This, of course, is a question entirely separate from that of how much autonomy a given public enterprise should, ideally, enjoy. It is one of evaluating relative responsibilities for an actual situation. But it necessarily carries with it certain important implications for political practice; for if one arrives at the conclusions (a) that the autonomy of enterprises has been reduced to an undesirable extent and (b) that this has been mainly due to pressures from parliamentarians, then the case for a deliberate limitation of parliamentary powers (either by way of self-denying ordinance or of firm refusal by the government, confident of its majority support, to pander to parliamentarians' importunities) is a strong one—particularly if the criterion of 'business efficiency' is to be regarded as dominant.

It almost goes without saying that parliamentarians are always reluctant to allow important areas of administration to pass wholly or partly outside their supervision. Indeed, it would be democratically very unhealthy if this were not the case. (Perhaps the comparative lack of interest shown by Western German parliamentarians in the uniquely autonomous public enterprises of their country may be regarded as one of the indices of the immaturity of West German democracy.) It is also obvious that a parliament which has equipped itself with various powers, whether over a public enterprise or over a more normal administrative agency, may grieviously misuse them. Other things being equal, such misuse is more likely to occur in a new and inexperienced democracy than in an older and more experienced one. India offers an example. There, according to Mr. Paul Appleby, Parliament 'is the chief citadel of opposition to delegation of powers, the need for which is the worst short-coming in Indian administration'.

'Its reluctance to delegate its power in detail, as it is essential to do if Parliamentary powers are to be important and positive, discourages Ministers from delegating their powers, discourages Secretaries from delegating their powers, and Managing Directors from delegating their powers.'[4]

[4] Paul Appleby: *Re-examination of India's Administrative System with special reference to Administration of Government's Industrial and Commercial* [footnote continued on page 179]

One might also quote, as an example of the pathology of parliamentary control, the manner in which Turkish parliamentarians influence the policies of their Maritime Bank (Denizçilik Bankasi) an operational agency which runs shipping lines.

> 'Inhabitants of a certain coastal town may wish the ships to call there, as a matter of local prestige, although they might easily get to a neighbouring town where ships are already scheduled to stop. In such cases, they can usually force the Bank, through their deputies, to stop.'[5]

Examples such as this are familiar enough to students of parliamentary practice in democratic or semi-democratic countries comparatively low on the scale of development. But what, in our view, has been insufficiently noticed is that there is no positive correlation between the extent of parliamentary powers and the extent of their misuse. There may, indeed, be some degree of negative correlation, in so far as there are fairly numerous examples of a parliament's attempting to impose inappropriate and restrictive *controls* precisely because it has felt frustrated at the inadequacy of its *powers*. One can attempt to shield the corporation from over-inquisitive parliamentary interest, but sooner or later any democratic parliament worth its salt will revolt against the restrictions that have been imposed. If it does so successfully, the danger is that it will *use* its powers with far less discretion than it would have done if these had been available to it from the beginning. Some are of the opinion that this has happened in the United States, through

---

[*footnote continued from page 178*]

Enterprises (Cabinet Secretariat, Organization and Methods Divisions, New Delhi 1956), p. 45. Without, however, having had Mr. Appleby's opportunities for on-the-spot study. I would guess that Mr. Nehru's reluctance to delegate powers is a far more potent cause of these 'short-comings'. 'He has never shown,' writes his latest and best-informed biographer, 'a capacity or inclination to delegate authority. The result has been the "administrative jungle" which he bemoans. When Nehru is out of the country the decision-making process comes to a virtual halt. And even when he is in Delhi the bureaucracy functions only as rapidly as Nehru can handle the vast amount of paper that crosses his desk.' (Michael Brecher: *Nehru, a Political Biography*, Oxford 1959, pp. 622–3.)

[5] Sevda Erem and Guthrie S. Birkhead: *A Study of the Administration of the Port of Istanbul*, Public Administration Institute for Turkey and the Middle East, Ankara 1956, p. 14.

the passing of the 'Ramspeck' Act of 1940 and the Corporation Control Act of 1945. Others, such as Mr. Harold Seidman, who must be regarded as the leading authority on this subject, think that these Acts simply tidied up a disorderly administrative structure and put the corporations in their proper place as governmental agencies.[6] But wherever the truth may lie in this controversy, there can be little doubt about the *motives* of Congressmen and Senators in passing legislation which, according to one critic, 'very largely destroys the advantages of government corporations which have been the principal inducement for their use'.[7] As I have written elsewhere of the Corporation Control Act:

'The general trend of this Act is unmistakable. Almost every line speaks of Congress suspicion of the corporate device, of its exasperation at previous failures to open the "closed book", and of its determination to bring into force what it regards as adequate controls, even at the cost of undermining much of that "business autonomy" which is supposed to be the corporation's unique virtue.'[8]

However, in attempting to use foreign experience to throw light on British problems, it is dangerous to pay too much attention either to under-developed countries, where parliamentary institutions are embryonic or unstable, or to the United States, which has a totally dissimilar governmental system and a set of public enterprises which play no more than a peripheral role in the national economy. European experience also needs to be used with great caution for reasons that are obvious enough. It is to the older countries of the British Commonwealth that one may turn most hopefully for usable comparative material; for these have broadly similar political systems, conventions and attitudes not too distant from our own, and public enterprises which, if not always as 'central' as Britain's, are at least important and well-established.

[6] See Harold Seidman: *The Government Corporation: its Place in the Federal Structure*, in Hanson: *Public Enterprise*, International Institute of Administrative Sciences, Brussels 1955.
[7] Albert S. Abel: *The Public Corporation in the United States*, in W. Friedmann: *The Public Corporation, a Comparative Symposium*, Stevens & Sons, London 1954, p. 356.
[8] Hanson: *op. cit.*, p. 33.

Of all Commonwealth countries, Australia offers the most fruitful comparative experience; for Australia has not only used the public corporation for a great variety of purposes over a long period, she has also produced a number of able writers, such as Sir Frederic Eggleston, Professors Bland, Sawer and Webb, and Mr. T. H. Kewley, who have dealt with that experience systematically and critically. Australia, moreover, is the only Commonwealth country where questions of the kind we are here considering have been the subject of detailed inquiry and report by a Government Committee.

The extent of ministerial control over Australian corporations, both Federal and State, varies considerably from corporation to corporation. In general, it has tended to increase, partly for reasons with which all countries are familiar, partly for reasons specific to Australia. Indeed, Professor Sawer has gone so far as to say that 'to some extent the incorporation of a public authority has become a drafting cliché, or automatic response by Parliaments to any suggestion that a body has a degree of isolation from the central executive government'.[9] The actual use of these powers of control depends upon numerous factors, including the respective personal qualities of the Minister and the Chairman of the Board concerned, the importance of the corporation's operations, its success in accomplishing its mission, the extent of its financial dependence on the government, etc. As in England, factors of this kind, rather than legal prescriptions, determine the nature of the minister-corporation relationship. There are, however, certain statutory provisions, having no exact parallel in England, which would seem to compel the minister to keep a tighter rein on the corporations than, in their absence, he might wish to do. For whereas the power to give general directions is not invariably embodied in the constituting legislation, requirements for specific ministerial approvals, sometimes of a rather pettyfogging kind, frequently are. Thus, for instance, the Australian National Airlines Commission has to obtain ministerial approval for the purchase of land costing more than £5,000, for entering into a lease of land for a period exceeding five years, for disposing of any 'property or privilege' having a book value in excess of £5,000, for entering into any contract for the supply, from outside Australia, of aircraft equipment or

[9] G. Sawer: *The Public Corporation in Australia*, in Friedmann: *op. cit.* p. 42.

materials costing more than £10,000, and for the payment to an officer of any salary exceeding £1,500 a year.[10] There is a similar provision regarding the salaries of officers in the Act constituting the Snowy Mountains Hydro-Electricity Authority, and also a requirement of ministerial approval for contracts of over £100,000.[11] The Overseas Telecommunications Commission is hedged in by ministerial 'approvals' at almost every point—so much so that its Chairman has said:

> 'In large Commonwealth Departments it is necessary for the Minister to delegate to his permanent head and to executive officers powers which are, in many respects, greater than those conferred upon the Commission by the Overseas Telecommunications Act.'[12]

It may be that the sheer extent of such powers, supplemented as they are in certain states[13] by the requirement that the corporation's exercise of its functions 'shall be subject in all respects to the control and direction of the Minister', is partly responsible for the fact that 'parliamentary questions about the activities of corporations tend to be treated in much the same way as questions about the activities of ordinary government departments.'[14] At least, that is what Mr. Kewley suggests, while recording that 'there has been little discussion about the principles which should relate to parliamentary questions on the affairs of the corporations' and no 'specific ruling' on the matter by the Speaker. But whereas the extent of ministerial control, together with the absence of any restriction on questioning, would appear to provide Parliament with ample *opportunities* for intervention, it has *used* these opportunities with considerably less vigour than the British House of

[10] Joint Committee of Public Accounts: 21*st and 22nd Reports: Australian Aluminium Production Commission*, Government Printing Office, Canberra 1955; Memo. by the Chairman of the Australian National Airlines Commission, p. 97.

[11] *Ibid*. Memo. by the Chairman of the Snowy Mountains Hydro-Electricity Authority, pp. 103–4.

[12] *Ibid*. Memo. by the Chairman of the Overseas Telecommunications Commission. p. 103.

[13] e.g. New South Wales. See T. H. Kewley: *Some General Features of the Statutory Corporation in Australia*, in *Australian Journal of Public Administration*, Vol. 16, No. 1 (New Series), March 1957, p. 23.

[14] *Ibid*. p. 25.

Commons has used its apparently more restricted ones. Again to quote Mr. Kewley:

> 'The statutes require the corporations to render annual reports and financial statements to the Minister who is usually, but not always, required to transmit these to Parliament. Usually neither these reports nor the Auditor-General's report on the financial statements provide an occasion for debate in Parliament upon the affairs of the corporation concerned.'[15]

Nor does any regular investigation of the corporations by special parliamentary committees compensate for this failure to give their affairs a periodical airing on the floor of the House. The conclusion seems inescapable: that whatever factors have been responsible for the enhancement of ministerial responsibility, with its concomitant extension of parliamentary powers, the desire of parliamentarians to bring the corporations persistently 'under the harrow' has not been one of them. Can it be that the absence of frustration has killed the desire to interfere?

Some evidence pointing in the same direction—although perhaps rather ambiguously—may be gleaned from the Report on the Australian Aluminium Production Commission. This body had some severe remarks to make about 'the trend away from the autonomy of statutory corporations, especially marked in Australia since World War I', which it ascribed to 'a desire to insist on ministerial responsibility'.[16] It condemned the 'blurring' of the distinction between corporations and ordinary government departments, expressed the opinion that 'statutory corporations should, with whatever modifications may be required by the particular circumstances of the corporation, enjoy a degree of autonomy', and supported 'the desire on the part of the seven major statutory corporations created by the Commonwealth and consulted by us to retain such a status'. In its opinion, understanding of the nature and purpose of statutory corporations in Australia was defective, with the result that there had been 'a failure to draw clear statutory lines of authority between the Corporation and the Minister'.[17] It was careful, however, not to ascribe

[15] *Ibid.* p. 25.
[16] *Op. cit.* p. 74.
[17] *Ibid.* pp. 62, 74.

this allegedly undesirable situation to Parliament's itch to interfere, and made no proposals for the limitation of existing parliamentary powers, except to the extent that some such limitation might be implied by any diminution of ministerial responsibility. Moreover, it was not particularly critical of those clauses in the nationalization acts which gave the Minister specific powers, but concentrated its fire on those that left the extent of ministerial responsibility ambiguous. Thus, for instance, it criticized the Aluminium Production Commission Act on the grounds that this measure did not clearly set out 'either the terms and conditions upon which Members of the Commission hold their office, or their duties and responsibilities as 'representatives' of the Commonwealth on the Commission'.[18] Such demands for a clearer definition of responsibilities, as we have seen in our account of the work of the Select Committee on Nationalized Industries in Britain, are usually made with a view to *enhancing* Parliament's supervisory powers, by reducing the Minister's opportunities to use the Board of the corporation as a screen.

Specifically opposed to any limitation of Parliament's right to question Ministers about the affairs of the corporations was Sir Richard Boyer, the Chairman of the Australian Broadcasting Commission, who presented a Memorandum to the Committee. Expressing his disagreement with the British practice of refusing 'to answer questions on matters which are clearly within the jurisdiction of the Authority', he wrote:

'Indeed, this is one of the legitimate and healthy means by which a Minister can have brought to his notice any action of the Authority which may require his attention. In practice, it is customary for the Minister to secure the answer to a question from the Chairman of the Authority concerned and convey it to the questioner and the House as the answer of the corporation, with or without his own comment. There appears to be no reason why this practice should involve the Minister in assuming responsibility for the action questioned if it is within the jurisdiction of the Authority.'[19]

[18] *Ibid.* p. 48.
[19] *Ibid.* pp. 93–4.

It is significant that Sir Richard saw no contradiction between this freedom and the 'high degree of independence' for the corporation which he stated elsewhere to be 'undoubtedly essential'.[20] It must be admitted, however, that in some respects his views are by no means free from ambiguity, for he also says that the Statutory Corporation is 'responsible, not *to* its Minister, but to Parliament *through* its Minister' and that therefore 'the controlling members of the Statutory Corporation' should be required 'to come up for re-appointment or rejection at set intervals, a procedure which is at the very heart of the principle of accountability, in much the same way as Cabinet Ministers'. How this is reconcilable with a 'high degree of independence' he does not explain.

Professor Leicester Webb is also, apparently, quite uncon-cerned about the alleged dangers of excessive parliamentary scrutiny of the public corporation. Indeed, although there may be some doubt about what his carefully-modulated arguments add up to, the Memorandum which he presented to the Commission is, in certain respects, considerably more radical than Sir Richard Boyer's. Much of it is devoted to what amounts to an exposure of the *mystique* of the corporation. He criticizes Mr. Herbert Morrison (and the Australian Solicitor-General, who, in his Memoranda, re-peated with approval the Morrisonian arguments) for underrating 'the level of managerial efficiency which can be achieved in govern-ment departments', which he considers to be 'as capable as other organizations of adapting themselves to the needs of new forms of activity', and expresses the view that comparative study fails to reveal that the public corporation possesses any 'natural superior-ity' as 'a recipe for managerial efficiency'. Business flexibility, he considers, is not 'incompatible with full ministerial responsibility'. 'Moreover, it should be noted that even in the case of government departments, full ministerial responsibility does not require or in practice entail ministerial control over details of management.' What he dislikes is not so much the width of ministerial powers (and, by implication, the extent of potential parliamentary super-vision they attract) as their uncertainty and lack of definition. The existing controls, he holds, display 'both redundancy and inade-quacy'. 'In some respects they restrict freedom of management

[20] *The Statutory Corporation as a Democratic Device*, in A.J.P.A. *loc. cit.* p. 34.

unnecessarily. Yet they are not sufficiently comprehensive to achieve their main purpose', which is 'to ensure certain minimum standards of probity and efficiency in administration' and 'to ensure that the activities of public corporations do not conflict with or nullify national economic policy'.[21] Like Sir Richard Boyer's, his arguments display certain internal inconsistencies, but these are not very relevant from the standpoint of our present investigation. What is important is that one of Australia's most distinguished students of public enterprise sees no inherent incompatibility between the conferment of extensive parliamentary and ministerial powers and the enjoyment by the corporation of necessary managerial freedoms. If he is right, then the dilemma which we have discussed at such length in earlier chapters is less sharp and less real than theorists in this country have been prone to imagine.[22]

New Zealand, like Australia, has had extensive experience in the use of the public corporation, but 'there has been little generalized discussion of government corporations as an administrative device' and virtually no controversy over the extent of ministerial and parliamentary powers. Professor Webb gives four reasons for this lack of interest in a problem which British politicians, political scientists and administrators have regarded as of major importance, viz. (1) that New Zealand governments are unusually strong and stable, with the result that there is little difficulty in 'securing continuity of management in state enterprises'; (2) that, with the elimination of patronage and corruption, government administration is 'reasonably competent'; (3) that, in such a small country, people are on 'familiar terms' with their politicians, and regard the state as a 'domestic animal' not likely to 'get out of hand'; and (4) that 'extensions of state activity have taken place piecemeal in response to particular situations rather than through the election of governments committed to programmes of socialization'. For these reasons, 'it would not occur to New Zealanders that the public corporation had inherent virtues as an administrative device'; in

[21] Memorandum in *op. cit.* pp. 94–6. See also Leicester Webb: *Freedom and the Public Corporation* in *Australian Journal of Public Administration*, Vol. 13, No. 2, 1954; and G. Sawer: *The Legal Status of Statutory Corporations*, in *ibid.*, Vol. 16, No. I (New Series), 1957.

[22] The latest discussion of Australian experience is S. Encel: *Public Corporations in Australia, Some Recent Developments* in *Public Administration*, Vol. 38, Autumn, 1960.

practice, the corporation 'has not established itself as the administrative form most likely to lead to efficient and enterprising management of state enterprises'.[23]

Hence it is hardly surprising that New Zealand has neither special provisions for nor special limitations on the supervision of public corporations by the legislature. As in Australia, the extent of statutorily-prescribed ministerial control varies from corporation to corporation, 'but there can be little doubt that . . . government companies and corporations are responsive to whatever influence Cabinet and ministers care to exert'.[24] Ministerial practice in dealing with parliamentary questions on the corporations is not entirely consistent,[25] but 'if the point at issue is important enough and the Opposition insists, a government spokesman will provide an answer rather than risk the possibility of a loss of public confidence through his party's failure to reply'. No attempt has been made to define ministerial responsibility, either in general or in particular, and Members of Parliament 'do not display any great interest in the activities of the corporations', confining themselves, in the main, 'to making short and superficial comments when annual reports come up for discussion'.[26]

Whatever general conclusions, then, can be drawn from the experience of Australia with the public corporation would appear to be reinforced by that of New Zealand.

The Canadian case is similar in some respects, different in others. It is similar in so far as Canadian parliamentarians, like their Australian and New Zealand counterparts, have escaped continuous exposure to a coherent public enterprise 'philosophy' such as

[23] Leicester Webb: *The Public Corporation in New Zealand*, in Friedmann: *op. cit.* pp. 267–8, 300. See also R. J. Polaschek: *Government Administration in New Zealand*, O.U.P., Wellington and Oxford 1958, p. 73. There are several examples of oscillation between corporation and departmental management, without 'significant difference to operating efficiency'. The outstanding example is the Railways Department. It was controlled by boards from 1889 to 1894, 1925 to 1928, 1931 to 1936, and 1952 to 1957. 'Before, after, and in between these periods management has been the responsibility of a single permanent head accountable to a minister' (*Ibid.* p. 56). There is a tendency, both in Australia and in New Zealand, for the socialist parties to prefer 'direct' and the non-socialist parties 'corporation' administration. The reasons for this are explained with admirable clarity by Professor Sawer in the article, already cited, which he contributed to the Friedmann symposium.
[24] *Ibid.* p. 69.
[25] Webb: *loc. cit.* p. 294.
[26] Polaschek: *op. cit.* pp. 69–70.

Mr. Herbert Morrison's, and shown no more than sporadic interest in the affairs of their country's corporations. As in Australia, the corporation has tended to become a 'drafting cliché'—so much so that, when pressed in Parliament, the most prolific progenitor of corporations, Mr. D. C. Howe, was quite unable to explain why the corporate should be preferred to the departmental form of organization.

> 'My honourable friend', he said, 'asked why this commission should take the form of a corporation. I shall have to get a more satisfactory answer to that question than I can give off-hand. All I can say is that for a commission to operate and do business it seems to be necessary that they be formed into a corporation. All the commissions I know of that operate around Ottawa are formed into corporations.'[27]

Although there are plenty of references to public corporations in general debates, their annual reports and accounts are not debated, and other occasions for discussing their affairs do not appear to be either eagerly awaited or persistently sought by parliamentarians. A few important corporations, such as the Canadian National Railways and the Canadian Broadcasting Corporation, whose operations impinge directly on the public, get their fair share of parliamentary attention, but the remainder are very much neglected. Even the power to establish committees to investigate corporation affairs has been very sparingly used. Of Questions, Mr. Lloyd D. Musolf, who has analyzed them, says: 'An average of approximately one question a day from a House of 265 members scarcely qualifies as an indicator of strong interest in the corporations as a group.'[28]

One reason for this apparent parliamentary quiescence is what Mr. Musolf calls the 'low level of visibility' of the majority of the corporations, which are not regarded as playing a key role in the economy. Another may be that business interests, well represented on the Boards, have in general accepted the need for the corporations

[27] Quoted from Canadian Parliamentary Debates in J. E. Hodgetts: *The Public Corporation in Canada*, in *Public Administration*, Vol. 28, Winter 1950, p. 284.

[28] Lloyd D. Musolf: *Public Ownership and Accountability—The Canadian Experience*, Cambridge, Massachusetts, 1959, pp. 103–5.

in the economic areas where they operate. A third may be memory of the reasons for the granting of a large measure of autonomy to the Canadian National Railways, the prototype of the Canadian public corporation, viz. (1) the abuses that had been associated with departmental railway administration; (2) the fact that the state railways were in competition with private lines. Such considerations may help to explain 'the relative calm with which Canadians have generally regarded public enterprise' and their lack of any marked 'ideological' interest in it. They certainly explain, at least in part, why systematic parliamentary attention to the affairs of the corporations is so infrequent as to cause Mr. Musolf some slight uneasiness.[29]

This, however, is not the whole story; for there is some evidence of parliamentary frustration, arising from the fact that the Government has deliberately attempted to restrict the House's opportunities 'in pursuit of the earlier ideal of managerial autonomy and freedom from partisan pressure'. Ministers, says Professor Hodgetts, 'have taken great pains when answering questions in the legislature to show that they are nothing more than passive channels of communication between the Corporation and the House'. The initial riposte to a Question is usually: 'This is a matter concerning the internal administration of an independent agency. I shall consult with the officials of the corporation to see whether they are prepared to provide the information requested.' If and when an answer is given, it is preceded by the formula: 'The corporation advises that . . .' Although answers are sometimes given quite readily, particularly to Questions about the affairs of the Canadian National Railways and the Central Mortgage and Housing Corporation, many Questions are turned down on the grounds that 'it would be disadvantageous to the corporation in business negotiations' to make public the information requested.

During the long period of the Liberal Government's tenure of office, these restrictions evoked periodical protest from the Opposition.

On one occasion, Mr. Diefenbaker complained of the Crown Corporations: 'Whenever they need money they come to parliament, but whenever we endeavour to ascertain whether they have overexpended or recklessly wasted, then they hide behind the

[29] *Ibid*. pp. 25, 137.

fiction that parliament has no right to know'. As Ministers possessed extensive powers of control, and frequently appointed civil servants as members of the Boards, this 'sealed lips' policy tended to suggest that something nasty was being concealed. As long as the Liberals remained in office, however, it was fairly logically pursued. Hence, in so far as Parliament took any active interest in the corporations, it tended to 'gyrate between alternate fits of despairing passivity and bouts of energetic but uninformed criticism'.

It was the advent to office of Mr. Diefenbaker's Conservative Government that appears to have revealed the strength of the former Opposition's feelings about the matter. Shortly after this event, Professor Hodgetts wrote:

> 'During its prolonged period as official opposition, the present Conservative Government had naturally built up a strong antagonism towards the agencies which seemed so particularly immune to their questions and criticisms . . . As a consequence, the present government has injected a new note of uneasiness into the even tenor of the lives of these Liberal-created and Liberal-supported corporations. Already the chairmen of three of the most prominent corporations have resigned, one quite openly because the government had not given him any assurance that it would be prepared to underwrite the programme of his agency for the coming year or to take up the many unsettled proposals for reorganisation made by a royal commission appointed during the previous régime of the Liberals. Even the Governor of the Bank of Canada and the Minister of Finance have engaged in written and verbal arguments which make no pretence at concealing the real differences of opinion on the Bank's so-called 'tight money' policy. Moreover, the Prime Minister and his leading lieutenants, while in opposition, had been ardent champions of the rights of parliament which, they often asserted, had nowhere been more flagrantly violated than in the excessive resort to the device of the crown corporations.'

How far the Conservatives' attitude was due to an enthusiasm for parliamentary liberties and how far to dislike of public enterprise itself is a moot point. Probably their motives were as mixed as those of British Conservatives during the period 1945–50. It is the result of that attitude which is important. Writing in 1958, Professor Hodgetts thought that there was a 'strong likelihood' that the public corporations would be 'faced with uncertainties which they had never before experienced'. He could not say whether these would 'have a stimulating or a stultifying effect on management', but saw signs that morale had already 'been somewhat undermined'. On the other hand, it was possible that more intelligent forms of parliamentary control would be introduced as a result of the Government's reactivation of parliamentary standing committees, including the Public Accounts Committee, and its re-establishment of the Select Committee on Estimates.

> 'This committee has had before it the accounts of the departments of Defence and Defence Production, along with those of five crown companies which come under them. The report on "certain weaknesses in accounting and procedural methods" used in crown corporations has been characterised as the most critical to come from a Commons committee since the second world war. This is clearly a most promising beginning and may mark a new stage in the development of parliamentary control.'[30]

More recent information, to confirm or refute Professor Hodgetts' prognostications, is not available to the author at the time of writing, and it must be admitted that, in many respects, the Canadian experience is much more ambiguous than the Australian or New Zealandian. In the main, however, it would seem to offer support to the view that restrictions of parliamentary powers over public corporations tend to defeat their object. A parliament, such as the Canadian, which has been denied facilities to establish what it regards as reasonable and necessary forms of supervision, may easily succumb to the temptation to run amok in the corporate sector as soon as someone unbolts the door, often with scant regard to those delicate conventions and understandings upon which

[30] The source of both of the above quotations is Professor Hodgetts' paper, *The Control of Public Enterprise in Canada*, presented to the Rome Congress of the International Political Science Association. See also the same author's *Responsibility of the Government Corporation to the Governing Body*, in *Proceedings of the Fifth Annual Conference, of the Institute of Public Administration of Canada*, Ontario 1953.

PARLIAMENT AND PUBLIC OWNERSHIP

the successful management of the enterprises so largely depends. It may be, indeed, that under a régime of nominally unrestricted parliamentary control the managers of public enterprises, in the long run, enjoy greater real protection from wanton political interference than under a régime which gives them formal protection against parliamentary inquisitiveness.

Before leaving Dominion experience,[31] some reference must be made to the untypical but interesting situation in Saskatchewan, where a Co-operative Commonwealth Federation Government has found in the Crown Corporation a 'useful tool' for the administration of the many public enterprises which it created to give effect to its socialist programme. The uniqueness of the Saskatchewan experience lies not only in the size and importance of the newly-created public sector, but also in the Government's well thought out attempt to give it systematic organization.

Each corporation is responsible to a cabinet minister, who, until very recently, has been invariably Chairman of its Board of Directors, but, in addition, all the corporations except two are controlled by a Government Finance Office, which is simultaneously a holding company and a cabinet committee. Consisting of the six cabinet ministers with responsibilities for the corporations, together with the Deputy Provincial Treasurer and the Secretary of the Economic Advisory and Planning Board, this 'Office' finances the corporations, co-ordinates their policies, and 'advises' them on accounting matters and industrial relations problems. Legislative control is effected mainly through a Select Standing Committee on the Crown Corporations, before which 'the responsible minister, advised by the corporation manager, accountant and other officials, answers questions on the activities of the corporation for the preceding financial year'.[32]

Clearly, the Saskatchewan corporations are subject to a political

[31] South Africa is deliberately omitted. Although these are one or two accounts of public enterprise in the Union (see, for instance, T. W. Price: *The Public Corporation in South Africa*, in Friedmann: *The Public Corporation*, London 1954; and *Public Enterprise in South Africa*, in Hanson: *Public Enterprise*, Brussels 1955), there is no study, as far as the author is aware, of enterprise-minister-parliament relations in that country.

[32] Allen E. Blakeney: *Saskatchewan's Crown Corporations, a Case Study*, in *Proceedings of the Fifth Annual Conference of the Public Administration Institute of Canada*. Other studies of this subject are to be found in Friedmann: *op. cit.* (Blakeney) and Hanson: *op. cit.* (G. W. Cadbury).

192

control so extensive and all-pervading that their distinction, in this respect, from ordinary government departments is by no means clear. The reason given for this extreme unorthodoxy, which was the product of a deliberate decision and not of accidental circumstances, is interesting.

> 'The Government', writes Mr. Blakeney, the Secretary of the Government Finance Office, 'did not stumble into government enterprise, all the while protesting its distaste for the whole process, as happened in most other Canadian jurisdictions. The establishment of the Crown Corporations was a major plank on the CCF Party's political program. Under these conditions it would have been useless for the Cabinet to endeavour to shelter behind independent corporations. The electorate clearly held the Cabinet responsible for virtually all acts of Crown Corporations. The degree of independence given to the Corporations was that which was considered by the Cabinet as likely to give the responsible minister the best opportunity to administer the operation efficiently under his personal direction.'

Evidently, the leaders of the C.C.F. decided that, under the circumstances, any attempt to give the corporation special 'protection' was unlikely to avoid trouble either for themselves or for the management. What is perhaps more significant is that, according to Mr. Blakeney, the corporations are enjoying greater *de facto* independence now that they are passing out of the sphere of political controversy and becoming 'accepted'. His comment on this situation is worth quoting, as it displays a realism much to be commended to those who are over-concerned with legal niceties:

> 'I am inclined to the view that much of our preoccupation with the form of the corporation is illusory. If we grant that policy matters must be controllable by the political heads, and if we grant that policy matters and administrative matters are merely two ends of the same stick, then it appears likely that the degree of policy and indeed of administrative independence is determined not so much by the corporation structure as by the political considerations in the mind of the responsible minister and his colleagues.'

In general, examination of both Dominion and other foreign experience reveals a trend of thought that seems to the present writer thoroughly healthy. No longer is the emphasis on the formal *limitation* of parliamentary powers over public enterprises. Attempts, where made, to treat parliamentarians as over-inquisitive and interfering schoolchildren are being abandoned. The elected representatives of the people naturally resent such treatment, and are liable to react to it by making the lives of public enterprise managers more difficult than they need be. Today, the emphasis is almost everywhere on providing parliaments with better opportunities to use their powers *constructively*. What they need is more understanding of the special problems of public enterprise, and a clearer realization both of their own capacities and of their own limitations. This involves providing them with facilities to obtain impartial and objective information about those aspects of public enterprise in which they are currently interested, and is greatly facilitated if opportunities are present whereby a small body of Members, specially concerned with the public sector, can become sufficiently well informed about its problems to be able to provide their fellow-members with authoritative or quasi-expert guidance.

These objectives *may* be attained by the establishment of special parliamentary bodies for investigation and inquiry, equipped with adequate powers. Experience is too short for one to be able to say that this is the best method, under all circumstances. But the record of the British Select Committee on Nationalized Industries is, to say the least, encouraging, and even the record of the French sub-committees, which has attracted a good deal of criticism from those who can find little that is commendable in the parliamentary experience of the Fourth Republic, is far less black than it is sometimes painted. True, these sub-committees have 'looked over the shoulders' of the managers of the French nationalized industries in a way that would be found intolerable in Britain; but one has to make allowance for a totally dissimilar political and administrative environment, which enables the French nationalized industries to bear without flinching—and even, in many cases, to welcome—a degree of external control and supervision which in many other countries would produce complete paralysis. At least, it is the opinion of the best-informed British student of French nationalization that the committees' investigations have been useful to

Parliament and harmless to the industries. Concluding a survey of the 'Parliamentary Control of Public Enterprise in France', Dr. F. Ridley writes:

'It will be seen that the French Parliament has powerful means at its disposal for the control of public enterprise. Where it wishes, it is exceedingly well informed. It can moreover investigate thoroughly any matters that have aroused public concern. It need only be added that there is little evidence that the efficiency of public enterprise has suffered or that the initiative of management has been impaired.'[33]

The present writer's own impression, based on conversations with politicians, civil servants and enterprise managers from many lands, is that the 'select committee' device is attracting increasing support, particularly in those countries whose political systems more-or-less follow the British pattern. Canada, as we have seen, is reactivating its Estimates Committee. India, which already has an Estimates Committee with frequently-used powers to investigate public enterprises, is now considering the establishment of a separate committee for this purpose, on the grounds that the Estimates Committee has too many other responsibilities and insufficient time.[34] At a Seminar organized by the Indian Institute of Public Administration in December 1959, attended by top-level civil servants from the economic ministries and by leading enterprise managers, this proposal, after full discussion, received unanimous support.

There is less agreement, however, on the scope of such a committee's inquiries, and on the methods that it should use. In England, as we have seen, there were fears lest the Select Committee

---

[33] *Parliamentary Affairs*, Vol. 10, No. 3, Summer 1957, p. 287. It should be noted, however, that some French students of nationalization are not as happy about the record of the sub-commissions as is Dr. Ridley. M. Chenot, in his *Les Entreprises Nationalisées* (Paris 1956) emphasizes the danger that 'parliamentary control' will turn into 'Assembly administration'. M. Delion, in his *L'Etat et les Entreprises Publiques* (Sirey, Paris 1959), while commending the sub-commissions for much of their work, considers that they have abused their powers of investigation to the extent of creating 'serious confusion in the organization of the *pouvoirs publics*'. (See pp. 63–5.)

[34] See *Parliamentary Supervision over State Undertakings*, being the Report of the Sub-Committee of the Congress Party in Parliament, New Delhi 1959.

on Nationalized Industries should become too powerful a body, to the detriment of ministerial responsibility and enterprise autonomy. These have now been allayed to such an extent that discussion has taken a new turn, being concerned with the question whether the Committee should not have its investigatory powers *enhanced*, by the attachment to it of expert assistants. This latter question may not seem to have any great urgency for us in England, because many of the Committee's own members, such as Sir Toby Low, Mr. Austin Albu, Mr. Ernest Davies and Colonel Lancaster, possess considerable knowledge and experience of both public enterprise and private. But even so the need for assistance of some kind is generally admitted. In countries where there is less knowledge and experience of this kind available among parliamentarians the need is correspondingly greater. The problem is how to provide it and yet restrain the parliamentary body from using it in such a way that enterprise managers become harassed and bewildered.

So far, in England, the question has been discussed in terms of giving the Select Committee *its own* experts: accountants, statisticians, economists and perhaps management engineers. But this is not the only possible solution. If the measurement of commercial efficiency is the crux of the matter, it may be better to create an entirely separate, expertly-staffed efficiency-auditing body. This would decide on its own programme of investigations, perform its work in a strictly professional way, and not be in any sense tied down to those subjects which were of current interest to parliamentarians. (Some of them, indeed, it would have to avoid.) It could, nevertheless, provide the Select Committee with most of the kinds of information of which the latter now feels the lack, and could even conduct certain investigations at the instigation and for the benefit of the parliamentary body.

On any showing, some kind of efficiency audit is desirable, particularly for public industries which enjoy a degree of monopoly or are otherwise protected from the blast of competition. Most of them, indeed, already employ a great variety of *internal* performance checks, the results of which are publicized through their Annual Reports in the form of operating statistics. But, as we have seen in connexion with the Select Committee's Report on the Civil Airways Corporations, these figures require a great deal of processing before they can yield any reliable information about the quality of the enterprise management, as distinct from all the other factors, internal and external, which affect its performance. It cannot be doubted that the industries themselves do some processing of this kind, but they can hardly be expected to do it *fore publico*. Hence, although measurement *may* be adequate, publicity is absent—and, in its absence, the adequacy of measurement itself remains conjectural. Moreover, the whole of administrative experience suggests that it is unwise to rely for the initiation of reforms on the body that may need reforming.

For these reasons, many countries are attempting to subject their public enterprise to some type of external efficiency auditing. Sometimes this amounts to no more than the production, by statutory financial auditing bodies, of sundry comments on Annual Reports and Accounts. These, it must be admitted, are rarely of great value, because Auditors-General or Courts of Accounts usually lack the capacity to interpret commercial statistics and understand managerial problems. Indeed, when such comments are conveyed to a parliamentary committee, which proceeds to treat them as authoritative, more harm than good may be done. Only two countries, as yet, have had fairly lengthy experience of efficiency audits conducted by outside bodies specializing in the affairs of public enterprises. Of these, one, Turkey, can hardly be used in evidence; for the body concerned, known as the Prime Minister's High Control Board, is expert only in theory, and has not conducted investigations which would be regarded by qualified accountants or management engineers as of any consequence. The other, France, has done very much better, as might be expected. Her *Commission de Vérification des Comptes des Entreprises Publiques* possesses a genuinely expert staff and produces reports which, by all accounts, are worth taking very seriously. Some description of the work of this body will therefore be apposite. Although not a parliamentary body, it is intended, *inter alia*, to facilitate parliamentary supervision, and is expected to take up questions referred to it by the sub-committees of the two Chambers.[35]

It was established by a law of 6th January 1948, which extended

[35] It should be noted that the following description, although in the present tense, is based entirely on the record of the *Commission de Vérification* during the *Fourth* Republic.

its competence to all state establishments of an industrial or commercial type, to nationalized enterprises and to 'mixed' companies with majority state participation. Although the precise limits of its jurisdiction subsequently caused some controversy, this need not detain us here, as there has never been any doubt about its right to investigate all the French nationalized industries which are comparable with the British ones. In respect of these enterprises, the 1948 law defined its duties as follows:

> "The Commission makes an annual examination of the operating accounts, balance sheeets, and profit and loss accounts of the enterprises . . . and from this draws conclusions about their financial results . . . It expresses opinions on the regularity and propriety of the accounts, suggests any amendments to the accounts which it thinks necessary, and expresses opinions on the competence of the enterprise's commercial and financial management . . . In the general report on the operations and performance of the enterprises which it supervises, it indicates, if necessary, the changes which it thinks ought to be made in their structure and organization, and expresses its opinion on their future prospects.'

Thus, although financial supervision is placed in the forefront of its duties, it has adequate powers to investigate all aspects of management.

For the conduct of its investigations, it makes use of two kinds of personnel: *rapporteurs*, who investigate *sur place et sur pièce*, and members, who deliberate. Of the *rapporteurs* whom it employed in 1957, 28 came from the Court of Accounts, 22 from the Ministry of Finance and Economic Affairs, 19 from inspectorial or supervisory bodies, such as the Council of State and the Inspectorate of Finance, and 17 from the technical *corps*. The members, numbering 25, were headed by a President who was one of the five 'Chamber Presidents' of the Court of Accounts. Of the remainder, two-thirds were Councillors of the Court and one-third were representatives of the Ministry of Finance and Economic Affairs. While, therefore, one might wonder whether sufficient of its personnel was qualified to examine the commercial efficiency as distinct from the financial regularity of the enterprises, there can be no doubt that it is staffed by men of high intelligence, good administrative experience, and adequate prestige. The diversity of their backgrounds, which was a matter of deliberate policy, is also an advantage. As M. Delion says:

> 'This makes it possible to assign certain investigations to men who are well acquainted with the matters in question, or, on the other hand, to officials with entirely different backgrounds, who look at the problems from new angles and produce highly original reports. Diversity of recruitment is also in the interest of the various administrative *corps* themselves, in that it enables them to widen the experience of their members.'[36]

According to the same authority, the presence of technically qualified people (even if in inadequate numbers) on the Commission raises its prestige with enterprise managers. The combination of technicians and administrators is, he considers, the secret of its success. 'Every member of a supervisory body', he writes, 'knows that supervision ought not to be conducted by technical experts in the matter under examination, but that it ought invariably to rely on their knowledge and experience.'

The major disadvantage from which the Commission suffers is that all its members and *rapporteurs* are part-timers, lent to it by the various administrative and supervisory agencies which are their real homes. This temporary status is particularly serious for the *rapporteurs*, who are all too often called away by their chiefs from important investigations. The priority inevitably given by them to their other work is described by M. Delion as 'une très serieuse menace', and the Commission itself, in its second General Report, stressed its need for more *rapporteurs*, more of their time, and greater stability of personnel. At the time of the Commission's establishment, the 'part-time' principle was justified on three grounds, viz. (1) that full-time personnel would be too costly; (2) that the authority of the Commission would be enhanced if a substantial number of its members and *rapporteurs* came from the

[36] *Op. cit.* p. 108. In this account of the Commission, I rely heavily on M. Delion's excellent study, which provides the best survey of its work as yet published in French. I have also had the advantage of reading, in typescript, the relevant chapter in Dr. Ridley's forthcoming book on the French nationalized industries.

prestigious Court of Accounts; and (3) that specific recruitment would be difficult, as 'precise doctrines on the supervision of public enterprises had not yet been formulated'. All three reasons were then valid, but none of them continues to have great force now that France has recovered from the economic difficulties of the immediate post-war years and the Commission has acquired a well-established place among the various control bodies and developed distinctive methods of work. As a *pis aller*, a decree of 14th August 1950, permitted the Commission to make use of the services of the *Contrôleurs d'Etat*, who are officers of the Ministry of Finance permanently attached to the enterprises. This it rejected as derogatory to its independence. Nevertheless, the *rapporteurs* do tend to liaise very closely with the *contrôleurs*, relying to some extent on their opinions and making use of the material that they have accumulated. Indeed, if this were not so it would be difficult for the Commission to get through its heavy annual task.

Structurally, the Commission is modelled on its main 'parent' body, the Court of Accounts. It has four specialized sections, each composed of three Court of Accounts magistrates and two other members, and dealing respectively with (a) power, (b) transport and communications, (c) credit, insurance and information services and (d) engineering and chemical industries, etc. Co-ordination is the task of the President, of the *rapporteur-général* (who acts as the President's second-in-command), and of the Plenary Session, where common problems are discussed, programmes of work formulated, responsibilities allocated, section reports considered, and a General Report annually adopted.

In the last resort, the value of the Commission's work depends on the intelligence and assiduity of its *rapporteurs*, who go into the enterprises to find out what is happening. Each *rapporteur* presents his completed report to the appropriate section, where it is discussed in the presence of the *contrôleur d'état* and of representatives of the *Commissariat au Plan*, the 'tutelary' ministry, other state services having relations with the enterprise, and the enterprise itself. Much of the business of the section consists of the oral examination of the enterprise representatives.

Reports which go out in the name of the Commission are of two kinds, Special and General. A Special Report, which deals in detail with the affairs of one enterprise, is addressed to the Court of

Accounts and to the tutelary ministry, and can also be sent, on request, to the appropriate parliamentary sub-committee. It is an entirely confidential document, not available—as far as can be discovered—even to *bona fide* research workers. A General Report consists of the Commission's observations on the whole of its annual exercise. Although it singles out individual enterprises, and particular aspects of their work, for approbation or criticism, it does not go into matters which we, on this side of the Channel, categorize as day-to-day, and much of it is usually concerned with relations between the enterprises and the Government. The General Report is addressed to the President of the Council of Ministers and the Presidents of the National Assembly and the Council of the Republic, and is published in the *Journal Officiel*. Lengthy and ill-printed, it constitutes a unique annual survey of the public sector, and contains a host of criticisms and proposals which, while not very different in kind from those embodied in the Reports of our own Select Committee, have the advantage of being based upon more thorough investigation. It is through this General Report that the Commission, if need be, can attempt to mobilize public and parliamentary opinion in favour of proposals which, if they remained locked up in the confidential Special Reports, might be entirely neglected.

M. Delion is of the view that 'this extraordinary privilege given to an administrative body helps to overcome one of the dilemmas of parliamentary régimes, in that it permits parliament and public opinion to judge the management of a public enterprise without getting themselves unduly involved in its day-to-day affairs.'

As for the Special Reports, it is impossible, without access to them, to estimate their value. At least some enterprise managers, however, appear to consider them useful. Speaking of the Commission, the General Director of the nationalized gas industry has said:

'Justice demands that tribute should be paid to the quality of its work and to the professional integrity and independent spirit of its personnel . . . I am not the only Director of a nationalised concern to recognise not only that the Commission's labours have imposed greater order and intelligibility on the accounting documents of the enterprises, but also that he derives great benefit from some of the analyses and proposals contained in the individual reports.'

Some analysis of the material contained in the General Reports will indicate the types of subject in which the Commission is more-or-less continuously interested. It has been very much concerned to ensure comparability between the accounts of the various enterprises. A *plan comptable* was supposed to be formulated by each enterprise in association with the *Conseil Supérieur de la Comptabilité* and then to be sanctioned by the tutelary Minister and the Minister of Finance. Delays and difficulties in the operation of this *plan* provoked strong criticism from the Commission, in its earlier General Reports. By the time of its Fourth Report, it was reasonably satisfied with the progress that had been made in this respect, but was still critical of delays in formulating a '*compatibilité analytique d'exploitation*', i.e. a series of statistics which would facilitate comparison of operational results, regarded by it as necessary for the stimulation of quasi-monopoly enterprises through 'paper competition'. In its analysis of the financial results of the enterprises, it has paid particular attention to such matters as conservation of assets, depreciation provisions, the liquidity position, the extent of auto-financing, stock policies, and the balance between short, medium and long term capital. In respect of price policy, it has directed its main criticisms, not at the enterprises themselves but at the Government, which has the ultimate responsibility. Cost control is very much its concern, and it has been particularly anxious to reveal the extent of cross-subsidization, by demanding that the accounts shall show the profit or loss made by each distinct operational unit. It has criticized both the enterprises and the government for errors and miscalculations in programming investments, has demanded better co-ordination between public and private sectors, and has expressed many doubts about the ministries' exercise of their tutelary responsibilities, suggesting, among other things, that the Government's agents in the enterprises, the *Contrôleurs d'Etat* and the *Commissaires du Gouvernement*, sometimes place unreasonable restrictions on the exercise of managerial discretion. Only in matters of organization has it shown some hesitancy about offering suggestions. While it has emphasized the need to secure economies through the concentration of productive facilities, and the importance of adequate devolution of managerial responsibilities, particularly in the larger enterprises, it has not attempted to penetrate at all deeply in the field of managerial techniques. M. Delion is of the opinion that this is due, not to any lack of qualifications for such studies on the part of its personnel, but to its reluctance 'to enter a new field of control, less clearly mapped out than the traditional field, and where the legal authorization for its jurisdiction may appear insufficiently well established'.

'In contrast', he continues, 'with textually-based criticism and legal analysis, or quantitative statements and comparisons, both relatively objective, organisational studies involve entering the very life of the enterprise itself, so to speak, and can become the subject of controversy. The hesitations of the supervisors are therefore quite understandable, but they will need to overcome them if they are to fulfil the whole of their task . . .'

These scruples, as M. Delion suggests, are partly the product of the close association between the Commission and the traditionally-minded Court of Accounts. There may be some doubt, however, whether he is right in holding that the personnel of the Commission is strong enough on the 'organizational' side. The predominance of members of the Court of Accounts, civil administrators and technicians does not suggest that it is very well equipped to undertake management engineering studies.

How relevant to our own problems is this French experience with the *Commission de Vérification*? Clearly, it needs to be used with great caution, for reasons that are obvious enough. Both the institutional setting and the attitudes of the people concerned are very different from ours. We have nothing equivalent to a Court of Accounts, and no official *corps* of technicians on the French pattern. Our nationalized industries are not saddled with *commissaires du gouvernement* or *contrôleurs d'état*. Our civil servants, in the Treasury and the Ministries of Power and Transport, would not consider themselves qualified, as do their French counterparts when attached to the Commission, to examine and report on public enterprise management. Nor would the managers of our nationalized industries be prepared to tolerate this kind of civil service interference; for in Britain the experience and assumptions of civil servants and businessmen respectively do not coincide or overlap to anything like the same extent. As Dr. Ridley says:

'In France there has never been a sharp distinction between public administration and big business. Many of the directors of large industrial undertakings or financial houses have come from the civil service. Many of the government representatives on the boards of public enterprise are in fact men who would be heartily welcomed to the boards of private enterprise.'

In fact, our whole conception of the relationship between a nationalized industry and the state is fundamentally different from the French. We tend to regard such an industry first and foremost as a commercial venture which, for certain special reasons, has been acquired by the state so that it may be reorganized and developed in accordance with the public interest. The French look at it very much more as a part of the state apparatus. Again to quote Dr. Ridley:

'The state as such has an inherent responsibility for public services. For the more convenient organisation of a particular service, it may either delegate functions to a *concessionnaire*, or set up a specialised institution. In the latter case, there is decentralisation of public service. The *établissement public* is defined as a specialised public service with legal personality and financial autonomy. While these terms might appear to describe a British public corporation as well, the similarity is superficial. The legal personality of the *établissement public* arises as a result of the dissection of the legal personality of the state. It remains part of the state. Unlike the British corporation, which owns property in perpetual succession, the property of the *établissement public* belongs to the state, and the board merely acts as administrator. Financial autonomy means only that its funds are distinct from those of the national budget: it does not mean financial independence. Indeed, special accounts within government departments may, as a matter of convenience, also be endowed with financial autonomy.'

Perhaps too much can be made of these differences, particularly in view of the fact that the autonomy of the British corporation has been considerably eroded. But they remain of sufficient importance to make institutional imitation extremely hazardous, if not impossible. Nevertheless, the work of the French Commission cannot but provoke thought, because the *need* for which it provides is one that we too experience. Even Mr. Morrison, the very last person who could be accused of wishing to undermine corporate autonomy, has urged the setting up of a common efficiency unit for the British nationalized industries, under the joint control of the various boards. Professor Robson, who can be described as of the 'Morrisonian' School, has consistently advocated over many years, the establishment of a public 'efficiency audit' commission, with functions in some ways analogous to those of the French body.[37]

There are, in fact, four alternative ways in which the measurement of public enterprise management could be organized in this country, viz. (1) by a common efficiency unit maintained jointly by the industries themselves; (2) by a research staff attached to the Select Committee on Nationalized Industries; (3) by specialized bodies within the responsible Ministries; and (4) by an entirely independent, but publicly appointed and financed, body.

The advantage of the first is that it would have the confidence of the managers, who, being responsible for its establishment and in joint control of its operations, could not complain that it was interfering with their day-to-day work. On the other hand, unless they agreed to the publication of its reports, it would constitute measurement without publicity. Moreover, its investigations would be mainly confined to problems of interest to the managers themselves, to the exclusion of those interesting the Ministry, Parliament, and the general public. The second would be free from these disadvantages, but would almost certainly be the object of managerial resentment, at least initially. It might also suffer the disadvantage of being tied too closely to a parliamentary body, with the result that, while it would help parliamentarians with their actual investigations, it would not be likely to discover, except incidentally or by

[37] For the latest expression of his views, see W. A. Robson: *Nationalized Industry and Public Ownership*, Allen & Unwin, Ltd., London 1960, Chap. VIII, Public Accountability.

accident, the new or less familiar problems requiring study, whether by the Committee or otherwise. Furthermore, it would be inhibited from dealing with, and would almost certainly be instructed to avoid, those day-to-day matters which would be bread-and-butter to the common efficiency unit. A departmental body would probably be freer in this respect, and might also inspire less resentment, as it would represent only a new way of enabling the minister to obtain information from the industries, which he is already empowered by statute to do. On the other hand—devotion to ministerial responsibility being what it is—there might be considerable difficulty about publishing the reports of such a body, or even of making them available to the Select Committee. Only the fourth type of body, the independent commission, would appear to have most of the advantages which we seek and to escape most of the dangers which we would avoid—that is, of course, if it is assumed, as I think it should be, that a multiplicity of separate investigatory bodies is undesirable.

The main difficulty about an independent commission, however, is that if it were equipped with the personnel and endowed with the authority to do a proper job (i.e. one broadly equivalent to that done by the French Commission) it would be highly unpopular with the industries themselves. Indeed, its very appointment might provoke the resignation of some of the best enterprise managers. No government, therefore, is likely to risk taking this step in the near future. Hence, if we are eventually to have such a commission, it will probably be necessary to move towards it rather slowly, as we moved towards the Select Committee, giving the industries ample time to accustom themselves to the idea and to overcome their fears. In the long run, an independent commission might evolve, by a series of stages, out of either a departmental investigatory unit or a research apparatus attached to the Select Committee. Perhaps the latter is the better 'bet', because it is already under active discussion and has won some support, at least in principle, from both Government and Opposition spokesmen. On the other hand, a departmental body might be easier to organize and more acceptable to the industries themselves. Admittedly, its services would not be straightforwardly at the disposal of the Select Committee, but arrangements could surely be made whereby the latter could see its Reports, without publishing them or divulging their contents, and, by way of informal representations to the Minister, could suggest to it subjects of investigation. At least, this would be a line of advance well worth exploring, and it is perhaps a pity that the Select Committee did not consider it during the discussions preceding their Special Report.

It would be presumptious to suggest that this chapter has mobilized all foreign experience relevant to a consideration of the relationships between our Parliament and our nationalized industries. Information on this aspect of public enterprise is as yet fragmentary for lack of adequate research. Enough has been said, however, to indicate that some enlightenment can be obtained from a study of foreign practice. Very much more, I believe, would emerge from a well-prepared meeting of parliamentarians, civil servants and enterprise managers from a variety of democratic countries. As yet, the subject has been systematically discussed only by a group of academics at the Rome Congress of the International Political Science Association. This is a beginning, but the growing importance of the problems there brought to light demands that they should receive further discussion by people who have closer practical acquaintance with them.

VIII

Some Conclusions

In the preceding chapters, there are many indications of the conclusions to which the author has been led through his study of the material. The purpose of this final chapter is to make them explicit and to embody them in a series of proposals that can be profitably discussed. This is a hazardous task, for in the so-called social sciences analysis, even should it approach the unattainable ideal of completeness and impartiality, is always capable of sustaining more than one set of conclusions. The temptation to follow the well-trodden path to academic respectability by refraining from giving advice is therefore strong. It must nevertheless be resisted; for the object of a work such as this is to clarify the discussion of certain *practical* issues, and this can best be done by presenting a series of proposals which the author, however mistakenly, considers supported by the factual evidence, in so far as they were by no means present in his mind when he began to study it. The process of shooting them down may then lead to the formulation of better proposals which he, unaided, was unable to conceive.

As we have seen, the present board-minister-parliament relationship is unsatisfactory for several reasons. Responsibilities are not clearly defined, with the result that the three parties are uncertain of the roles that they are respectively called upon to play. The Minister can use the Board as a screen, and often does so. The Board, if it wishes, can ascribe its failures to government interference. Parliament, glancing from the one to the other like a spectator at a tennis match, does not know whom to blame and is deeply suspicious that something which it ought to know is being concealed. In normal times, of course, the frustrations inherent in this uncertain situation are mollified by the operation of half-formulated conventions, which work reasonably well when the

208

performance of the industry is giving general satisfaction. But times are never normal for all the nationalized industries simultaneously, with the result that, to date, there has always been at least one industry at the centre of a crisis which raises these frustrations to an acute point. It may be admitted that, from Parliament's point of view, the situation has been improved by the appointment of the Select Committee on Nationalized Industries; but this specific, although useful, is certainly not powerful enough to cure the fundamental malaise.

Of remedies currently sought, the most popular is a clearer definition of the respective responsibilities of Minister and Board and hence, by the automatic operation of our most respected constitutional doctrine, of the responsibilities of Parliament itself. It is suggested, in fact, that we should go back to the original ideas of the Founding Fathers of the public corporation, and insist that ministerial interference should be exclusively by way of directions and approvals, of a kind clearly specified by statute. This is the tendency of the Select Committee's line of thought. In the 'Coal' Report, it demanded that the Minister's power over prices, at present resting on the so-called 'gentlemen's agreement', should be statutorily defined and exercised by means of 'specific directions'. In the later Air Corporations Report, it demanded that this relationship should be extended to cover all exercises of ministerial authority.

> 'Your Committee consider it essential to the efficient running on commercial lines of the Air Corporations that there should be a clear cut division of responsibility between the Chairmen on the one hand and the Minister on the other. When the Minister wishes, on grounds of national interest, to override the commercial judgement of a Chairman, he should do so by a directive, which should be published.'

This doctrine was by no means new when the Select Committee stated it. Two years previously, it had been the theme of Part VI of the 'Herbert' Committee's Report, entitled 'The Powers and Duties of the Minister'. The Herbert Committee, moreover, had clearly explained the theoretical foundation on which they considered that it rested, viz. that the national interest normally demanded that the Board should be left free to pursue a commercial policy, and that departures from that policy, when required, should be made at the Minister's specific behest.

'We have expressed the view', reported the Committee, 'that the less the principle of commercial operation is invaded the better it will be for the efficiency of the industry. Taking the long view we believe this to be of the greatest importance to the success of nationalisation. But it must be recognised that unless Parliament and the Government are prepared to deny themselves the power, always and in every particular, to require the industry to act on other than purely economic considerations, the Minister must be armed with the necessary authority. We would, however, urge that the lines of demarcation between the industry and the Minister should be clear. There should be no doubt as to where the responsibility lies when the industry is acting on other than purely economic considerations.'[1]

In the light of this principle, the Committee saw the principal duties of the Minister as follows:

(a) to make appointments to the Central Authority and the Boards;

(b) to satisfy himself through the reports of the Central Authority and the individual Boards that the industry is being run efficiently as a commercial concern or, to the extent that it is not run as a commercial concern, in accordance with the directions issued by him;

(c) to authorize the amount of capital to be raised and the terms of issue;

(d) to give the industry precise instructions if and when it is required to act in some way different from what would be dictated by purely economic considerations;

(e) to decide whether or not to give consent to the issue of directions by the Central Authority in the rare cases in which this is likely to be required.

[1] *Report of the Committee of Inquiry into the Electricity Supply Industry*, Cmd. 9672, pp. 136–7.

All this sounds clear enough, and the Herbert Committee make out a good case for equating 'commercial operation', as defined by them for the Electricity Supply Industry, with the 'national interest'. Even so, it is difficult to concede that there are unique principles of commercial operation which apply to an industry which works in conditions which, to say the least, are less than fully competitive and which does not aim primarily at making a profit. If there were, the anguished discussions of rival schools of economists as to what are the right investment, pricing, and production policies for nationalized industries in various circumstances would be pointless. The purpose of a nationalized industry is presumably to provide the best possible service to the whole national economy, and there is no reason to imagine that this can be done by following certain previously-defined principles of commercial operation, only to be departed from on those rare occasions when the minister steps in and gives an order. It is obviously important that a nationalized industry should be commercial in the sense of providing its services as economically as possible, but simply to say this does not take us far along the road to defining the policies that it should pursue. Used in any other sense, 'commercial' cannot be much else than a convenient shorthand for 'economically desirable', and what is economically desirable varies from time to time and from industry to industry. If the coal industry, for instance, had attempted during the post-war years to relate its charges as closely as possible to unit costs of production, as the Herbert Committee—with considerable justification—said that the electricity industry ought to do, the result would have been either that a great deal of coal would have been offered at virtually prohibitive prices or a very large number of uneconomic pits closed down. In either case, the national economy would have been gravely damaged. Hence no one, at the time, suggested that the National Coal Board should pursue this type of commercial policy except to the extent that it was specifically ordered by the Minister not to do. Indeed, the best way of seeing the weaknesses of the Herbert Committee's *general* doctrines about nationalization is to imagine them being applied to the coal industry. For their revival of the idea of the 'invisible hand'— 'behave commercially and thereby do the best for everyone, including yourself'—is curiously anachronistic in the context of a modern, controlled economy. In the special case of electricity supply, it may produce the kind of result that the government and the public want, but to apply it indiscriminately to all nationalized industries, or to suggest that it is a principle from which departures have to be specially justified, can only make for confusion.

 So-called commercial behaviour, in fact, is a matter of convenience rather than of principle and subject to judgement by results. If it simply means that the industry should be enterprising, cost-conscious and business-like there can be no argument, for these qualities are always desirable. Indeed, we would like to have more of them not only in nationalized industries but in government departments and local authorities. If it means that the industry should invariably pay its way and as far as possible relate unit prices to unit costs, then we are on more debatable ground. In so far as this type of behaviour results in the optimum allocation of factors of production it would appear clearly desirable. But what *is* the optimum allocation? Are we considering the interests of the industry itself or those of the whole national economy? Do they invariably coincide? May it not be good policy in some circumstances to permit losses to be made ('taking one year with another') and to provide certain services to certain consumers below cost? What is cost, anyway? Average or marginal? This is only the beginning of the series of questions that needs to be asked. Simply to ask them indicates that there should be no presumption that commercial behaviour, as interpreted by the Board, will necessarily produce the best results. Nor, on the other hand, should there be any presumption that it will not. In so far as it does, the Government is obviously justified in pursuing a policy of non-interference, the desirability of which is not likely to be seriously questioned in Parliament. In so far as it does not, the Government may have to interfere, unless the Board chooses spontaneously to adjust its policies to national needs and is in fact able to do so without requesting financial or other assistance. That such interference will be exceptional, that it needs to be specially justified, and that it will never concern itself with so-called day-to-day matters is one of the legends that has grown up around the nationalized industries.

This is the first difficulty that confronts those who favour a 'clear cut division of responsibility between the Chairmen on the one hand and the Minister on the other'. But it is not, of course, essential that the advocates of such a clear cut division should commit

212

themselves to the theories of the Herbert Committee. If those theories were correct, it would certainly be easier to define the *occasions* on which the Minister should intervene and those on which he should abstain from intervention. It is quite possible, however, to be thoroughly sceptical about the Herbert Committee's distinction between 'purely economic considerations' and 'other than purely economic considerations', and still hold that the present informality of ministerial intervention is wrong and that his relations with the nationalized industry should invariably—or at least usually—take the form of giving a direction or according a statutory approval. This, indeed, sounds reasonable enough. It is based, not on a controversial view about the way the national economy should be run, but upon a perfectly understandable desire to know who is responsible for what. The trouble with it is simply that it is quite impracticable. For no power on earth, apart from actual physical separation and interruption of postal and telephonic communications, can prevent the Minister from *consulting* with the Board members whom he has appointed and whom he is able to dismiss. They do not want such a severance, and he cannot afford it politically. It is through such consultation that the policies of the nationalized industries are in fact made and that the operation of these policies is continuously watched and checked by the man who, in the last resort, cannot avoid taking responsibility for them in the House of Commons, whatever the theories of the Founding Fathers may decree. But the distinction between consulting with a Minister and receiving a ministerial order is so fine as to be almost imperceptible. For the Minister, in virtue of those reserve powers which he never employs, has the whip hand. Admittedly, he may be restrained from using it as he would wish by threats of resignation or of a politically-damaging public exposure of the differences that have arisen. But the 'old boy' atmosphere which surrounds the relationship between him and his appointees makes this unlikely, and to the extent that the Board members become 'career' men recruited from within the industry, the likelihood of any kind of revolt is still further diminished. Not only British but foreign experience goes to show that this type of relationship can be neither prohibited nor regulated. The reason is obvious. The industries which have been nationalized are, in every sense, basic to a national economy for the direction

213

of which the Government of the day cannot escape responsibility. If they are performing satisfactorily it is the Government that takes the credit; if they are performing badly it is the Government that will receive the blame. Hence the Ministers directly in contact with them cannot confine themselves to sporadic interventions. Nor can they afford to make nice distinctions between general policy and day-to-day administration, however much they may pretend to do so in their replies to parliamentary Questions and their contributions to parliamentary Debates.

Much effort has been devoted to the clarification of this alleged dichotomy, and most of it has been wasted. As early as 1933 Professor Marshall Dimock, in a pioneer work, pointed out the impossibility of distinguishing 'superficial' from 'larger' issues.

'Is it desirable', he asked, 'that the Post Office should have to explain why two employees were discharged from a Post Office factory? Should an artist be permitted to object to the placing of a red telephone kiosk on the bank of the Thames, where it was said to detract from the landscape? These are actual instances of so-called superficial questions which were recently addressed to the Postmaster-General in the House of Commons. It may appear on first thought that such questions are merely a nuisance, and that small matters are none of the public's business. However, reflection usually reveals that there is a larger issue involved: in the above questions one aspect of the merit system and aesthetic values were affected.'[2]

As Mr. I. J. Pitman said in a letter to *The Times*: 'Most important issues of principle arise over matters of apparently only trifling importance.' The closing down of a small branch line, the restriction of a railway workshop to 'care and maintenance' functions, the refusal to extend electricity supplies to a rural consumer, and the introduction of a new method of charging by an area gas or electricity board are all day-to-day decisions which involve fundamental questions of policy. General principles, as every administrator knows, are not always specifically formulated at the highest level, but often arise from a host of small decisions of the day-to-day kind. The process of policy-formation takes place at a number

[2] Marshall E. Dimock: *British Public Utilities and National Development*, Allen & Unwin, Ltd., London 1933, pp. 160-1.

of different levels and no one can clearly say where the 'general' ends and the 'day-to-day' begins. The famous case of the occasionally late and the persistently late train illustrates the curious scholasticism in which the most well-meaning efforts to elucidate this alleged distinction become involved.

That the Minister cannot, in fact, divorce himself from the performance of the Board that he 'generally' directs is confirmed by the course of those debates in the House of Commons to which reference has been made. Even while formally denying his own responsibility, he is always manœuvred into a position where he has to defend the Board's record, in general and in particular. Even when he justifies a decision, as he often does—and in many cases rightly so—on grounds of 'sound commercial policy', what he is saying in effect is that the pursuit of such a policy by the Board, in respect of the particular matter under discussion, is the *will* of the Government, and that it is in accordance with the national interest. When he refuses to intervene it is not because he is constitutionally inhibited from intervention but because he considers that it would be *undesirable* to do so. Hence the oft-repeated use of the formula: 'I *think* that we *ought* to leave that matter to the discretion of the Board.'

Why then should we not decide to cut the Gordian knot by simply abandoning a 'public corporation' idea that has become little more than an inconvenient and frustrating constitutional fiction? Why not decide that the experiment in autonomy has failed, and return to straightforward departmental forms of administration, using the Post Office as our example? Surely we now have the experience which would enable us to adapt the department to the needs of a governmental function which is commercial in the sense that it involves producing, buying and selling? Would not this be the best way of preventing the use of the Board as a screen, of clarifying the relationships between Ministers and managers, and of ending the frustrations that make Members of the House of Commons increasingly restive?

At present, opinion certainly seems to be moving in this direction. Even Lord Morrison has not renounced his publicly-expressed opinion that the 'departmentalization' of gas and electricity is a possibility worth considering, and there is a powerful current of opinion among Labour Members, and to a lesser extent among

215

Conservatives, in favour of sweeping away the present restrictions on ministerial responsibility. As usual, controversy has been centred on the refusal of Questions, and there has been comparatively little coherent discussion of the wider implications of the demand, voiced by Mr. Mellish on behalf of 'many' Labour Members and some 'hon. Gentlemen opposite', that the Minister 'should accept full responsibility in Parliament for these Questions, and now'.[3] Only Mr. Thorneycroft has presented a stark alternative between the concept of commercial autonomy, to be realized through the public corporation, and that of public service, to be realized through the government department. But, in transport at least, support for the 'public service' idea appears to be increasing, and with it, one may reasonably assume, will grow the demand that the British Transport Commission should be taken into the Ministry of Transport.

There is a close connection between the demand for departmentalization and the view that the commercial aspects of a nationalized industry should be subordinated to its public service aspects, just as there is a close connection between support for the public corporation and the view that commercial considerations should be kept in the forefront. In neither case is the connection a logical or necessary one, but it is obvious that the demand for departmentalization is strengthened if those who voice it can prove that the public interest requires that the provision of coal or electric current or transport should be neither more nor less commercial in character than the carrying of letters or the conveyance of telephonic or telegraphic messages. Undoubtedly, transport offers the strongest case for departmentalization, through a Ministry which would simultaneously run the railways and exercise control over the carrying of goods and passengers by road. For social, economic and strategic reasons, the provision of transport services of a certain kind, scope and quality *must* be made, whether it is commercially viable or not, and those who suggest that free competition is the answer are only arguing—what is almost certainly a losing case—that such provision may *best* be made by this method. They do not and cannot argue that if the job cannot be done commercially it ought not to be done at all, and most of them are prepared to admit that there are certain commercially marginal

[3] H.C. Deb. Vol. 612, col. 1206.

services which, in any case, will have to be provided at a loss. For their critics, it is not at all difficult to make the retort that wider economic and social considerations in this field demand that the 'service' aspect should not be marginal but central, and that in view of this the departmental form of organization is the most appropriate one.

Similar arguments, although not equally strong ones, can be applied to other nationalized industries. It may be doubted, for instance, whether the coal industry, since nationalization, has even been run on genuinely commercial lines. Until the last few years, maximum productivity has been given absolute priority over costs of production, while today social considerations, reinforced by long-term economic and strategic factors, are preventing the contraction of the industry at a rate that ordinary commercial calculations would appear to demand.

Experience, therefore, would appear to show that the arguments in favour of departmentalization are very much stronger than the original advocates of the public corporation were prepared to allow.

Yet even those who are most ready to admit the force of these arguments still hesitate to advocate the scrapping of the public corporation. For a strong commercial element is necessarily present in the manner of performing the functions that the nationalized industries exist to discharge, and it can reasonably be argued that this will tend to be *unduly* subordinated, at the cost of wasting valuable resources, if the managers of these industries are denied an appropriate measure of autonomy. Commercial behaviour, as we have seen, is not easy to define, but there can be no doubt about the existence of a commercial *spirit* or about the need for it in a nationalized no less than in a private industry. The plain fact is that the nationalized industries are *both* public service institutions and commercial businesses. This is what all the trouble is about. As the Chairman of the National Coal Board said in evidence:

'I would like to put it to the Select Committee that one of the things they might consider is this kind of half world in which we live as the National Coal Board. What are we? We are not flesh, fish or good red herring. We are not a commercial undertaking; we are not a public service; we are a bit of each . . . It would not be a bad thing if you were just to say to the Coal Board—and how I would welcome it!—"From now on, you are free to act as a commercial concern". Then I think we might be able to show some rather different results. But full employment might suffer, and British industry would not be subsidised with the price of coal at the level it is at the moment as compared with what we can get abroad. However, if we are to act as a public service, let it be quite clear that we are such; and that we are not going from time to time to be tripped up, as attempts are made to trip us up, in relation to our balance sheet.'[4]

It is in view of this dual nature of the nationalized industry that, if departmentalization were attempted, it would have to be carried out with great care and skill. Undoubtedly, major modifications of the normal departmental pattern would be needed. To impose detailed estimating and accounting procedures, to give the Treasury control of establishments, to introduce ordinary departmental rules about the making of contracts, etc., would be fatal. Moreover, a wide delegation of authority to some kind of internal board, composed of top managers, would be almost essential, for the simple reason that the organization to be managed would be too big and complex 'for one or two men only to hold the whole of it before their minds as an entity and at the same time to control it in the requisite detail'.[5] Theoretically, there is no reason why these necessary modifications should not be made. As Professor Dimock has said, 'if sufficient improvements could be made among the departments in the direction of greater autonomy and flexibility, there would be little or no justification for public corporations at all'.[6] But as he has also pointed out, powerful internal and external resistances render these improvements very difficult to make in practice. Furthermore, there is still the view to be considered that full ministerial responsibility, which is the *sine qua non* of departmentalization and indeed one of its purposes, would inevitably reduce commercial flexibility below the essential minimum.

[4] H.C. 304 of 1957, p. 128.
[5] R. A. Lynex, in G. E. Milward: *Large Scale Organisation*, Macdonald & Evans, London 1950, pp. 163–4.
[6] *Government Corporations, a Focus of Policy and Administration*, in *American Political Science Review*, Vol. 43, p. 1163.

It is therefore worth inquiring whether between the public corporation, as at present conceived, and the government department
there is a half-way house where all the various and apparently
contradictory *desiderata* might receive reasonable if not complete
satisfaction. But before doing so it will be necessary to remind
readers that we are not here concerned with all the industries that
might be nationalized, but with those that *have* been nationalized,
which are basic to the national economy. The arguments advanced
and the proposals made relate, in fact, to coal, gas, electricity,
transport and civil aviation, and to attempt to refute them by
applying them to hypothetically nationalized motor-car, chemical,
aircraft, textile or cosmetics industries will be a redundant exercise.

In a sense, such a half-way house already exists, in so far as the
original conception of the public corporation has been profoundly
modified. But it is a house which seems to give us the worst of several
possible worlds, rather than the best.

Are there, then, any changes in law and convention which might
improve the situation, without the need to take the drastic step of
destroying the public corporation itself and thereby endangering
the perpetuation of the undoubted merits that it possesses?

To answer this question, we must inquire a little more closely
why the built-in safeguards of public enterprise autonomy have not
worked in the way they were supposed to work.

The odd thing, to which attention has rarely been drawn, is that
limitations on parliamentary control and ministerial responsibility have operated smoothly only when they were not needed,
i.e. when the industry concerned has been financially successful,
administratively and technically efficient, and giving reasonably
adequate satisfaction to consumer demand. By and large, this has
been the case with the gas industry since nationalization and with
the electricity industry since the overcoming, in the early 1950s,
of the serious shortages of supply. Under these conditions, the
comparatively smooth working of the present régime is due, not
to the inherent efficacy of the safeguards, but to the fact that no one
seriously wants to violate them. When an industry is doing well,
a Minister has every incentive to be reasonably liberal in his response to parliamentary requests for information, for the content
of that information will generally rebound, rightly or wrongly, to
his and the government's political credit. As most people are in

favour of letting well alone, the industry suffers little from either ministerial intervention or parliamentary inquisitiveness. Hostile Questions—of which there will inevitably be some, if only for political or constituency reasons—do virtually no damage at all and hence there is no reason why they should not be accepted, even if they are well within the field of the day-to-day. The industry, indeed, may receive encouragement rather than discouragement from proceedings in the House, which publicize its successes. The frequent congratulations which are now showered, from both Government and Opposition benches, on the leaders of the electricity supply and civil airways industries must make them the envy of the unfortunates responsible for transport and coal. It is difficult to imagine that even if the Minister's responsibilities were made complete and Questions freed from restriction the situation would be any different.

Conversely, the limitations work least satisfactorily when, according to the theory on which they are based, there is most need for them, i.e. when the industry is financially unsuccessful, less efficient than it ought to be, and failing to provide the consumer with the satisfaction which he thinks it his right to expect. Coal and transport are the obvious examples. In these circumstances, the ministerial attention is continuously engaged, both publicly and behind the scenes, and Members are anxious for information of all kinds, intensely critical, full of ideas for righting what is wrong, and suspicious that they are being fobbed off with something that is less than the truth. Inevitably, the protective devices break down. Ministerial refusals to give information or to take responsibility seem equivocal or downright dishonest. Constantly under pressure, the Minister is compelled alternatively to take refuge in the wording of the Act (or in his own interpretation of imperfectly-established conventions) or to defend things for which, according to his own admission, he is not fully responsible. Sometimes he even achieves the remarkable feat of doing both simultaneously, within the limits of a single speech. The industry itself cannot fail to be conscious of this anomalous situation, and will make as much effort as any government department to protect its Minister, and thereby itself, from embarrassment. If Questions are being refused, it will certainly know all about them, because they will go direct, by letter, to the Chairman of the

Board.[7] Moreover, any query or criticism to which he is unable to reply satisfactorily may at any time be brought openly into the parliamentary arena on the occasion of an Adjournment debate, Supply debate, private Member's resolution or some other way. Debates on the affairs of the industry are bound to be more frequent than usual, whatever steps may be taken to limit them, if only because the Government will be producing a succession of plans which it cannot prevent Parliament from discussing, even if it wished to do so. The only effect of the restrictions is to make parliamentarians frustrated and suspicious, and in this mood they can be dangerous. Sooner or later a significant number of them will come to the conclusion that commercial flexibility is so much moonshine and to demand that the public corporation be scrapped.[8]

If, then, it is unnecessary to protect the nationalized industries from political interference when they are doing well and impossible so to protect them when they are doing badly, why should we worry about protecting them at all? Would it not be possible to preserve the form and something of the spirit of the public corporation and yet hold the nationalized industry entirely responsible to its Minister, thus abolishing the artificial distinction between general policy and day-to-day administration and putting an end to the present equivocal board-minister-parliament relationship? This possibility is at least worth considering. Perhaps it might be made the subject of a major government inquiry. Even better, it might be tried experimentally with one of the nationalized industries to see how it worked and to provide those charged with such an inquiry with something better than speculation on which to base their recommendations.

There are plenty of reasons for believing that this new dispensation, despite disadvantages which have been pointed out *ad nauseam*, might be more satisfactory than the present one. Once

[7] According to the Reports of the B.T.C., the Board of this industry deals each year with well over 1,000 queries and representations from M.P.s.

[8] American experience may be relevant here. The Ramspeck Act of 1940 and the Corporation Control Act of 1945, which severely cut down the autonomies that the American public corporations previously enjoyed, were a direct result of the efforts of a suspicious legislature to open the 'closed book' for its inspection. There have also been other occasions, in other countries, when a legislature, lacking adequate means of supervising the work of a corporation, has decided to 'bring it under the harrow', as Lord Morrison would say.

the distinction between the general and the day-to-day was, abandoned, it would become incumbent on the Minister to decide in the light of the actual situation, just *how much* ought to be left to the discretion of the Board, and to *defend* his decisions to abstain from intervention just as wholeheartedly as he now defends his decisions to intervene. 'I think that we ought to leave this to the Board', a formula which, as we have seen, is already frequently used, would then completely replace denials of responsibility and refusals to answer Questions. Members, who now try to obtain information by the back-stairs method of asking the Minister why he has not issued or whether he intends to issue a general direction, would be entitled to information as of right. The Board could no longer be used as a screen, and the problem of who decided what would no longer give rise to angry exchanges across the floor of the House and mounting suspicions in Members' minds that some form of disreputable concealment was being practised.

In ordinary circumstances, the Minister would be able to leave as much to the discretion of the Board as he does now—perhaps more. To him, and to the majority of reasonably-minded Members, the policy of letting well alone would appear an obviously sensible one; for parliamentarians of all parties are by now genuinely anxious that nationalized industries should perform well, and can hardly fail to be acquainted with the conditions necessary for good performance. Inevitably, there will always be Members who wish to bring up specific grievances, however generally satisfactory the industry's record may be; but such representations are unlikely to cause serious embarrassment, and it is right that they should be freely made and properly answered. In more critical circumstances, as we have seen, the Minister is already compelled to interfere in such a way that he becomes, *de facto*, a participant in top-level management. This situation would become formally recognized, with the result that he could no longer take refuge behind the smoke-screen generated by the 'commercial' decisions of the 'Board'. It would still, however, be possible and indeed necessary for him to protect the Board from pettyfogging and malicious criticisms. This he could do by the use of the familiar formula, confidently relying on the support of the Government's automatic majority and of the common sense normally displayed by Members on both sides of the House.

What is being proposed, in fact, is the development of a new set of conventions, by the formal recognition of practices that have already arisen, *sub rosa*, within the framework of the old set. It would be upon these conventions, rather than upon any formal rules, that one would rely for the protection of the nationalized industries against excessive bureaucratization. Experience from Commonwealth countries, such as Australia and New Zealand, where such conventions are actually in operation, does not suggest that any damage to the nationalized industries would result. One might surmise that, on the contrary, the settling of this matter in the only way in which—according to the author's judgement—it can be reasonably settled might be a great relief to them.

If, however, these proposed new conventions are to work well, something else is needed. The Webbs called it 'Measurement and Publicity'. At present we do not have nearly enough of it. If we had more, both Ministers and Members would be able to exercise their powers more intelligently and constructively.

The 'Parker' Tribunal revealed, to the surprise of most people, how casually and capriciously some of the major decisions affecting our national financial policy were taken. It would be unjust to a handful of very intelligent and hard working civil servants to suggest that decisions relating to the nationalized industries are similarly taken. One may seriously doubt, however, whether these men and women have either the time or the skill to gather and to analyse all the data on which decisions should be based. Few of them have had any special training in economics or statistics. Practically none of them has had first-hand acquaintance with industrial life. Much of their time is taken up with drafting ministerial answers to questions, making inquiries on the Minister's behalf, and preparing, often against severe time limits, the briefs on which he will base his rulings, 'advice' and public pronouncements. This, of course, is day-to-day work of the highest importance, but it is not enough. The evidence that it is not enough, if evidence is needed, may be found in the verbatim transcripts of those sessions of the Select Committee on Nationalized Industries to which civil servants from the Ministries of Transport and of Power and from the Treasury were called as witnesses. These men speak as intelligent and informed amateurs. To their credit, they never claim to be anything more.

If there was some kind of automatic guarantee, such as that alleged to be provided by free competition, that a nationalized industry would always give of its best, or if ordinary commercial behaviour were all that was required of it, this would not matter. Questions of public interest would come up only occasionally, as envisaged by the Herbert Report, and could be dealt with on a basis of informed common sense and political calculation. But this is not the situation. The Minister and his civil service aides are more-or-less continuously engaged in the making of policy, in consultation with the Board, and for this purpose they need a stream of reliable, objective and carefully sifted information, specifically oriented towards the problems that are under discussion. The Board, of course, is itself supposed to be providing them with this, and there is no reason to suppose that it does not do its honest best. But 'control' information provided by the controlled organization is always suspect, for obvious reasons, and the Board, with the best will in the world, can look at the problems only from its own point of view. One result of this is that the Minister is often groping about, if not in the dark, at least in the twilight. Another is that Members of Parliament, knowing this, tend to adopt the view that their ideas about what ought to be done are as good as his. It is a matter of one amateur opinion as against another. Parliament has attempted to improve this situation, from its own point of view, by appointing the Select Committee. This has had the advantage of enabling a few Members to specialize in nationalized industries, to discover, in some detail, what both ministerial and board policies really are, and to advise their less well-informed colleagues on these matters. But although, as a channel for conveying information about the nationalized industries, the Committee is extremely useful, as a tool for investigating them it is less satisfactory; for it is a tool that lacks a sharp cutting edge. Hence the Committee's own tentative request that it should be equipped with some kind of investigatory staff, however modest.

Sooner or later, I believe, we shall have to establish some definite organ of measurement, comparable in function, if not in outlook, method or personnel, to the French *Commission de Vérification*. An alternative, of course, would be to increase the number and variety of specially-qualified people in the Ministries themselves, and this would be desirable in any case; for no one who visits the

Ministry of Transport or the Ministry of Power can fail to be surprised and shocked at the fact that great national enterprises are being supervised by an exiguous staff of Administrative Class civil servants, assisted by a handful of Executive and Clerical officers. But the real solution is not to increase the number of anonymous civil servants, working in secrecy on problems discovered by themselves or referred to them by the Minister or brought to their attention by various interest groups. If measurement is to be properly organized, and combined with publicity, it needs its own specific agency, independent of Ministry, Board and Parliament alike, and exclusively devoted to the production of high-quality information and the provision of reasoned advice.

Such an agency would not be at the exclusive disposal of Ministers, although they perhaps would give it most of its assignments. It would also place itself at the disposal of the industries themselves, of the Select Committee, and of the Consumers' Councils.[9] The objection will be made, of course, that this body would have as its function the impermissible one of looking over the shoulders of management. If it undertook a complete examination of all the nationalized industries every year, as the French *Commission de Vérification* does, this objection would have real force. For it is quite true that British managers are not prepared to tolerate the amount of supervision and inspection which their French counterparts apparently take in their stride. But there is no reason why it should work in this way, and plenty of reasons why it should not. Its proper function would be the examination of definite problems which had been referred to it or which it had decided to take up on its own initiative: problems of public importance either specific to one industry or common to them all. The investigation of these would undoubtedly involve some looking over of shoulders, but not everyone's shoulders all the time. Moreover, as its purpose would be not to catch people out but to help them to improve, the exercise of looking might even be welcomed, eventually, by those subjected to it. Plenty of looking over shoulders goes on already, particularly in respect of those industries whose problems

[9] The Councils are almost crippled by lack of independent expert advice. See W. A. Robson: *Nationalized Industry and Public Ownership*, pp. 264–6; G. Mills and M. Howe: *Consumer Representation and the Withdrawal of Railway Services* in *Public Administration*, Vol. 38, Autumn 1960.

cannot fail to attract attention. The sensible thing, one might well suggest, would not be to try to stop it but to make it more informed and purposeful.

Another possible objection is that the publicity afforded to the agency's recommendations would make difficulties for the Minister, in so far as if he decided not to accept them he would have to explain his reasons to an Opposition unusually well armed with counter-arguments. Such a situation, however, would not be without precedent, for it has been created by the reports of innumerable committees of inquiry. Moreover, there are several examples of advisory bodies from whose published recommendations the Minister is required to state the reasons for his dissent, if any. Such procedures may indeed be justified as injecting a much-needed element of reason into political life. But if a Minister were not prepared to tolerate publicity in every case, as might well be so, the publication of reports requested by him might be made conditional upon his permission. If he chose to refuse, they would remain confidential, like the 'industry' reports of the French *Commission de Vérification*.

In some cases, it would definitely be desirable to insist that a problem be referred to the agency, and its advice received, before action is taken. In transport, for instance, it might well become forbidden to sanction the withdrawal of existing facilities until its opinion, based on investigation, had been obtained. This might involve some extra delay, but would be much superior to the procedures at present in vogue. Proposals from the Transport Commission to close railway lines are now referred to the area Transport Users Consultative Committees, which, after inquiry, almost invariably support them. As the Committees have no clear terms of reference in dealing with such matters and no source of independent, expert advice, their deliberations are inevitably amateurish. Moreover, in taking evidence from members of the public, they have restricted themselves to inquiring into questions of alleged hardship, and have not encouraged (and sometimes have even forbidden) any challenge of the economic calculations produced by the Commission in justification of its proposals. Indeed, it has become practically impossible for an objector to know the figures upon which such calculations are based, as the Central Transport Consultative Committee, incredibly enough, has endorsed the

226

Commission's view that, since the Committees 'themselves sufficiently represent and guard the public interest, . . . there is no need to provide information for anyone else, particularly regarding figures of savings, costs or losses, which can only be explained with difficulty to those unfamiliar with them, and can be distorted by facile but unsound reasoning'.[10]

The Minister, for his part, has powers, so far unused, to give directions to the Commission in the light of Consultative Committee recommendations. In practice, when challenged in the House, he supports the 'commercial judgement' of the Commission, and shelters behind the Consultative Committee's endorsement of it. Additionally, he may claim that the Commission's decision, taken solely for reasons of profitability, will entail virtually no personal inconvenience or social diseconomies. If it does, he will 'look into' the matter. Closing railway lines is, of course, a very sad thing, but part of the inevitable cost of transport rationalization, economic progress, etc.

What would surely be more sensible than this untidy approach to the problem, which leaves everyone dissatisfied except the Minister and the Commission, is to have a proper, impartial investigation of the *facts*—all and not merely some of them—to discover what course of action is most likely to be conducive to the long-term interests not merely of the Transport Commission but of the locality and the nation. One might begin by stating, as a matter of principle, that no facility would be withdrawn until its lack of necessity was considered proved or until evidence was available that the cost of providing it outweighed the benefits that it brought. Information and advice on the subject would then become the responsibility of 'agency' experts skilled in the difficult art of 'costs-and-benefits' calculations. Having considered their conclusions, the agency would then present its report to the Minister, who would have to decide what action to take. If he decided that the balance of advantage lay in withdrawing the facility, he would have to consider, if necessary, ways and means of providing a substitute, and not merely express his confidence either that no substitute was needed or that somehow it would materialize. If he decided against withdrawal, he would need to consider, on

[10] C.T.C.C. *Annual Report for* 1957, para. 7, as quoted in Mills and Howe: *loc. cit.*

227

the basis of the agency's advice and in consultation with the Transport Commission, to what extent the latter's losses in providing the facility ought to be met by a subvention from the Exchequer.

A similar type of procedure might be followed in respect of unremunerative services demanded by consumers but not yet provided. Such demands might be made of the Transport Commission. They are actually being made, for rural electrification, of the Electricity Boards. In the latter case, the details of the procedure would necessarily be different but the course of events would be the same, viz. (a) a consumer demand; (b) an impartial and expert investigation of it; (c) a report, leading to (d) a decision, based upon a broad and informed view of social and economic needs and possibilities; and (e) a subsidy, if necessary.

Another and much more important subject on which an expression of 'agency' opinion might be mandatory is price policy. It has long been recognized that an industry which provides a basic service cannot be left entirely free to determine its own prices, particularly if it occupies a monopolistic or quasi-monopolistic position. When coal, gas, and electricity were nationalized, this seems temporarily to have been forgotten. For railway transport, however, the Tribunal was retained, with amended powers, and through the operation of the 'gentlemen's agreement' coal prices were in practice kept under ministerial control. How far the Minister has intervened to influence gas and electricity prices we do not know. In respect of the fares charged by civil airways, he is in practice bound to respect those agreed on through international negotiations.

At present the Transport Tribunal provides the only formal method of rate-fixing, and it has come in for some heavy criticism. It works so slowly that its decisions are often outdated before they enter into force. Its procedure, which is of the quasi-judicial kind, may enable some kind of justice to be done as between the John Doe of the Transport Commission and the Richard Roe of the transport user, but is hardly adapted to the determination of what constitutes the national interest. Some say that in any case it is useless, as the railways no longer possess any kind of monopoly and ought to be allowed freely to compete (after suitable adjustments have been made to ensure that each form of transport bears the real costs of its overheads) with their road-borne rivals. Others, while conceding that the Tribunal has faults which ought to be rectified, have taken precisely the opposite view, holding not only that it ought to be retained but that the 'price court' principle should be extended to other nationalized industries. As this is not an essay in applied economics, we cannot go deeply into these matters. What seems reasonably clear is that unless the Government decides to adopt the views of our neo-classical economists (which would involve, so far as the nationalized industries are concerned, much more than merely giving them the freedom to fix their own prices), pricing policy will continue to be a political matter, either openly or *sub rosa*. The question, therefore, is how the decisions involved can be made more intelligent and informed than one strongly suspects they are at present.

In the last resort, of course, it is the Minister who has to decide, and there are very strong grounds against his being hamstrung by the judgement of a quasi-judicial body. It may be that in certain cases, such a body has a useful function to perform, but the arguments for giving it an advisory rather than a mandatory role are very strong. What the Minister surely needs is the advice of an agency which has both the facilities and the time to engage in continuous study of pricing policies, with particular reference to the nationalized industries—an agency which, having the necessary material at its disposal, could present the necessary facts and figures without delay and indicate the probable results of different kinds of decision. If such an agency were in existence, it would become possible to place the ultimate control of pricing policies squarely in the hands of the Minister, with the proviso that before issuing a direction or giving an approval, he received the agency's opinion. It might even be desirable to impose a time-limit within which that opinion had to be received.

Constitution-building *in vacuo* is not a very useful exercise, and enough has now been said to indicate (a) what types of work the agency whose creation has been proposed could usefully do, and (b) in what manner it could help both Ministers and parliamentarians to discharge their respective duties *vis-à-vis* the nationalized industries more competently and consequently with less purely wasteful friction. As to the composition and structure of such an agency, we can only give the most general indications. As we conceive it, it would consist of a small nucleus of full-time members, selected for the width and variety of their experience of industrial and public affairs. These would be responsible for appointing such full-time experts as they considered necessary, in the light of the character and extent of the agency's long-term commitments and of the limitations of its budget. They would also be empowered to employ suitably qualified outsiders, for limited periods or specific jobs, on contract terms. Reports of individuals or teams would be made, not directly to the authority which had requested the information or advice, but to the governing body of the agency, in whose name each report, amended or unamended, would be sent to the appropriate place. Such, at least, might be the initial plan. If the experiment proved successful and the functions of the agency underwent expansion, its organization would necessarily become more complex. Eventually, a government might see advantage in extending its terms of reference considerably beyond the nationalized industries. One can envisage, for instance, that it might be able very usefully to examine proposals for the subsidization of private industries, so that they would no longer be placed before parliament with the sketchy justification which the Minister now chooses to vouchsafe.

As has been suggested in Chapter VII, it would hardly be practical politics to propose the immediate establishment of the type of agency that we have in mind. Except under emergency conditions, proposals for constitutional or administrative innovation receive a chilly welcome in this country, and ideas for improvements have to undergo a lengthy period of gestation before an institutional birth is finally achieved. Moreover, in this particular case there is likely to be very strong opposition to the proposed new institution not only from the nationalized industries themselves, which would be predisposed to fear and resent it, but from civil servants, who would tend to regard its existence as an implied criticism of their own abilities, and from all those who consider that the best thing to do with nationalized industries is to leave them alone. The probability, therefore, is that if anything even faintly resembling an agency of the type we have envisaged eventually materializes, it will be the result of the development of 'information and advice' functions within an existing institution to the point where it seems necessary or reasonable to hive them off. As we have suggested, the most obvious growing points are the Select Committee and the Ministries themselves. What needs to be emphasized is that we are *not* proposing a régime in which Ministers and parliamentarians would be perpetually and wantonly interfering with the nationalized industries. The point has been fully conceded that the more a nationalized industry *can* be left alone to get on with its business, the better it will be for all concerned. The virtue of having an investigatory agency is not that it would enable Ministers to do more and parliamentarians to talk more, but that it would direct action and talk towards the points where they were really needed. Indeed, other things being equal, the 'silent persuasiveness of ascertained fact' should have the effect of removing from the sphere of political debate a good many subjects which are only controversial to the extent that they are not properly understood. Already there is evidence, admittedly not conclusive, that the Reports of the Select Committee are having a salutory effect, in this sense, on the course of parliamentary discussions. If this is so, the acceptance of our proposals should permit further progress in the same direction. One can only speculate how any proposed change will work out, but at least it seems likely that the diffusion of information and of adequately-informed ideas about current problems will afford better protection to a nationalized industry against wanton interference than any of the so-called protective devices on which we have vainly relied up to the present.

There are two things that Parliament can do supremely well. One is the broad discussion of important issues of public policy; the other is the ventilation of individual grievances. If it is to do either with maximum effectiveness, some kind of preparatory or 'filtering' process is necessary, so that its attention may be directed towards what is of real importance. For the former it needs the very best information that can be obtained. At present its broad discussions of the nationalized industries take place mainly on the annual Reports and Accounts, sometimes supplemented by a Report from the Select Committee. If these debates are unsatisfactory—and no one, I think, would claim that they represent the House of Commons at its best—it is partly because no point of concentration has been provided, partly because information is deficient, and partly because many Members, instead of devoting their attention to the big issues, seize the opportunity to expatiate on constituency grievances which they find difficulty in raising at Question Time. One cannot, of course, prevent them from using a Report and Accounts Debate as a grievance session, if they wish to do so, but one can at least provide alternative opportunities; and it should not be past the wit of parliamentary man to devise forms of motion which would impose a greater coherence on the debate and to ensure that documents summarizing all the relevant information should be supplied to Members well ahead.

If these things were done, many of the complaints that Parliament lacks time to give adequate attention to the nationalized industries would die a natural death. Inevitably, when a debate is a 'free for all', in which most Members begin their speeches with apologies for not being able to follow up the interesting points made by their predecessors, nobody is satisfied that anything has been properly discussed, and everyone who has spoken feels that there ought to be some other occasion when the important subject he has so inadequately dealt with can be further ventilated. To some extent, of course, this malaise is an occupational disease of parliamentarians, which no changes in procedure can cure. But most M.P.s, one imagines, feel happier after a debate in which a few points of major public importance have been intelligibly discussed than after one in which a large number of bits and pieces have been incontinently thrown into the air. Time itself is not a problem; the use of time is. Parliamentarians are better employed in devising ways of using their time to better effect than in deploring its inefficiency. If, when provision has been made for using more adequately the time at present devoted to discussing the nationalized industries, it is found that more is genuinely needed, then Members have the remedy in their own hands. Greater use of committees is one solution as yet insufficiently explored. It might also be suggested that a Parliament which spends about six hours debating an almost uncontroversial bill for the provision of cattle grids on the highways and an equal time debating an equally uncontroversial bill to increase the number of High Court judges has no right to complain when it finds that it has no more than a day to devote to the affairs of the National Coal Board.

The more that discussion of the nationalized industries can be confined to well-prepared parliamentary occasions, and the more productive of enlightenment these occasions can be made, the better will the requirements of genuine supervision be satisfied. This is the perfectly valid point that has been endlessly reiterated by the 'Morrisonians' and which they have attempted to secure, mistakenly in our opinion, by attempting to limit ministerial responsibility to matters of major policy. But the discussion of specific grievances is also important, for Parliament ought not to divest itself of its role of a final court of appeal. To our mind, the suggestion that over the whole vast field of administration covered by the nationalized industries it should attempt to renounce this essential function is utterly absurd. If a person has a strongly-felt grievance against a nationalized undertaking, and after exhausting all the possibilities of representation, both direct and through the Consumers' Council, cannot secure what he considers adequate remedy, he quite naturally and rightly contacts his Member of Parliament, whom he expects to 'do something'. The Member will then make inquiries of the Chairman of the Board and endeavour to get the wrong righted—if he considers that a genuine wrong has been done. If he fails in this attempt, he may try writing to the Minister. In the last resort, he should be able to table a Question. Under the present dispensation, he does not normally possess the right to do so, because his constituent's grievance is almost inevitably a day-to-day matter. Hence, unless he considers it important enough to raise on the Adjournment, and is successful in the ballot, the ultimate step in the grievance-ventilating and grievance-correcting process is lacking. The elimination of this ultimate step is not a matter of small importance. It is a deliberate withdrawal of one of the most vital of democratic rights, a serious limitation on the liberty of the subject and an affront to the dignity of the legislature.

The current justification of this practice is by now all-too-familiar. If Members were free to take up matters of this kind, we are told, Parliament would be overwhelmed with minor and perhaps frivolous grievances, 'adopted' by Members for constituency or political reasons, with the result that the Minister would be compelled to intervene to such an extent that the commercial flexibility of the nationalized industry would be virtually eliminated. To this argument several replies may be made. Firstly, there is little evidence that the freedom which Members have to ask questions about all other aspects of central administration is seriously or consistently misused. Secondly, if the extension of such freedom to questions about the nationalized industries *did* result in a flood of complaints, it would indicate the existence either of serious mismanagement by the members of the Boards and their subordinates, or of gross inefficiency in the machinery of consumer representation at the lower levels. Thirdly, if the Minister on examination of the complaint, decided that it was trivial or that it had already been dealt with to the best of the Board's ability or that, for one reason or another, it was irremediable, he could say so. For, as we have already suggested, it should be the duty of the Minister not only to answer on behalf of the Board but in doing so to *protect* the Board against unwarranted interference with the discharge of its functions. If he cannot do this then no one else can.

What needs to be emphasized, in this connection, is that Parliament must normally act as a 'court' of *final* appeal, not one of first instance. To fulfil this role to the best public advantage, it needs assistance. Just as, in discussing matters of Board policy, it requires the help of well-developed organs of information and advice, so, in discussing grievances, it requires the help of an effectively-functioning machinery of consumer representation, which would ensure that only those matters which could not be disposed of at lower levels would reach the parliamentary level. Machinery of a kind, of course, already exists, in the form of the various consultative committees. But no one has much confidence in it, and perhaps only a few of those who might wish to use it are even aware of its existence. For our whole approach to consumer representation has been so tentative and hesitant that the *Economist*'s characterization of consumers' councils as 'worthy, windy and weak' has hardly been seriously challenged.

The defects of the present machinery are thus summarized by Professor J. A. G. Griffith:[11]

'First, the consumers' councils and committees are too closely linked to the administering corporations . . . Second, there are too many different systems. This raises the problem of personnel, for the number of people who have the time, energy and ability to do the kind of work which is required is

[11] See *The Voice of the Consumer*, in *Political Quarterly*, Vol. 21, No. 2, April–June 1950.

limited. The country is becoming littered with advisory committees of one sort or another, and the standard seems to be
declining. Above all, unity is strength and division is weakness.
Thirdly, the individual consumer suffers from being unorgan-
ised . . . (He) is much too easily brushed aside, whether in-
tentionally or not; indeed he often feels so helpless that he
does not trouble to make his complaints. He needs a champion
—someone over whom he has some influence . . . Fourth,
the present consumers' bodies are too inaccessible to the
individual consumer. This is particularly true in the case of
coal, and seems likely to be true for transport also.'

To meet these defects, he suggests:

'That one hierarchy of authorities should be established to
represent the consumer and user of services and facilities provided by *all* nationalized industries. At the top a Cabinet
Minister without departmental responsibilities should represent consumers' interests. The most obvious choice would be
the Lord President of the Council. There should be one central
consumers' council and, at the lower level, one county consumers' council for each county and county borough area.
In adddition there should be a central consumers' tribunal
and county consumers' tribunals.'

Professor Griffith goes on to amplify these suggestions. He
distinguishes between 'general representations and complaints',
which should be made direct to the county consumers' councils
and 'particular complaints by individual consumers or industries',
which would be made in the first instance to the local office of the
corporation concerned and on appeal to the county consumers'
tribunal. He emphasizes the importance of enabling individual
consumers with 'general' complaints to get them sponsored by the
local authority, which would have the right of making representations to the county consumers' councils. He deals with the machinery for taking appeals from the county bodies to the national ones,
and with the functions that would be performed by the Cabinet
Minister.

235

The details of his scheme do not concern us here. All we wish to do is to indicate that at least one reputable authority has produced a plan designed, as he himself says, 'to meet the principal weaknesses in the existing system and to enable the voice of the consumer to carry further and more strongly down the corridors and into the rooms of the administering corporations'. It may not be the best possible plan.[12] Some might prefer a further simplification, by which, what Professor Griffith calls 'particular complaints' would be referred for investigation and report to an Ombudsman. He certainly does not link his plan, as we have done, with the suggestion that parliamentary questioning should be freed from its present limitations; but he does clearly envisage for Parliament the role of a 'court of last resort'.

If we had an efficient system of consumer representation, it would be possible to impose a rule whereby Questions relating to day-to-day matters could not be asked until the resources of the representative machinery had been exhausted. Such a rule, however, would not be desirable, because there would be great difficulty in applying it fairly or consistently. Moreover, there will always be the exceptional case where the short-circuiting of the machinery, to bring up what seems an urgent matter at the highest level, will be necessary. One can envisage, however, that the practice would be established whereby Members would be prepared to accept an answer from the Minister to the effect that a matter which was being inquired about was receiving the attention of a council or a tribunal. One can also envisage that, as soon as the new machinery was working properly, Members would receive far fewer representations from aggrieved consumers and consequently would need neither to indulge in so much correspondence with the Boards nor to ask the Minister more than an occasional Question that was concerned with matters other than those of general policy. That, indeed, would be one of its main purposes.

It is freely admitted that the arguments upon which the above proposals have been based are of a speculative order. No one can

[12] Interesting alternative proposals for strengthening the system of consumer representation have been made by Professor G. Sargant Florence and Mr. H. Maddick (*Political Quarterly*, Vol. 24, p. 259) and by Mr. L. Freedman and Mr. G. Hemingway in their *Nationalization and the Consumer* (Fabian Research Series, No. 139). Chapter X of W. A. Robson's *Nationalized Industry and Public Ownership* contains an excellent discussion of the whole subject.

prove that the dire results which some consider to be the inevitable consequence of any expansion of ministerial responsibility and parliamentary control would not actually materialize. The best that one can do is to suggest that a more liberal régime, particularly if buttressed by reforms designed to secure better measurement and publicity and to strengthen the voice of the consumer, would not automatically reproduce in the administration of a nationalized industry those bureaucratic characteristics which it must at all costs avoid. The only *evidence* to which one can appeal is the Post Office, and this is admittedly inconclusive. But it is at least worth noting that, since the early 1930s, the 'total' responsibility of the Postmaster-General has not prevented his department either from embarking on an imaginative public relations policy or from effecting a considerable—and highly necessary—measure of decentralization. It is also worthy of note that most students of management are of the opinion that 'bureaucratic' tendencies are by no means exclusively, or even mainly, a product of the device of ministerial responsibility. They are partly a function of size (a matter which we have deliberately refrained from considering here), and partly of the temptation experienced by an organization immune or partly immune from competitive pressures to preserve and to elaborate its well-established routines. It is at least possible that parliamentary criticism, if well-informed and intelligently directed, might actually help the nationalized industries to save themselves from this hardening of the arteries.

At any rate, the whole question is still a very open one. We have not solved the dilemma which has been stated in the first two chapters of this study, and there is as much room for experiment as ever. As has been suggested, it is unlikely that we shall ever *solve* it, for the problem of 'bureaucracy', in its various senses, is likely to be a permanent one in modern political democracies. Inevitably, there has to be some form of compromise between a number of conflicting *desiderata*. All we have suggested, by putting forward what seems a viable alternative to the present British compromise, which is not working very satisfactorily, is that fresh thinking is needed.

APPENDIX

Adjournment Debates on Nationalized Industries

Sessions 1951–2 to 1957–8

20th November 1951. Losses, due to Theft, from British Railways (Half-Hour), Vol. 494, cols. 349–58.

30th November 1951. Railway Branch Lines (Closing) (Half-Hour), Vol. 494, cols 1983–94.

21st March 1952. Railway Worshops (Employment) (Half-Hour), Vol. 497, cols. 2834–44.

3rd April 1952. Railway Branch Lines (Diesel Cars) (Half-Hour), Vol. 498, cols. 2141–52.

10th April 1952. Railway Branch Lines, Northumberland (Closing) (Half-Hour), Vol. 498, cols. 3078–84.

30th May 1952. Rural Electrification (Whitsun Recess), Vol. 501, cols. 1787–98.

19th June 1952. Railway Pensioners (Half-Hour), Vol. 502, cols. 1704–12.

12th June 1953. Rural Electrification (Half-Hour), Vol. 516, cols. 684–704.

6th April 1954. National Coal Board (Ex-Employee) (Half-Hour), Vol. 526, cols. 322–30.

25th June 1954. Rural Electricity Schemes (Wales) (Half-Hour), Vol. 529, cols. 860–8.

8th July 1954. Civil Aviation Pilots' Service Conditions (Half-Hour), Vol. 529, cols. 2485–96.

22nd December 1954. Airways Corporations (Trade Unions), (Christmas Recess), Vol. 535, cols. 2809–19.

8th February 1955. Railway Pensioners (Half-Hour), Vol. 536, cols. 1857–64.

11th February 1955. Continental Air Services (Southend-on-Sea), (Half-Hour), Vol. 538, cols. 907–18.

13th July 1955. Battery Rail Cars, Scotland (Half-Hour), Vol. 543, cols. 2069–80.

14th November 1955. Railways (Long Service Recognition) (Half-Hour), Vol. 546, cols. 159–68).

20th December 1955. Railway Branch Lines (Closure) (Christmas Recess), Vol. 547, cols. 1575–615.

2nd May 1956. Rural Electrification (Half-Hour), Vol. 552, cols. 554–62.

21st November 1956. Trolley Buses, London (Replacement) (Half-Hour), Vol. 560, cols. 1896–904.

23rd November 1956. Transport, North-East Essex (Half-Hour), Vol. 560, cols. 2100–8.

27th February 1957. Rural Transport (Half-Hour), Vol. 565, cols. 1353–64.

28th February 1957. Electricity Supply Industry (Pensioners) (Half-Hour), Vol. 565, cols. 1524–36.

1st April 1957. Coal (Domestic Consumers' Complaints) (Half-Hour), Vol. 568, cols. 194–204.

8th April 1957. Coal Industry (Organisation) (Half-Hour), Vol. 568, cols. 914–34.

30th October 1957. Electricity Supply (Torridon Area) (Half-Hour), Vol. 575, cols. 355–64.

31st October 1957. Railway Stations, Manchester (Half-Hour), Vol. 575, cols. 520–30.

4th December 1957. British Transport Commission (Purchasing Procedure) (Half-Hour), Vol. 579, cols. 576–84.

10th December 1957. Transport (Consultative Committees) (Half-Hour), Vol. 579, cols. 1229–38.

12th December 1957. Railways (Coniston-Foxfield Branch Line) (Half-Hour), Vol. 579, cols. 1621–8.

17th December 1957. Bo'ness Dock (Future) (Half-Hour), Vol. 580, cols. 379–88.

27th January 1958. Coal (Prices and Grades) (Half-Hour), Vol. 580, cols. 167–75.

27th June 1958. North-West Electricity Board (Rural Programme) (Half-Hour), Vol. 590, cols. 843–52.

8th July 1958. Railways (Building, Repair and Maintenance Programme) (Half-Hour), Vol. 591, cols 357–68.

16th July 1958. Port of Cardiff (Half-Hour), Vol. 591, cols. 1404–14.

1st August 1958. Passenger Train Services, Wales (Withdrawal) (Half-Hour), Vol. 592, cols. 1883–92.

Index

Index

Acton Society, *The Powers of the Minister*, 42; *Nationalized Industry*, 43

Acts of Parliament:
Air Corporations Acts (1953, 1956), 43
Air Navigation Acts, 41
Civil Aviation Act (1946), 41
Coal Industry Acts (1949, 1951, 1956), 43
Coal Industry Nationalization Act (1946), 38, 55, 125
Coal Mines Act (1911), 55
Coal Mining (Subsidence) Act (1950), 43
Electricity Acts (1947), 38; (1957), 39*n.*, 43, 75, 91
Electricity Reorganization (Scotland) Act (1954), 43
Gas and Electricity (Borrowing Powers) Act (1954), 43
London Passenger Transport Acts (1933), 18, 22, 40; (1947) 40
Ministry of Fuel and Power Act (1945), 55
Statutory Instruments Act (1946), 42
Transport Acts (1947), 92, 95, 97; (1953), 43, 91, 100–1
Transport (Borrowing Powers) Act (1955), 43
Transport Charges (Miscellaneous Provisions) Act (1954), 43
Transport (Disposal of Road Haulage Property) Act (1956), 43

Ad hoc bodies, 13–16, 27
Air Corporations, Select Committee Report on, 154–62, 209
Albu, Austin, 143, 196
Allen, Sir Carlton, 9, 11; *Bureacracy Triumphant*, 8
Alport, C. J. M., 80
Appleby, Paul, 178

Area Traffic Commissioners, 13
Attlee, Clement, 22
Australia, 181–6, 223
Australian Airlines National Commission, 181–2
Australian Aluminium Production Commission, 183–4
Australian Broadcasting Commission, 184
Ayres, R. J., 151

Baird, Mr., 51, 132
Bank of England, 19
Barber, Anthony, 116–17
Barnes, Alfred, 59, 96–7
Barton, Sir Harold, 128
B.B.C., 20; ministerial responsibility for, 29–30; finance, 129
B.E.A. (Airways), 158–62
Beswick, Frank, 160, 161
Blakeney, Allen E., 193
Bland, Professor F. A., 32, 181
B.O.A.C., 156–62
Bo'ness Dock, 85
Bonham-Carter, Mark, 108
Bowen, Roderic, 87
Bowman, Sir James, 151, 166
Boyd-Carpenter, Mr., 53, 80
Boyer, Sir Richard, 184–6
Boyle, Sir Edward, 66–7, 70
Bracken, Brendan, 39
Braddock, Mrs., 88
Bridges, Sir Edward, 135
British Coal Utilization Research Association, 151
British Electricity Authority: the Central Electricity Authority and the Area Boards, 38–9; the 'Clow' dispute, 47–9 ; and Ministerial responsibility, 68–9, 74–5; Debates on, 80–1, 83–4, 87–91; and rural electrification, 228

243